T0341652

A Guide to Galatians and Philippians

SPCK International Study Guide 40

A Guide to Galatians and Philippians

Kim Huat Tan

First published in Great Britain in 2009

Society for Promoting Christian Knowledge
36 Causton Street
London SW1P 4ST

British Library Cataloguing-in-Publication Data
A catalogue record for this book is available from the British Library

ISBN 978–0–281–06081–8

10 9 8 7 6 5 4 3 2 1

Produced on paper from sustainable forests

Contents

Contents

Contributors

Dr Kim Huat Tan is the Chen Su Lan Professor of New Testament and Dean of Studies at Trinity Theological College, Singapore. His scholarly interest is in the emergence of Christianity from a Jewish matrix. He has published *The Zion Traditions and the Aims of Jesus* with Cambridge University Press. He is a Baptist who worships at a Presbyterian church.

Born in Ecuador, **Juan Carlos Cevallos** is Supervising Editor of the Baptist Spanish Publishing House, a pastor in Texas, and author of several books and articles. His Ph.D. is from the Seminario Bautista Internacional de Colombia. He was President of the Seminario Bautista del Ecuador and member of the translation team of the Nueva Versión Internacional.

Mark L. Y. Chan is Lecturer in Theology and Coordinator for Faith and Society with the Centre for the Study of Christianity in Asia at Trinity Theological College, Singapore. He studied at Fuller Theological Seminary and completed his Ph.D. in hermeneutics and Christology at the University of Nottingham. He worships at a non-denominational Singaporean church.

Sam Tsang, Vice Principal of Overseas Theological Seminary, California, received his Ph.D. from the University of Sheffield, UK. He publishes widely in Chinese, including an award-winning book on John in 2007. He has spoken on biblical studies in every continent, except Australia.

Lousiale Uasike is a native of Tonga and an ordained minister of the Free Wesleyan Church of Tonga (Methodist). She taught at Sia'atoutai Theological College of the Methodist Church in Tonga and is currently a D.Min. student of San Francisco Theological Seminary.

The SPCK International Study Guides

The international Study Guides (ISGs) are clear and accessible resources for the Christian Church. The series contains biblical commentaries, books on pastoral care, church history and theology. The guides are contextual and ecumenical in content and missional in direction.

The series is primarily aimed at those training for Christian ministries for whom English is an alternative language. Many other Christians will also find the ISGs useful guides. The contributors come from different countries and from a variety of church backgrounds. Most of them are theological educators. They bring their particular perspectives to bear as they demonstrate the influence of other contexts on the subjects they address. They provide a practical emphasis alongside contemporary scholarly reflection.

For over forty years, the ISG series has aided those in ministerial formation to develop their own theology and discern God's mission in their context. Today, there is a greater awareness of plurality within the universal Christian body. This is reflected in changes to the series that draw upon the breadth of Christian experience across the globe.

Emma Wild-Wood
Editor, International Study Guides

Acknowledgements

The writing of this Study Guide has given me immense joy, and I am grateful to the Series Editor, Emma Wild-Wood, for the opportunity to be involved in this important work. True to her responsibility as the Series Editor, she has expertly guided the whole process from start to finish, and offered many pertinent suggestions on how the manuscript might be improved.

This work is in many ways a collaborative enterprise. I am acutely aware I am standing on the literary shoulders of David H. van Daalen and John Hargreaves. Their Study Guides on Galatians and Philippians contain much that is helpful to the fledgling student and the struggling pastor, because they endeavoured to make things clear and applicable. Such gems must not be wasted, and the reader should not be surprised that much of what they wrote has been retained. Juan Carlos Cevallos, Mark Chan, Samuel Tsang and Lousiale Uasike enrich this work by contributing theological essays on important topics confronting Christians today. They also make this collaborative enterprise truly international.

It would be greatly remiss of me not to mention here the contribution of Professor Graham Stanton. Not only has he taught me much of what I know of the New Testament, but also he has always had a keen interest in all that I write. The work would be much the poorer if not for his insightful comments.

As always, I am indebted to my dear wife, Michelle, for making it possible for 'Daddy' to type his precious little without much interference from our precious little.

To all the above-mentioned, I want to say a big 'thank you', because you have taught me what it means to have *koinōnia* in Christ.

Kim Huat Tan

Using this Guide

The plan of this Guide follows much the same pattern as that of other biblical Guides in the series.

In his **introduction** the author sets the scene for our study of the biblical book that is selected by providing a brief note on its background. Its relationship with other biblical books may also be explored.

The study of the biblical book itself has been divided into short sections according to natural breaks in the text. But before beginning their work readers may find it helpful to consider how they can make the best use of this Guide.

Each section consists of:

 1 **A summary** of the passage, briefly indicating the subject-matter it contains. Of course the summary is not intended as a substitute for the words of the Bible itself, which need to be read very carefully at each stage of our study.

 2 **Notes** on particular words and points of possible difficulty, especially as relating to the purpose of the writing, and to the situation which gave rise to the writing.

 3 An **interpretation** of the passage and the teaching it contained, both as it applied to those to whom it was addressed, and as we should understand and apply it to our own situation today.

 ## Special notes

Special notes give extra attention to important biblical words that are often found throughout Paul's Letters.

 ## Theological essays

Topics that warrant extended attention because of their implication for theology and the current situation of many churches today are covered as 'Theological essays'. The authors of these essays show one way in which a theme, a biblical text and a particular context can be read together to discern God's will in our world today.

 ## Study suggestions

Suggestions for further study and review are included at the end of each section. Besides enabling students working alone to check their own progress, they provide subjects for individual and group research, and topics for discussion. They are of four main sorts:

1   **Word study**, to help readers check and deepen their understanding of important words and phrases.

2   **Review of content**, to help readers check the work they have done, and make sure they have fully grasped the ideas and points of teaching given.

3   **Bible study**, to link the ideas and teaching of the biblical passage with related ideas and teaching in other parts of the Bible.

4   **Discussion and application**, to help readers think out the practical significance of the passage being studied, both to those to whom the biblical author was writing, and for the life and work of the churches and of individual Christians in the modern situation. Many of these are suitable for use in a group as well as for students working alone.

The best way to use these study suggestions is: first, reread the Bible passage; second, read the appropriate section of the Guide once or twice: and then do the work suggested, either in writing or in group discussion, without looking at the Guide again unless instructed to do so.

The **Key to study suggestions** at the end of the Guide will enable you to check your work on those questions which can be checked in this way. In most cases the Key does not give the answer to a question: it shows where an answer is to be found.

Please note that all these suggestions are only **suggestions**. Some readers may not wish to use them. Some teachers may wish to select only those most relevant to the needs of their particular students, or may wish to substitute questions of their own.

A list of books suggested for **further reading** is provided on p. xvii, and a **map** of the countries around the Eastern Mediterranean at the time when Paul was writing may be found on p. xix.

Index

The Index includes only the more important names of people and places and the main subjects treated in the Letters or discussed in the Guide. Bold-type page references are provided to show where particular subjects are treated in detail.

Bible versions

The English translation of the Bible used in the Guide is the New Revised Standard Version (NRSV). Reference is also made to the following versions, where these help to show the meaning more clearly:

● the New English Bible and Revised English Bible (NEB, REB)

● the New International Version (NIV)

- the Jerusalem Bible and New Jerusalem Bible (JB, NJB)
- the Good News Bible (GNB or TEV)

In a few cases, reference has also been made to the Authorized (King James) Version (AV).

Further reading

As far as possible, only books published within the last 25 years will be listed. This is to ensure that students will not find it too difficult to purchase or refer to these books. Those marked with an asterisk (*) are books that are written at a more advanced level, but may contain discussions that are useful for the first-year student or the beginner.

Books on Galatians

*Barrett, C. K. *Freedom and Obligation: A Study of the Epistle to the Galatians.* London: SPCK, 1985.

Cousar, C. B. *Galatians.* Interpretation: A Bible Commentary for Teaching and Preaching. Atlanta, Ga.: John Knox, 1982.

Dunn, J. D. G. *The Epistle to the Galatians.* Black's New Testament Commentaries. London: A. & C. Black, 1993.

*Dunn, J. D. G. *The Theology of Paul's Letter to the Galatians.* New Testament Theology. Cambridge: Cambridge University Press, 1993.

Fung, Ronald Y. K. *The Epistle to the Galatians.* New International Commentary on the New Testament. Grand Rapids, Mich.: Eerdmans, 1988.

Jervis, L. N. *Galatians.* New International Bible Commentary. Peabody, Mass.: Hendrickson, 1999.

Matera, F. J. *Galatians.* Sacra Pagina. Collegeville, Minn.: Liturgical Press, 1992.

McKnight, S. *Galatians.* NIV Application Bible Commentary. Grand Rapids, Mich.: Zondervan, 1995.

*Witherington III, B. *Grace in Galatia: A Commentary on St Paul's Letter to the Galatians.* Grand Rapids, Mich.: Eerdmans, 1998.

Ziesler, J. *The Epistle to the Galatians.* Epworth Commentaries. London: Epworth, 1992.

Books on Philippians

Bockmuehl, M. *The Epistle to the Philippians.* Black's New Testament Commentaries. London: A. & C. Black, 1998.

Bruce, F. F. *Philippians.* New International Bible Commentary. Peabody, Mass.: Hendrickson, 1989.

Craddock, F. B. *Philippians*. Interpretation: A Bible Commentary for Teaching and Preaching. Atlanta, Ga.: John Knox, 1985.

*Donfried, K. P. and Marshall, I. H. *The Theology of the Shorter Pauline Letters*. New Testament Theology. Cambridge: Cambridge University Press, 1993

*Fee. G. D. *Paul's Letter to the Philippians*. New International Commentary on the New Testament. Grand Rapids, Mich.: Eerdmans, 1995.

Marshall, I. H. *The Epistle to the Philippians*. Epworth Commentaries. London: Epworth, 1992.

Osiek, C. *Philippians, Philemon*. Abingdon New Testament Commentaries. Nashville, Tenn.: Abingdon, 2000.

Witherington, B. III. *Friendship and Finances in Philippi: The Letter of Paul to the Philippians*. New Testament in Context. Valley Forge, Pa.: Trinity Press International, 1994.

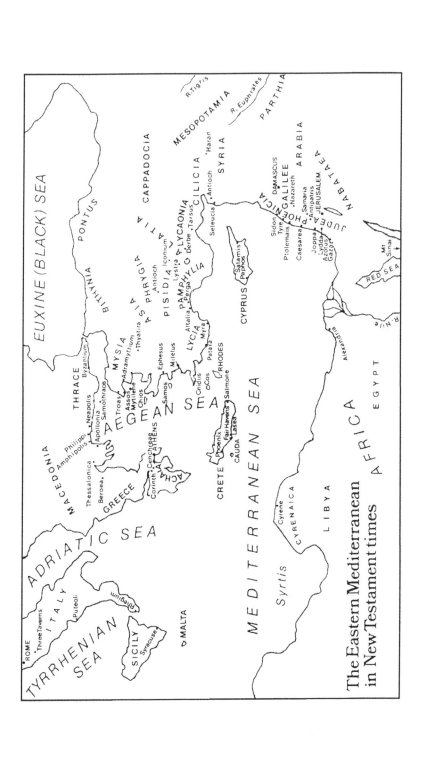

The Eastern Mediterranean
in New Testament times

Reading Galations and Philippians together

The tone of Paul in his Letter to the Galatians is combative, and sometimes bordering on being rude and crude. Take for instance the harsh words of Galatians 5.12: 'I wish those who unsettle you would castrate themselves!' 'Anathemas' are pronounced against these agitators in 1.8–9, and the Galatians are called 'foolish' in 3.1. Almost as the opposite of this tone is that of the Letter to the Philippians. There he strikes the note of 'joy' frequently and speaks to his readers as 'friends' and 'partners'. Perhaps this is one reason why, if Paul's Letters have to be broken up into parts by commentators, no commentary has put Galatians together with Philippians. In other words, if Galatians needed a 'partner', it would not be Philippians. However, this Study Guide goes against the grain by putting them together. We will make a modest case for so doing and point out the wisdom that comes with it. Many of the following points will be best appreciated after a thorough study of the two Letters.

1 The illumination of opposites

The first thing to note is a maxim: that it is only when we get to see apparently contrasting presentations or revelations of people's characters that we gain a better appraisal of their personalities. Enlightenment or clarity often comes through a juxtaposition of opposites. We understand people better if we know their 'likes' and 'dislikes', what makes them happy and what makes them sad, or how they act in a friendly situation and how they react in a hostile situation. If the maxim is accepted, then reading Galatians and Philippians together is *unavoidable* if we want to study the personality of this great apostle. This is so because there is no Letter of Paul that is harsher in tone than Galatians, and there is no Letter of Paul that has a more endearing tone than Philippians. To be sure, all Letters must be taken into account if we want a complete picture of Paul. But if we have to choose only two, a good case may be made for choosing Galatians and Philippians.

Second, the Letters come from the initial and final phases of Paul's ministry. There are indeed many debates over the precise dating of Paul's Letters. But almost every scholar will accept that Galatians is one of the earliest – if not the earliest – and Philippians is to be grouped together with Paul's last Letters (this becomes even more evident if the pastoral Letters are regarded as having been written by Paul's disciple). By taking Paul's writings from the earliest and the latest phases of his apostolic ministry and viewing them together, we can see what endures through time with respect to Paul's teaching, emphasis and concerns. Were there issues that dogged Paul throughout his missionary career? Did Paul change his views on important matters over time? Did his personality also undergo change? Hence, our reading strategy affords us the opportunity to catch a better glimpse not just of Paul's personality but also of the essential shape and concerns of his ministry, and the issues he had to face.

We will now look at some of these aspects.

2 Is Paul a Dr-Jekyll-and-Mr-Hyde?

There is a famous story in the English language about a doctor who, because he took some potion, was transformed into another person, with a drastically different character. Many English speakers today refer to people whose personalities swing from one extreme to another as a Dr-Jekyll-and-Mr-Hyde. So then, if we look at the personal traits emerging from the two letters under consideration, does Paul come across as a Dr-Jekyll-and-Mr-Hyde?

Such a conclusion would be hasty. We have to bear in mind that Paul was tackling different problems called forth by different situations. The situation of the Galatian churches was critical. Troublemakers had infiltrated those churches. These Jewish agitators brought with them a brand of 'gospel' that would have given prominence to one ethnic group to the detriment of others. Worse, the focus would be on deeds and not grace, and the significance of the cross of Christ would be nullified. In other words, the issue concerned what was fundamental to the existence of the Christian Church (i.e. people are justified by faith and are one in Christ) and the meaning of the gospel (i.e. it is of grace and not of works). Paul must show in no uncertain terms that this teaching must stop. But the situation in Philippi was different. Paul was addressing a church that was only beginning to be divided. This matter was certainly important but it was not critical in the sense that the fundamental nature of the Church's existence or the meaning of the gospel was being threatened. Furthermore, Paul wrote also to thank the church at Philippi for the gift sent through Epaphroditus. This church had always been supportive of Paul's ministry. Not surprisingly, the tone of this letter is different from that of the Letter to the Galatians.

Of course, we may still agree that Paul might have sometimes overstepped the bounds of propriety when he wrote to the Galatians. We know from Acts 15.36–41 how uncompromising Paul could be. Paul parted ways with Barnabas over whether Mark should be allowed to join them in their missionary journey, even though Barnabas was the one who introduced Paul to the churches at Jerusalem and Antioch (Acts 9.27; 11.25). We are told that the quarrel between them was very sharp (Acts 15.39). Such fiery characteristics are certainly evident in Galatians.

That said, we have still to remember that Paul did not refrain from using some offensive language in Philippians 3 (see next section). The fiery characteristics were still present. However, compared to what was said in Galatians, these appeared to have been toned down. In fact, no other surviving letter of Paul contained such language. A process of mellowing had probably taken place. In short, there was still a consistency to his personality although we may also speak of a process of maturing or development.

3 Paul and the gospel of God's grace

The understanding of the gospel as being given by God's grace and how this led to the idea that nothing counted except faith in Christ was a burning concern of Paul. This is clear in Galatians, which was written primarily to treat a serious misunderstanding of it. But a similar occurrence is also found in Philippians, and at a literary juncture which is most fascinating. At Philippians 3.1, Paul states that he is about to conclude the Letter but he then goes on to warn his readers about Jewish agitators (Philippians 3.2–4). Most probably, Paul decided that he must treat this before ending the Letter because either there was an incipient threat or this had always been one issue on his mind, or both. If there was such a threat, it meant that this problem was found not just in Galatia but also in Philippi, separated by hundreds of miles and a time span of about a decade. Whether actual or imaginary, the mention of these Jewish agitators in Philippians shows us that this problem dogged Paul *throughout his whole ministry*. Even in prison and with the prospect of death facing him, he would still be confronted with or thinking about it. What needs to be emphasized again is that this problem concerned the fundamental meaning of the gospel. The gospel is a gospel of grace, leading to freedom. It is a gospel that is made possible because of what Christ has done for humankind and not because of humankind's effort or merit. Concerning this, Paul never wavered. As the apostle to the Gentiles, Paul must ensure that the Gentiles were really free through the gospel, and not shackled by Jewish ways, even if these appeared to be supported by the Old Testament.

Interestingly, harsh language could also be found in the Letter to the Philippians: the Jewish agitators were called 'dogs' and 'mutilators of the flesh' (Philippians 3.2). Paul even described his 'Jewish achievements' as 'refuse' or 'rubbish' (Philippians 3.8). The Jewish achievements mentioned in the Letter were highly prized by Jewish society and it was certainly offensive to call such prestigious achievements 'refuse'. In this sense, Paul's apparently rude language had not quite left him. We come to understand then that Paul's tone in Galatians was not something he came to regret wholly. All this means that it was when Paul thought the fundamental meaning of the gospel was being threatened that he would not mince words, and sometimes resorted to harsh words in order to get the severity of his point across. His harsh tones were reserved for those he perceived to be 'enemies of the gospel'. This is so because of the importance he gave to the gospel. The one true gospel must not be corrupted: so, even if an angel – i.e. someone supposedly sent by God – were to preach a different gospel, he is to be anathematized.

People who believe strongly in something can sometimes behave this way. We think, for example, of angry protesters against the destruction of our fragile environment. It is good that they feel passionate about a serious problem. People who do not feel strongly about serious problems are not being nice: they are just indifferent or uninformed. But we must also note that as harsh as Paul might be in his tone, he never once resorted to using violence to make people conform. His anger, if it is the right way to put it, was confined only to discussion and debate.

4 Paul and the harmony of humankind

Arising from Paul's fundamental understanding of the gospel as a gospel of God's grace through the faithfulness of Christ (and faith in Christ) is the concept that all human beings are one in Christ. As there is one God, there can be only one family of God. This family cannot be split into different 'classes'. In this family, the virtues are love, forbearance and humility, which are great aids in bringing people together and making them stay together. Such an emphasis is found in both Galatians and Philippians.

In Galatians, this teaching is offered in the context of preventing the Galatians from following Jewish ways, even though these appeared to be supported by the law. Indeed, Paul stood up to Peter because Peter withdrew from having table fellowship with the Gentile believers (Galatians 2.1–14). In Paul's view, all who believe in Christ may sit at table and have fellowship together, regardless of cultural scruples or otherwise. Paul expressed a most profound and astonishing statement in Galatians 3.28, which covers all important distinctions that separate one person from another: racial, social and gender.

The fight for the harmony of the Church that is found in Galatians is also present in Philippians. It was for the sake of getting the church at Philippi to be harmonious (Philippians 2.1–4) that Paul appealed to the example of Christ. In the same passage (Philippians 2.5–11), Paul argues from the standpoint of the divine character, and concludes that service leading to harmony must be the way to go for humankind. What also needs to be noted is that Paul appealed for harmony in Galatians 5.15 and 6.1–5.

Paul's vision for humankind, then, is breathtaking. It is featured prominently in both Letters, spanning many years and expressed in different contexts: combative and friendly. He saw the harmony of humankind as being both *possible and required in Christ*.

5 Paul the pastor

We may risk putting Paul in too good a light – but it is worth it – when we say that beneath his harsh tone was a heart that was full of pastoral love and concern for the people who were under his care. If Paul was angry, it was because he was fighting for their spiritual welfare or the 'truth' of the gospel, upon which people depended for their relationship with God. However, if accusations or slanders were directed against him, he could take them in his stride and even rejoice, as long as Christ was being preached (Philippians 1.15–18).

Good pastors are people who care for others more than they care for themselves. This does not mean all pastors must purposely neglect their own welfare; rather it is to say that they put the welfare of others above theirs. In so doing, they exemplify the character of Christ, the good shepherd (John 10.11–15). In Philippians 2.5–11, Paul presents a picture of Christ that speaks volumes about love: Christ, although having the status of God, did not exploit it or use it to exploit others; instead he humbled himself to serve. Similarly in Galatians 3.13, Christ is described as having been cursed in order that the curse of the law may be neutralized.

Caring for others means standing up for those we have charge over and defending them, especially against evil people and debilitating forces. The story of Oscar Romero is illuminating in this connection. He was a shy man who became the Archbishop of El Salvador. At first he supported the government and had no sympathy for Christian priests who opposed it. But as he watched government soldiers killing very poor people rather than feeding them, he changed his mind. He said to soldiers, 'When you hear the words of a man telling you to kill, remember instead the words of God, "Thou shalt not kill." God's law must prevail.' Friends tried to persuade him to be silent. He said, 'As a shepherd I am obliged by divine law to give my life for those I love.' He was shot through the heart at 6.30 p.m. on 24 March 1980, as he was saying the words of the Mass in a small hospital chapel: 'This is my body which is given for you.' A pastor who is 'benign' and does not speak up against evil may appear 'gentlemanly', but he does not really have a pastor's heart.

6 Conclusion

By viewing Galatians and Philippians together, it shows that there is, surprisingly, much in common between them even though they were written for different occasions and separated by at least a decade. Paul came across as a man of strong convictions, very driven and fiery. But this fire was tempered by love, and surfaced only when there was an urgent need to defend the truth of the gospel and protect the people under his care. It is just possible that he mellowed with age. Even so, his convictions did not waver. We may thus speak of Paul as exhibiting 'consistency and growth'. He was certainly a very consistent person. But this does not mean that he stagnated. Indeed, amid this consistency, he also grew: the convictions remained the same but the fiery energy became better controlled and directed. For Paul we may say that, at the end of a long and hard 'road' of life, we find a man not broken but refined, whose faith in Christ remained intact.

There are also important interlocking themes in the two Letters. This shows that, although many years had elapsed, Paul's central concerns were still consistent. Some critical issues troubled Paul throughout his missionary career. Indeed, some of these are still present today: the harmony of humankind in Christ, and the understanding of the priority of grace over race or works. The European Reformation owed much to the rediscovery of this Pauline emphasis. We have Paul to thank for treating these matters from the standpoint of what God has done in Christ. His writings are truly a legacy for us all.

Galatians

Introduction

The Letter and its writer

The Letter to the Galatians is one of the earliest writings of the New Testament, and, though it is short, it is a very important work. It was written by the apostle Paul, who also wrote many other Letters, which are now collected together in the New Testament. Thirteen have been attributed to him although some scholars debate whether this number should be trimmed down to seven (Romans, 1 Corinthians, 2 Corinthians, Galatians, Philippians, 1 Thessalonians, Philemon). This debate need not detain us here. It is enough to know that there is no dispute over Paul's authorship of the Letter to the Galatians.

Paul's ministry is recorded in the Acts of the Apostles (Acts 9; 11.25–30; 12.25; 13—28). However, we must be careful in our use of the Acts as a guide to Paul's life and teaching. When Luke wrote the Acts, he wanted to tell about the progress of the gospel from Jerusalem to what he called the furthest parts of the earth, meaning Western Europe (see Acts 1.8). Paul played a large part in this, so Luke paid a lot of attention to Paul and his work. But Luke was more interested in the Church as a whole than in the biographies of individual people.

To Luke the important thing about Paul was not so much that he travelled all over the Roman Empire, but that he did so in order to spread the gospel. Luke's account of Paul's travels gives us an impressive and interesting picture of his ministry; the sermons show that this was a ministry of the gospel. They show the gospel as Luke had received it from Paul and the other apostles, but not the particular way in which Paul presented it. The good news has been, and still is, presented in many different forms. However, if we want an accurate account of Paul's presentation we must rely above all on his own writings.

Even so, we must remember that Paul's writings are letters, written in view of particular circumstances. All of them were addressed to people who were already Christians, and some of the Letters, including this one, were to people Paul knew or churches he had already visited. In each case he wrote what the occasion demanded, and we should not expect them to provide a handbook of Christian doctrine, nor try to draw too far-reaching conclusions from what he did not write. For example, Paul said little about Jesus' earthly life, and some people have thought that he did not know much about that, or did not think it very important. But we do not really know how much or little he knew; he could certainly have asked other Christians all he wanted to know. Nor do we know how much Paul told his churches about Jesus' ministry. He may have told them much, but we just do not know. What we do know is that the institution of the Lord's Supper, Jesus' death on the cross, and his resurrection were events which he had to mention in his Letters. In Paul's day, writing was a time-consuming job, and paper was very expensive, so people kept their letters short. Paul's letters are among the longest known from the ancient world, but even he would not have cared to write more than he needed to.

So the Letter to the Galatians was a real letter, written on a particular occasion, to specific people, and in view of particular circumstances. What those circumstances were, we can only find out from the Letter itself, and we shall discuss them as matters arise. But what Paul wrote was always important. He always saw the deeper significance of events and people's reactions to them, and what he wrote is never trivial. In responding to the situation in the Galatian churches, he dug down right to the root of the matter. This Letter is not just an interesting historical document from which we can learn something about a small part of the history of the early Church; it has a lasting significance, and contains much that we need to relate to the context of our own lives and apply in our own churches.

Galatians 1.1–5

Greeting

 Summary

Paul, stressing that he is an apostle, greets the churches of Galatia, conveying to them grace and peace from God the Father and Jesus Christ.

 Notes

1.1. An apostle: The Greek word *apostolos* means 'someone who has been sent' or a 'messenger'. The Gospel writers sometimes used it to mean messengers in a general sense, e.g. in Luke 11.49 and John 13.16. But more often they used it specifically to mean the 12 disciples of Jesus, whom he sent out to preach (Matthew 10.2; Mark 6.30; Luke 6.13; 17.5; 22.14; 24.10). In the Acts of the Apostles Luke nearly always uses the word only for the Twelve (the 12 apostles named as such in the Gospels, minus Judas Iscariot, and plus Matthias: Acts 1.2, 26; 2.37, 42, 43, 4.33, etc.); but in Acts 14.4 he also refers to Paul and Barnabas as apostles. Both in the Acts and in this Letter it is stressed that an apostle must have been appointed by Christ.

Neither by human commission nor from human authorities The Greek text simply reads 'neither from humans nor through humans'. The NRSV translation makes clear Paul's intention. Paul emphasizes the divine origin of his calling to be an apostle. It came from Jesus Christ directly and did not depend on human initiative or power.

1.2. And all the members of God's family: Paul was not working alone, but in fellowship with the Church and in close co-operation with some fellow-preachers.

The churches in Galatia *Galatai*, 'Galatians', is the Greek name for Celts, and Galatia was called after three Celtic tribes who had settled in the area round Ancyra (present-day Ankara in Turkey) in the third century BC. But the Roman province of Galatia was much larger than the area inhabited by the Galatians themselves, and its southern half was peopled largely by Phrygians, Lycaonians and Pisidians. Scholars are divided on the question whether Paul wrote this letter to churches in northern Galatia, or to

11

those in southern Galatia mentioned in Acts 13—14, that is to say, Pisidian Antioch, Iconium, Lystra and Derbe (refer to the map on p. xix). On the one hand, the people in southern Galatia were not actually Galatians, so it may seem strange for Paul to have addressed them by that name (3.1). However, we should note that in Paul's time people were also addressed according to the Roman provinces to which they belonged. On the other hand, we do not know that Paul ever visited northern Galatia; some people think that Acts 16.6 refers to northern Galatia, but 'the region of Phrygia and Galatia' probably means the border area between the two provinces, that is to say, the region of Pisidian Antioch. On the whole it seems more likely that this letter was addressed to the churches mentioned in Acts 13—14. Paul may have thought it easier to call them 'the churches in Galatia' and their members 'Galatians', rather than use such a clumsy expression as 'O foolish Phrygians, Lycaonians and Pisidians' (3.1).

1.3. Grace to you: Paul uses the Greek word *charis*, meaning 'grace', instead of the usual Greek greeting, *chaire*, which means 'be happy'. He wished them God's favour, which does give happiness, but is much more.

And peace This harks back to the Jewish greeting, *shalom*. It sounds rather solemn in English, and may have been unusual in Greek, but to Paul it was no more solemn than the equivalent *salaam* or *salama* is in many countries today. However, when Jesus greeted his disciples with 'Peace' (John 20.21, 26), he wanted to say more than 'Good evening', and really did give them his peace. So Paul too wanted to convey the full meaning of God's peace, which is based on the security which comes from being in the right relationship with God and our fellow human beings (see Special note I).

From God our Father and the Lord Jesus Christ The apostolic greeting does not come from Paul and his companions, but from God. Paul was an apostle, and therefore a person under orders, like a messenger: unimportant in his own right, but authorized to speak and to act in God's name.

1.4. Who gave himself for our sins: Paul stresses that Jesus offered himself of his own free will (see John 14.30–31: 'the ruler of this world ... has no power over me; but I do as the Father has commanded me'). He is also hinting at what the true gospel is so as to prepare the readers for the important discussion later.

The present evil age The biblical writers did not think in terms of the contrast between time and eternity, but of the contrast between the present 'evil' age and the 'age to come', when God will not only *be* King, but *be seen* to be King. The age to come was expected to be in the future; but several New Testament writers stress in various ways that those who belong to Christ have already been delivered from the present evil age.

Christians already belong to the age to come. They are citizens of the New Jerusalem (Galatians 4.26; Philippians 3.20). The kingdom of God is among them (Luke 17.21).

 ## Interpretation

Every nation has its own particular way of beginning and ending a letter. The French are probably the shortest in their beginnings: in a formal letter they just write *Monsieur*, 'Sir', or *Madame*, 'Madam'. The Chinese and English write, 'Dear So-and-so', even if they do not know the person to whom they are writing. Arabs begin with a long string of greetings. Iranians apologize for presuming to write at all. In Paul's world it was the custom to begin with the name of the writer, followed by the name of the addressee, and a wish of 'joy' or 'happiness', so the normal beginning of this letter would have been, 'Paul to the churches in Galatia, joy'. Paul did not alter this pattern, but he did alter the words, for he had more to give than merely a wish for the Galatians' happiness.

Paul also wished to stress first of all that he was an apostle, duly appointed by God the Father and Jesus Christ as the others had been. Even though Paul had not followed Jesus during his ministry on earth, Jesus himself had called him to be an apostle, and had done so directly. No one else was involved in Paul's apostolate. So he was not a representative of the earlier apostles, nor their 'successor'; and because he had been appointed and commissioned by Christ, he had the same authority as the other apostles.

Paul had good reason to state that God raised Jesus Christ from the dead (v. 1): it was the risen Lord himself who had appeared to him on the road to Damascus (see Acts 9.1–9). So if anyone in the Galatian churches was questioning his apostolate, they were criticizing what Christ had done to him.

The churches in Galatia had been founded by Paul. He had worked there, some people had gladly accepted the gospel he brought, and a number of young churches had come into being. When we read the Acts of the Apostles, it may seem surprising that Paul and his companions seem to have worked in each town for only a short time, appointed some people to lead the congregations, and then left them as young but independent churches. We should not assume that in most cases all this took only a few weeks, but certainly the foundation of many early churches took only a few years at the very most.

These young churches were not left entirely to themselves. There was regular coming and going between the churches, and between them and the mother church in Jerusalem. The young churches had the advantage of regular contact with other churches. Moreover, missionaries kept in touch with the churches they had founded. Paul's Letters show how much he cared for the people to whom he had preached the gospel. If there were any problems in any of those churches, he would write to them, or even visit them again. But he seems to have interfered only when it was really necessary. He did regard the members of those churches as his spiritual 'children', but as grown-up children (see note on Galatians 4.19). So Paul allowed them to get on with their Christian lives, and to make their own decisions.

However, events in the Galatian churches had led to a situation in which Paul could not continue to let them carry on alone. These churches had been visited by other so-called Christian preachers who had caused a great deal of confusion. They seem to have been convinced that they alone knew the whole truth, and they did not approve of Paul's presentation of the gospel. Their preaching probably ran more or less on these lines: 'We know that Paul preached the gospel to you, and you ought to be grateful to him. But it is only fair to tell you that he has not told you the whole truth. For one thing, he does not know the whole truth, for he never followed Jesus when he walked on earth. Moreover, he has no authority to preach the gospel, for he is not an apostle, and he was not sent by the apostles. Also, he has tried to make things easy for you, by leaving out some awkward truths, and that is not good enough. Now we will tell you the whole truth ...'

This is what made it necessary for Paul, right at the beginning of his letter, to stress that he had been commissioned directly by Christ, without any intermediary.

Paul's greeting to the Galatians was thus more than just a pious wish. As a representative of Christ, he had something to offer. He was in a position, not merely to *wish* them, but to *offer* them 'grace and peace from God our Father and the Lord Jesus Christ'. A person who is commissioned to carry the good news of Christ can speak and act with authority. Paul does not explain this in detail, but the authority implied is the same as that which is described more fully in John 20.23a: 'If you forgive the sins of any, they are forgiven them.' The offer, of God's grace in the one case, of the forgiveness of sins in the other, is a genuine offer from God, and can be accepted.

Paul ended his greeting by praising God.

 # STUDY SUGGESTIONS

Word study

1 (a) What is the exact meaning of the word 'apostle'?

   (b) In what two ways was it chiefly used by writers in the NT?

2 (a) What is the meaning of the Hebrew word *shalom*?

   (b) How should we normally translate it into English?

Review of content

3 In what way and for what reason did Paul alter the usual way of beginning a letter in Greek, when he wrote to the churches?

4 Why was Paul particularly anxious to establish his authority as an apostle?

5 What sort of relationships were there between the various young churches in Paul's time, and what was their relationship with their 'missionaries'?

Bible study

6 Read the following passages, and say in each case whether the writer was referring to **(a)** messengers generally, or **(b)** one or other or all of the 12 apostles whom Jesus appointed to preach and heal.

(i) Luke 6.13; **(ii)** Luke 11.49; **(iii)** Acts 1.26; **(iv)** Acts 14.14; **(v)** John 13.16; **(vi)** Revelation 2.2; **(vii)** Revelation 21.14.

Discussion and application

7 Paul's opening words clearly emphasize the authority of his words for the Galatians. What does this mean for us who read his words today?

8 Some Christian ministers and missionaries today are appointed and authorized by the central organization of the church or denomination to which they belong; some by the state; and some by the individual congregation which they serve.

(a) By which method are ministers and missionaries appointed and authorized in your own church, and what do you see as the advantages and disadvantages compared with other methods?

(b) How far do you think it is important for a minister to have such authority? In what circumstances, if any, can a person 'minister' without such authority? Give reasons for your answers.

9 What did Paul mean by the phrase 'the present evil age'? In what way, if any, do you think that the 'present age' is any better or worse today than in Paul's time?

Galatians 1.6–10

Paul's reason for writing

 Summary

Astonished that the Galatians were attracted so quickly to a different 'gospel', Paul insists there is no other gospel than that which he has already preached to them.

 Notes

1.6. I am astonished: This is rather different from what Paul usually wrote after his greetings: e.g. 'I thank my God' (Romans 1.8; Philippians 1.3; Philemon 4), or similar words of thanks (1 Corinthians 1.4; 1 Thessalonians 1.2; 2 Thessalonians 1.3), or a word of praise to God (2 Corinthians 1.3).

The one who called you That is to say, God. In using the verb 'call', Paul always meant that it is God who calls.

1.6–7. A different gospel – not that there is another gospel: Paul deliberately distinguishes between the two words, 'different' and 'another', to emphasize that what the Galatians were tempted to accept was not the actual gospel. It was something entirely different. The word 'gospel' comes from the Greek *euangelion* and means basically 'good news'. It was used in the early Christian communities to sum up the message they heard and the new life they experienced in Christ Jesus. It has its roots in Isaiah, where it is used to refer to God's rescue of his people from exile and his victory over evil (see e.g. Isaiah 52.7; 61.1). In this sense, the word spoke of the fulfilment of Old Testament prophecy. Furthermore, it was also used to counter the propaganda of the Roman Empire. The empire used the word for the birthday and accession of the emperor, and proclaimed these events to be good news for the whole world. The early Christians claimed otherwise: 'It is only in Jesus Christ that the true good news may be found.' All this being the case, it is clear that agreement over what the gospel was became very important in the early Christian communities. What the 'another gospel' that Paul accuses his opponents of preaching is will be made clear in the later chapters of Galatians.

Confusing you The Greek word *tarassō*, taken by the NRSV to mean 'to confuse', actually means to 'disturb' or 'toss about' as by the waves of the sea. Paul thinks of these people as agitators or troublemakers.

To pervert The Greek word means 'to change into its opposite'. The opposite of good news is bad news.

1.8, 9. Accursed: The Greek word *anathema* means 'something given to a god'. Outside the Bible this usually means a gift to a temple in fulfilment of a vow, but the translators of the Old Testament into Greek used it for something, or someone, that had been cast out of the community and left to God's judgement. The REB translates it appropriately as 'Let him be banned'.

1.10. Still pleasing people: Before his conversion Paul had been 'pleasing' the Jewish authorities by persecuting the Church, but now that he was a servant of Christ he only wanted to please God (see Acts 8.1b–3; 9.1–2).

 ## Interpretation

Paul usually thanked God for the faith and life of his readers, but in this case he could only express his amazement and alarm at the fickleness of the Galatian Christians. The very strong words which Paul used here show that he considered the matter was extremely serious.

The preachers who had caused the trouble in Galatia seem to have been convinced that they had the whole truth, and that anyone who disagreed with them was distorting the truth, or not telling the whole truth. We shall see later that they also believed they had the backing of tradition and the Old Testament. So they saw it as their first duty to convert other Christians to their particular sort of Christianity. Their chief aim was, not to convert unbelievers to the Christian faith, but to convert Christians to their particular point of view, and to their way of life.

This sort of thing has always been happening in the Church. People who have put their trust in Jesus, but are not able to put their beliefs into clear words, can be very disturbed if somebody tells them that they are all wrong in their beliefs. It is no secret that Christians differ in some of their beliefs, and in the ways in which they conduct their worship and their lives. This was already happening in Paul's time. These differences are serious, and we should discuss them, and try to reach an agreement about them. But we also have to accept that we know imperfectly, and only in part (see 1 Corinthians 13.9, 12), so maybe we shall continue to differ in our beliefs, our worship, and our ways of life, and must seek to achieve Christian unity in spite of our differences.

However, the belief that one has the whole truth, and that everybody else is wrong, is a great danger to the unity of the Church. It has, in fact, led to deep divisions among Christians. Christians who believed that they alone had the whole truth have often persecuted other Christians with whom they did not agree. The doctrinal debates during the Reformation are a sad testimony to this.

So the activity of these preachers in Galatia was harmful, quite apart from the question of what they actually preached. But the aggressive words with which Paul attacked his Galatian opponents show that he thought that in this case there was more at stake than a difference of opinion. Paul himself had very precise views on many matters of faith and life. His other Letters show that he was used to controversy, and also that he could use fairly strong language to express his views and to counter his opponents. But nowhere else in his writings do we find such fierce language as in this Letter. In his view the Galatians had been led astray, not by a different interpretation of the gospel, but by something that was not a gospel at all. His opponents were preaching the very opposite of the gospel, not good news, but bad news, and the Galatians were tempted to accept this bad news! This could only mean that they were beginning to turn away from God. But no one who preaches such bad news must be accepted in the Church. Even if Paul himself, or an angel from heaven, brought a message contrary to the gospel of Jesus Christ, he must be cast out of the Church, and left to God's judgement.

Paul did not expect the Galatians to like him for writing such strong words. But he was not trying to make himself popular by speaking soft words, and certainly not by misleading them. Nor was he trying to give them what they wanted by telling them what they wished to hear. He was a servant of Christ, so he had to act and speak as his Master told him.

 ## STUDY SUGGESTIONS

Word study

1 Which *three* of the following words are nearest in meaning to 'pervert' as used in v. 7?

   convert purvey distort revise deform misteach reform

2 **(a)** What meaning did the translators of the Old Testament into Greek give to the word which is translated as 'accursed' in the NRSV (vv. 8–9)?

   (b) Write a short sentence to show its meaning as used by Paul in those verses. (You may find it helpful to look, if you can, at the way the word is translated in other modern versions of the Bible.)

3 **(a)** What did 'gospel' mean to early Christians?

   (b) In what sense may we understand it as being used to counter imperial propaganda?

Review of content

4 What was the chief aim of the preachers who had been causing the Galatians to disbelieve Paul's teaching?

5 Paul accused the Galatians of 'turning to a different gospel … contrary to what we proclaimed to you'. But he also said 'not that there is another gospel'. If the preaching of Paul's opponents was not 'another gospel', what was it?

Bible study

6 **(a)** What is the chief difference between what Paul wrote after his greeting to the Galatians (v. 6), and what he usually wrote after his greetings in letters to other churches, e.g. in Romans 1.8; 1 Corinthians 1.4; Philippians 1.3; 1 Thessalonians 1.2; 2 Thessalonians 1.3?

   (b) How would a present-day preacher or teacher be likely to start a letter to a congregation he had visited?

Discussion and application

7 Describe what happens when Christians who believe that they alone have the whole truth try to convert other Christians to their ideas and way of life. How is such preaching likely to affect (a) individual Christians, and (b) congregations or other groups of Christians?

8 Paul said that the Galatians should treat as 'accursed' anyone whose preaching was 'contrary' to what he had taught them. Today there are deep divisions between the churches, but some Christians say 'We all preach the same gospel; disagreements over religion are a waste of time, we should live and let live.' How far do you agree with this view? Give your reasons.

Galatians 1.11–24

How Paul became an apostle

 Summary

Paul recounts how the gospel came to him: directly from Christ and independent of any human contribution, including the prominent apostles.

 Notes

1.12. I received it through a revelation: That is, through a *direct* revelation in which Jesus himself showed Paul the truth of the gospel: no other human being was involved in it. Paul is probably referring to the Damascus Road experience (see Acts 9.3–6).

1.13. I was violently persecuting the church of God: This accords with the picture given by Luke, e.g. in Acts 9.1.

Life in Judaism See Acts 22.3. The word 'Judaism' occurs only twice in the New Testament and both occurrences are found in Galatians 1.13–14. This word came into currency only in the second century BC, during the period when Israel had very turbulent relations with her Gentile rulers because of the pressure to adopt Greek customs and ways (the Maccabean revolt). Based on that context, we may understand the word as singling out the Jews who were faithful to their ancestral traditions over against the Jews who were not. Paul is emphasizing his distinctive zeal for his ancestral traditions, especially the kind that separated the Jews from the Gentiles. He is also preparing his reader for the discussion to come by hinting at what precisely the problem is.

1.16. Reveal his Son to me: The Greek actually says 'reveal his Son *in* me'. Paul writes in this way probably because he wants to stress the personal transformation that took place when he met Jesus Christ on the road to Damascus. What he received was not just 'head knowledge'.

Proclaim him among the Gentiles The word 'Gentiles' means 'nations'. Used in biblical passages, it almost always means 'non-Jews'. Paul understands his encounter with Jesus Christ also as a call to proclaim the gospel to the nations.

1.17. Arabia: This word in Paul's day could refer to anywhere east and south of Syria and Palestine, including also the Sinai peninsula. The mention of 'Damascus' in the same verse may indicate that Paul is referring to the Nabatean kingdom, located immediately to the south of Damascus. It is quite probable that Paul was engaged in evangelizing activity while being there, which he refers to in 2 Corinthians 11.32.

1.18. After three years: Biblical references to time are difficult to interpret, because in those days people counted inclusively, that is to say, they included both the beginning and the end. For example, any period that started in the year 800, and ended in the year 802, would be called 'three years'. So, this could mean the 366 days from 31 December 800 till 1 January 802, or the 1094 days from 1 January 800 till 31 December 802, or anything in between. Paul's information therefore does not give us precise dates for these events.

Cephas That is, Simon Peter. In Aramaic (the everyday language of Palestine at that time) *kefa* means a 'rock'; this was the new name which Jesus gave to Simon (John 1.42). Most New Testament writers translated the name into Greek as *Petros*, but Paul usually called him 'Cephas' (except in 2.7).

1.19. James the Lord's brother: This James had not been a disciple during Jesus' ministry (see Mark 6.3; Matthew 13.55), but became a disciple after Jesus' resurrection (1 Corinthians 15.7), and soon became a leading figure in the Jerusalem church (Galatians 2.9; Acts 12.17). When Peter left Jerusalem, James became the leader of the church there (Acts 15.13; 21.18).

1.21. The regions of Syria and Cilicia: This covers a wide area, including both Tarsus and Antioch (see Acts 11.25–26).

 Interpretation

Paul's purpose in writing this section was to give evidence for the claim he had made in v. 1, that Christ himself had made him an apostle. So he did not give a detailed account of his conversion such as we find in the Acts of the Apostles (Acts 9.1–19; 22.3–16; 26.9–18). Instead he stressed that both his conversion and his call to the ministry were due to God's grace. It was not his choice, but God's choice that he should be an apostle to the Gentiles.

His words also had another purpose. His opponents insisted on the Jewishness of the Christian faith, and the importance of certain commandments of the Jewish law. Paul could beat them at their own game. He was himself a Jew, brought up in the Jewish faith, and he knew more about the Jewish law than his opponents. Indeed, he was fully prepared to defend Jewish distinctives. Hence, his becoming a Christian and an apostle was totally unexpected: God had chosen him, even before he was born (v. 15). We must not exaggerate this, as if Paul had no decision to make at all: he had to *respond* to God's calling. But the deciding factor was God's decision (see also John 15.16). And Paul had received the gospel directly from Christ through a revelation, not through any human being.

When Paul wrote, 'I did not confer with any human being' (v. 16), he did not mean that he never spoke to any other Christians about the Christian faith. Of course he did. But he did not have to ask them to confirm his authority as an apostle, for this was something Christ had already given him, with a special commission to the Gentiles.

So he did not hurry to meet the other apostles after his conversion. He did not go up to Jerusalem until some years later, when he met Peter and John. The church in Jerusalem had neither called Paul, nor ordained him. All that the churches in Judea did was to take note of what God had done, to appreciate that he was now preaching the faith that he had previously tried to destroy, and to praise God because of him.

 ## STUDY SUGGESTIONS

Word study

1 (a) How was the term 'Judaism' understood in the first century?

   (b) How would this shed light on the issue that Paul was facing in the churches in Galatia?

Review of content

2 (a) What was Paul's chief purpose in writing this passage?

   (b) What did he write in order to achieve that purpose?

3 Why did Paul remind the Galatians that he had been 'advanced in Judaism' and 'zealous' for Jewish traditions (v. 14)?

4 Why did Paul emphasize:

   (a) that after his conversion he 'went away into Arabia';

   (b) that he did not meet any of the other apostles until three years later, and then only Peter and James;

   (c) that the churches in Judea had 'glorified God' because of him?

Bible study

5 Read Acts 9.1–22, and then say:

(a) How did Paul know that what had happened to him on the road to Damascus was 'a revelation of Jesus Christ' (v. 12)?

(b) What was the 'gospel' which came to Paul through that revelation?

6 Compare Galatians 1.15–24 with Acts 9.19b–31. How do you account for the differences between the two descriptions of Paul's activity following his conversion? How important do you consider those differences? Give your reasons.

Discussion and application

7 (a) Do you think that Paul was chiefly concerned to defend his own authority as a person against the accusations of his opponents, or the authority of the gospel he preached, as opposed to their preaching? Give reasons for your answer.

(b) What would be your own reaction if someone questioned your 'authority' to speak of the gospel as you do?

Special note A
Grace

The gospel is the message of God's grace. This is therefore an important word in the Christian vocabulary, and much has been said and written about it. But if we want to understand what Paul meant by 'grace', we must turn to the Old Testament, where 'grace' is expressed chiefly by two Hebrew words.

The first of these, *hen*, is translated in various ways, but the phrase 'to find favour in someone's sight' shows its meaning most clearly. This phrase was used in petitioning a ruler or overseer to grant some request, as when Joab was grateful that he had 'found favour' in King David's sight (2 Samuel 14.22; see also Esther 8.5). It always assumed inequality between the person who asked and the person who granted the favour. It was not given automatically, but required an act of condescension.

Some people today regard such subservience on the one hand and condescension on the other hand as 'paternalism', and argue for or against it. We could point to many situations in the modern world where all the power is on one side, and people hope for 'favour' from 'top management', or the boss or foreman, in business or industrial enterprises. And whatever we think about inequalities between humans, there can be no doubt about the absolute distinction between God and us. We are sinners, who have offended him. The amazing thing about God's grace is that he should know and love and be concerned about us at all.

Besides this condescension, there is also an element of kindly humour in the word *hen*. In Amsterdam, where the local speech contains Hebrew words, many people use the word only for that sense of humour which enables them to smile at their own troubles. It suggests that people who take God seriously should beware of being too serious about themselves. We should not actually translate *hen* by the word 'humour', but in this sense it reminds us that God bestows his grace with a smile, and that those who enjoy his favour can see themselves in a sunny light. So when Abraham 'found favour' with God, and Sarah at last bore him a son, they very properly called the boy 'Isaac', meaning 'laughter' (Genesis 17.19–20; 18.1–5).

The second word is *hesed*, which the NRSV usually (but not always) translates by 'steadfast love'. *Hesed* means a loyalty, love and kindness that is undeserved, and that remains constant and steadfast, whatever happens. When it is used of human beings, it often means an act of kindness which we might not have expected, or a good deed which most people would not regard as a duty. God wants people to practise *hesed* (Micah 6.8). The action of the Good Samaritan was an act of mercy (Luke 10.37).

The word *hesed* contains an element of surprise, and when it is used of God, it stresses that his mercy is *amazing* grace. We have offended against his love, and keep on offending him. Yet he continues to care for us and surround us with his love. In the Psalms the singers never cease to be amazed at God's steadfast love.

The two words *hen* and *hesed* are never used as if they meant exactly the same, but they both emphasize that God's unfailing goodness is not something he owes us: he grants us his grace entirely of his own free will.

The Greek word *charis*, which Paul used for the grace of God, means 'that which pleases', but in New Testament times it was used for the 'favour' granted by a ruler to his subjects. Like *hesed*, it emphasizes that God's kindness is undeserved and unexpected. In Galatians 1.15 Paul makes it clear that he had not deserved his calling to be an apostle, and in Romans 3.24 he stressed that God's goodness is not a reward for what people have done.

However, God's grace is not merely one of his attributes: it is God himself making his undeserved and unfailing love known to his people, a love that springs entirely from him.

Galatians 2.1–10

Paul's agreement with the Jerusalem apostles

 Summary

Paul describes another visit to Jerusalem. The leaders there did not compel Titus – a Gentile Christian who was with him – to be circumcised, and acknowledged that Paul had been called to be an apostle to the Gentiles.

Notes

2.1. After fourteen years: This is not a precise figure, see note on Galatians 1.18. Moreover, Paul does not say whether he is reckoning from his conversion or from his return to Syria and Cilicia.

I went up again to Jerusalem Such a statement would not occasion much discussion if not for the scholarly interest in comparing Luke's account of Paul's career with Paul's own testimony. So, if we want to harmonize Luke with Paul, which event is Paul referring to in this verse? There are two possibilities. The first is to think of the 'famine visit' recorded in Acts 11.27–30. This will then mean that Paul's conflict with the troublemakers took place before the Jerusalem Council of Acts 15. The second is that this visit of Paul is the same as the one recorded in Acts 15, i.e. the Jerusalem Council. The majority of commentators favour this. The implication of this is that the issue discussed at that council was not fully resolved as there were some Christians who did not follow the directives that were agreed upon.

Barnabas was a Cypriot Jew, who had joined the church in Jerusalem, where he became noted for his generosity (Acts 4.36–37). According to Luke he introduced Paul to the earlier apostles (Acts 9.27). Later the Jerusalem church sent him to Antioch in Syria, to see what was happening in the church there, where so many members were Gentile Christians (Acts 11.19–26). He seems to have approved of what he found there (Galatians 2.13). While at Antioch, he sent for Paul (Acts 11.25), and afterwards he went with Paul and John Mark on a mission to his native land of Cyprus (Acts 13.1–12). He also accompanied Paul during the mission to southern Galatia (Acts 13.13—14.28), but they quarrelled over whether John Mark should continue to accompany them, and parted before their next missionary journeys (Acts 15.36–40). However, they seem to have made up and worked together again later (see 1 Corinthians 9.6; Philemon 24).

Titus was probably known to Paul's readers. He is not mentioned in the Acts of the Apostles, and scholars differ as to whether this was the Titus to whom the letter of that name was addressed.

2.2. In response to a revelation: It is difficult to be precise about what this revelation was because the information is scanty. The scholars who believe that Galatians 2.1-10 does not refer to the same event as recorded in Acts 15 will think that the revelation here refers to the prophecy of famine in the Roman world in Acts 11.27–30. Even though we do not know the precise event Paul is referring to, his point is clear. He went to Jerusalem in obedience to divine direction and not human ideas. This stresses further Paul's independence of the Jerusalem apostles.

Private meeting There was no meeting with the church as a body.

To make sure that I was not running, or had not run, in vain Paul had received his commission from Christ himself, so he did not need anybody's approval. But he wanted to come to an arrangement with the other apostles, so that they would not be in each other's way or hinder each other's work.

2.3. Titus ... though he was a Greek: Paul actually wrote, 'Titus ... being a Greek' (AV), which could mean either 'though ...' or 'because he was a Greek'. A 'Greek' here means a Gentile, i.e. anyone who is not a Jew.

Was not compelled to be circumcised Many people think that this shows that Paul could not have urged Timothy to be circumcised as stated in Acts 16.3. But the two cases were different. Timothy's mother was a Jewess, so he was already a Jew (according to the rabbis everyone born from a Jewish mother is a Jew, no matter who the father is). The circumcision of Timothy would have shown that a Jew who became a Christian still remained a Jew. But Titus was not a Jew, and did not have to become one in order to be a Christian. This is the first time the word 'circumcision' is used in the Letter and it prepares the reader for the very important issue Paul wants to discuss and defuse. Male circumcision was a key indicator of Jewish identity. It was commanded in Genesis 17 for all Abraham's male children to observe. It was thus understood as the sign of the covenant between God and Israel. Its importance was heightened in the Maccabean crisis of the second century BC, when Antiochus IV banned circumcision for all his Jewish subjects. The Old Testament support for circumcision's significance would be one challenge for Paul in his attempt to nullify the divisive effect of the teaching of his opponents. Not surprisingly Galatians 3 is devoted to a discussion of some key scriptural passages.

2.4. But because of: This sentence does not run very well in Greek, and is awkward in English. The REB translation shows more clearly what Paul means: 'That course was urged only as a concession to certain sham Christians, intruders who had sneaked in to spy on the liberty we enjoy in the fellowship of Christ Jesus' (REB). Apparently, some people whom Paul calls 'false believers' have been sent furtively to observe what was going on in the church at Antioch. Verse 12 suggests that these people have been sent by James or the Jewish authorities in the church at Jerusalem.

That they might enslave us Paul was implying that to make Gentile Christians keep the Jewish law – especially the regulations that made Jews distinctive such as food laws and ceremonies – would be the same as making slaves of them, instead of setting them free.

2.6. God shows no partiality: Paul meant that the grace which God had shown to the other apostles was no greater than the grace he had shown to Paul himself.

2.7. Gospel for the uncircumcised … gospel for the circumcised: That is, the gospel proclamation to the Gentiles, the uncircumcised, and the gospel proclamation to the Jews, the circumcised. Such an expression indicates how important circumcision was as an identity indicator to Jews of Paul's day.

2.9. Pillars: That is, people in responsible and important positions who are honoured and respected by their fellows. Paul is referring particularly to James, Peter and John.

The right hand of fellowship This is a pledge of friendship. This custom existed among both Jews and Greeks, just as it still does in many countries today.

2.10. Remember the poor: The church in Jerusalem had many poor members, and needed the support of wealthier Christians (see Acts 11.29; 2 Corinthians 8—9).

 Interpretation

Having established that Jesus himself had called him to be an apostle, Paul now makes it clear that the other apostles had accepted him as their equal, and had agreed with him on the way in which he conducted his ministry. In a private discussion with the leading apostles, James, Peter and John, it had been agreed:

1 That Titus need not be circumcised. This was a very significant decision, for it meant that Gentiles who became Christians remained Gentiles. This implied that they were not expected to observe the law

of Moses, especially the regulations that made Jews outwardly distinctive. In this the apostles simply followed the views of the rabbis: the law was God's special gift to Israel. Gentiles also ought to do God's will, but God's will for them was expressed in the commandments given to Noah (Genesis 9.4–7).

2 That Paul and the others would each work in their own mission field, and they would not interfere with each other. Peter and his friends would work among Jewish communities, and Paul and his companions would work in Gentile territories. Each would be free to follow his own practice.

3 That the fellowship between the various churches would be maintained, and the Gentile churches should give support to the poor in Jerusalem.

There is some question as to the precise occasion when Paul reached this agreement with the Jerusalem apostles. Many scholars believe that Paul is here referring to the meeting recorded in Acts 15. There are great differences between the two accounts, but neither Paul nor Luke was giving a detailed account, and Luke allowed himself considerable freedom when writing Acts. If the two accounts refer to the same event, we must accept that Paul's is the more accurate.

The chief reason for thinking that Paul and Luke are referring to the same meeting is that the decisions made are the same. All that Luke did extra was to explain the implications.

But there are also reasons for thinking that Paul may *not* be referring to the same meeting as Luke. The participants are not the same. According to Paul, he and Barnabas and Titus met James, Peter and John privately. Peter was clearly still in Jerusalem. But in Luke's account Peter had already left Jerusalem (Acts 12.19), and only came to support Paul and his helpers. Moreover, the decisions were taken by the whole church, not by the leaders only at a private meeting.

Though we must allow for the possibility that, when Luke wrote, some of the details may not have been remembered accurately, we must also point out that Luke mentions an earlier visit by Paul and Barnabas to Jerusalem (Acts 11.30; 12.25). He does not say much about this visit, but he does mention that they brought John Mark with them (Acts 12.25), who shortly afterwards accompanied them on their mission to Cyprus (Acts 13.1–12). It seems reasonable to assume that they brought him for that very purpose and, if that is so, it would have been very strange if they had not discussed their plans with the other apostles. This visit seems to have been the ideal opportunity for the sort of agreement mentioned in Galatians 2.1–10.

However, we must not overrate the importance of such questions, and forget the chief points which Paul wanted to make:

- It was important for the Galatians to know that the Jerusalem apostles had accepted that Christ himself had called Paul, who was thus their equal in the sight of God, because that refuted his opponents' attacks on his authority.

● It was equally important that the apostles had agreed that a Gentile Christian was not a Jew, for that counteracted the claim that Christians must obey the Jewish law, or at least such commandments as Paul's opponents thought necessary. His opponents were acting against the policy of the mother church in Jerusalem, and, worse, against the will of Christ.

The agreement clearly left some important questions unanswered. The Christian life must be lived within the community of the Church, and this cannot very well be done without some rules. So the Church did gradually adopt some rules for the conduct of the members' lives, for the conduct of its worship, and for its organization. Some of these rules were derived from the law of Moses, such as the Ten Commandments (Exodus 20.2–17); some from the teaching of Jesus, such as practices about marriage and divorce (Mark 10.1–12; Matthew 5.31–32); others again from the practice of the apostles, such as the way in which to celebrate the Eucharist (1 Corinthians 11.23–26). Differences between the churches about the way in which they do these things arise very often from different interpretations of what we read in the Bible.

Paul was soon to discover that the agreement could be interpreted in more than one way. This also led him to concern himself with a much deeper question: what actually is the validity of the law?

 # STUDY SUGGESTIONS

Word study

1 In the New Testament, a 'Greek' does not necessarily mean someone belonging to the Greek nation. What else can it mean?

2 What did Paul mean by the word 'enslave' in Galatians 2.4?

Review of content

3 Although Paul's authority was not dependent on the Jerusalem apostles, he did want to come to an agreement with them. Why did he think this necessary?

4 How does Jewish teaching distinguish between those who are Jews and those who are not?

5 Briefly summarize the agreement reached at the meeting of Paul with the leading apostles in Jerusalem, as regards:

(a) the validity of the Jewish law for Gentiles, and

(b) the division of missionary work as between Paul and Barnabas on the one hand, and Peter and the other apostles on the other hand.

Bible study

6 What is the connection between Galatians 2.10 and Acts 11.29; 1 Corinthians 16.1–4 and 2 Corinthians 8—9?

Discussion and application

7 Paul wanted to come to an agreement with the other apostles. Find out some of the ways in which churches and Christian groups in your country 'come to an agreement' when there are differences either within or between them. In what circumstances do they give each other 'the right hand of friendship'?

8 'False believers secretly brought in … that they might enslave us' (Galatians 2.4). Imagine that you are one of Paul's opponents, and write a letter to tell the Galatians why you believe Paul's teaching was wrong, and what you think they should think and do instead.

Galatians 2.11–21

Conflict between Peter and Paul

 Summary

Paul describes how he stood up to Peter because the latter stopped eating with Gentile Christians when some people from Jerusalem came. Paul explains why Peter was wrong: justification comes to both Jews and Gentiles not by works of the law, but through the 'faith of Jesus Christ'.

 Notes

2.11. Antioch: Antioch in Syria (now Antakya in southern Turkey) was one of the largest cities of the Roman Empire. It had a large Jewish community, and became an important centre of the Christian Church (Acts 11.19–26). It must not be confused with other cities of the same name, such as Pisidian Antioch (Acts 13.14).

2.12. Certain people came from James: See note on Galatians 1.19. Who these people were is not clear. Most scholars think they are not to be identified with Paul's opponents, mentioned in 2.4–5. James was well-known for his Jewish piety and he would have strictly obeyed the Mosaic law. Perhaps James sent some people either to investigate or to advocate caution.

Eat with the Gentiles In many ancient societies a shared meal was a demonstration of acceptance and fellowship. However, between Jews and Gentiles, even if both parties were Christians, this could be a problem because Jewish meals were governed by the Mosaic food laws. The food provided by Gentiles would not have been prepared according to these rules and so it would have been regarded as 'unclean' by Jews. It might even include such forbidden meats as pork. If Jewish and Gentile Christians could not sit at the same table and share a meal, it would signify a breakdown in fellowship. All this indicates why this became such a problem at Antioch.

The circumcision faction Paul actually wrote, 'those of the circumcision' (see AV). The NRSV makes Paul's meaning clear by referring not to every

Jew, but only to those Jewish Christians who wanted to impose circumcision on the Gentile believers in the Galatian churches.

2.13. Hypocrisy: The Greek word *hypokrisis* means basically 'play-acting', i.e. referring to people who were pretending to be what they were not. To Paul, what took place at Antioch was an unfortunate 'play' or charade, where truth was suppressed.

2.14. They were not acting consistently: Most English translators interpret Paul's Greek expression, *ouk orthopodousin*, as meaning, 'not walking in a straight line'. As no Greek writer had used the word before, it is difficult to know what it means. *Orthopous* means 'standing upright', so Paul may have meant that they were not walking uprightly (see AV), but limping, and this makes more sense. They were limping on two unequal ideas (see 1 Kings 18.21).

2.15. Not Gentile sinners: This seems to imply that Peter and Paul continued to observe the Mosaic law in so far as this did not interfere with the Christian fellowship. Paul was not opposed to the law, but to what he regarded as a wrong use of the law.

2.16. Justified: see Special note C.

By works … through faith Paul used two different prepositions: *by* works, *through* faith. *By* refers to the cause: those who believe that they are justified by works of law think that their deeds make them acceptable to God. *Through* refers to the means: those who believe that they are justified *through* faith believe that God has already accepted them; their faith is the means by which they receive the gift: 'for by grace you have been saved through faith, and this is not your own doing; it is the gift of God' (Ephesians 2.8). The Letter to the Ephesians may or may not be by Paul, but this verse expresses his message admirably. However, Paul was not always so careful with his use of 'by' and 'through' (see the second half of v. 16, and also v. 21).

Works of the law This is a crucial phrase in the letter and it appears here for the first time. It means basically 'the deeds required by the Jewish law'. However, some prominent scholars suggest that the meaning may be narrower if we take into account the context, i.e. the issues between Paul and his opponents. They suggest the 'works' in the phrase refer to the special requirements that made a Jew visibly distinctive from the Gentiles. We may think of ceremonies, the observance of the Sabbath, special food laws and circumcision. These are things that erected a boundary between the Jews and Gentiles and may be known as boundary markers. We may then think of these Jews as emphasizing the social function or social effect of the law. One implication of such a suggestion is that the battle between Paul and his opponents is basically over entrance requirements and not legalism, i.e. on what basis do people become members of God's family (or the Church)? Must everyone adopt the Jewish way of life to be accepted by God? Even if the meaning is broader than Jewish boundary markers it does not mean Paul was fighting legalism. He was actually viewing the issues from the perspective of the covenant; i.e. how the Mosaic covenant has been fulfilled and its requirements – including those that made Jews visibly distinctive – should not be imposed on Christians in a manner that made them obligatory for belonging to God's family or experiencing the salvation of Christ. We will be in a better position to choose between these alternatives after we have studied the whole Letter to the Galatians.

Faith in Jesus Christ The Greek could also be translated, 'the faithfulness of Jesus Christ', see Special note B.

2.17. In our effort to be justified: A better translation of what Paul wrote is, 'in seeking to be justified' (NEB, REB, NIV).

We ourselves have been found to be sinners In order to maintain the Christian fellowship, Peter and Paul had transgressed against the Mosaic law, so according to the letter of the law they had become 'sinners'.

Is Christ then a servant of sin? If eating with the Gentiles meant that Paul and Peter became sinners, Christ becomes the servant of sin. This is so because Christ came to reconcile the world, i.e. to bring Jew and Gentile together at the same table through the salvation he offers. The point is that this sort of table fellowship is patterned after Christ and inspired by him.

2.18. The very things that I once tore down: This could mean either (a) those provisions of the law which interfered with the Christian fellowship, and which Paul no longer observed, or (b) the belief that obedience to the law justifies a person before God, a belief that he no longer held; or it could mean both.

Then I demonstrate that I am a transgressor This is not clear. It could mean (a) 'Then I prove that my conduct had been wrong', that is to say, if Paul (or Peter) returned to a strict obedience to the letter of the law, he would show that it had been wrong for him to have given up his strict obedience at first. Or it could mean (b) 'Then I would be really sinning', that is to say, returning to a strict obedience to the letter of the law would be the real sin. This seems more likely to be what Paul meant.

2.19. Through the law I died to the law so that I might live for God: The thought here is very compact and may be unpacked as follows. 'Through the law' refers to the effect of the law. This could mean possibly Paul was encouraged by the law to persecute the Church, which in turn led to his encounter with Christ, which set him free from the law. So, 'through the law' he 'died to the law', i.e. became no longer bound to the law because he found Christ, and lived for God. Alternatively, we may use Romans 7.1–6 as a guide since the passage contains similar language and themes. In his effort to keep the law, he discovered that he was actually condemned by the law because he could not keep all the

requirements. 'Through the law' he was condemned ('died'). This sever-
ance of the relationship between Paul and the law allowed him to be
joined to another, i.e. Christ, in order to live for God. In this case we may
think of the law as pointing to its own obsolescence. The first interpretation will mean Paul spoke of himself only, while the second will mean
that he spoke for Jews. The next clause in the verse suggests that the
second interpretation is closer to Paul's meaning.

I have been crucified with Christ Paul now thinks of his 'through death
to life' experience as being patterned after Christ. Together with Christ,
Paul was crucified. The Jews regarded someone who was crucified as
having been cursed by the law (3.13). The law has pronounced its
condemnation on Christ and all those who are joined to him. But the
pattern does not end here. Together with Christ, Paul and all who are
joined to Christ are also raised to new life. This life is possible because
Christ lives in them. Verse 20 continues this thought.

2.21. Justification: Paul wrote 'righteousness' (NIV, REB). Paul is not
simply repeating that the law does not justify us, but goes further:
obedience to the law does not make us righteous (see 3.9).

Then Christ died for nothing If the Mosaic law was the gateway to God,
then the death of Christ would not have served any purpose. But, as Paul
was to argue later (3.6–18), the law never was the gateway to God.

 ## Interpretation

Paul continues his letter by describing a conflict between Peter and
himself, which had taken place at Antioch in Syria some time after the
agreement mentioned in vv. 1–10. Paul told the Galatians about this for
three reasons:

1 to show once more that he was not a mere follower of the earlier
   apostles;

2 to illustrate how interference in the life of a church is likely to break
   up the Christian fellowship; and

3 to lay a foundation for his argument against his opponents.

Antioch was probably the first church in which there were both Jews and
Gentiles in significant numbers, and it had become the custom for Jews
and Gentiles 'to eat together'. The practice probably developed quite
naturally out of the Christian fellowship, without much conscious
thought. It was really unthinkable to have separate Communion services
for different sets of people; and when people are close to each other, they
will also have meals together.

When Peter arrived at Antioch, it probably did not occur to him to act
differently from the other Christians there, so he did the same. But

afterwards some visitors arrived from Jerusalem, and they were horrified at seeing fellow Jewish Christians sharing meals with Gentiles. They persuaded the local Jewish Christians to abandon the practice. Paul's words, 'for fear of the circumcision faction' (see note on v. 12) suggest that the visitors had pointed out that, by having meals with Gentiles, they were breaking their ties with their fellow-Jews, and particularly with the Jewish Christian church in Jerusalem. The description also suggests that circumcision was regarded by this faction as indispensable for belonging to God's true family. One can also surmise that they would be interested in emphasizing the distinctive markers that separated Jews from Gentiles (e.g. the food laws).

The situation was different from ours today, because the Church had not yet become divided into a number of different 'churches'. They were not faced, as we are, with problems about the differences between churches governed by 'bishops' and those with a 'presbyterial' form of government, or between churches with an ordained ministry and those with no ordained people. They did not belong to 'another denomination', but were members of a sister church which had different customs and applied different rules. They felt the same sort of surprise that is felt by people from churches where the congregation participate in the services by spontaneous shouts of joy and hand-clapping, when they attend a service in a church where the congregation remains quiet. Only in this case the matter was more serious, because the visitors believed that what the people at Antioch did was positively wrong and advised their fellow Jewish Christians to change their ways.

This problem had not been foreseen in the agreement between Paul and the Jerusalem apostles. That had dealt with different practices in various churches, on the assumption that each church would be either Jewish or Gentile. A Jewish Christian church in Jerusalem could live happily in harmony with a Gentile church in Caesarea, without being worried about the differences between them. Here the differences existed within the same church, and Paul saw clearly what other people did not see, that the demands of the visitors would split the church. If Jewish and Gentile Christians each followed their different customs, then they would become segregated. The Gentile Christians would then soon be regarded as second-class Christians; and the only way out of the problem would have been for them to become Jews by circumcision.

Paul had been particularly upset because Peter and Barnabas gave in to the visitors. These two were leading figures in the church, and their example counted for much. Moreover, they did not give in because they thought the visitors were right, but because they were afraid of what the visitors and the people in Jerusalem might say. No wonder Paul accused them of hypocrisy!

We cannot be sure where Paul's account of his rebuke to Peter ends and his argument with the Galatians begins: much of vv. 15–21 could be directed either at Peter or at the Galatians. Many interpreters regard this passage as evidence that Peter and Paul were habitual opponents, who preached very different gospels. There were certainly differences among the early Christians, and Peter and Paul did probably present the gospel in different forms. But we have no evidence that they were enemies, or that they headed two parties in the early Church. In this case Paul was not attacking Peter on a matter of principle: Peter had already been living by the principle that Paul advocated. Paul was urging him to act consistently, and in accordance with his beliefs.

Paul now comes to the heart of the matter. We are not justified 'by works of the law'. He meant the law of Moses: even if a person is a good Jew, who knows the law and keeps it, that does not justify him before God. It cannot make him acceptable to God, if God has not already accepted him. The good news is that God *has* accepted him.

However, Paul's words apply to any law, whether God-given or of human origin. All communities have their laws, and every church has its laws by which its affairs are conducted, and by which its members live. Such rules are necessary, and we should abide by them. But the visitors from Jerusalem made two mistakes, which Peter and Barnabas ought to have recognized. They regarded the ways of the church in Jerusalem as the only valid ones, at least for Jewish Christians; and they seemed to believe that obeying those rules, which were 'divine laws', justified them before God. But laws are made for people; people are not made for the laws (see Mark 2.27). 'The law is holy, and the commandment is holy and just and good' (Romans 7.12), and God gave it for a purpose (Galatians 3.19), but its purpose is not to put us right with God. What justifies us before God is his grace (v. 21); this is God's free gift, and we can receive the gift only if we accept it through faith (v. 16; see Special note B).

But some people would say that if Jewish Christians disobey the Mosaic food laws, they disobey a divine law, and become 'sinners'. Surely, this means that Christ encourages them to sin, which makes him a 'servant of sin' (v. 17). Paul's answer is an emphatic, 'certainly not'. He does not argue the case. His idea may have been that the more important command cancels a lesser one. This was a common rabbinic argument. In this case the will of Christ, that his people should be one body (1 Corinthians 12.12–13), cancels any less important command.

When Paul was younger he had regarded the law as a means of being accepted by God. But that was a wrong use of the law, and he had abandoned it. It would be a grave sin to return to it. He had 'died to the law'. So the law no longer had any power over him, for the person who had been governed by the law was no longer there. Now that he has been baptized, he is a new person (Romans 6.3–4). His past is dead and buried. He has been 'crucified with Christ', and raised to a radically new life.

This new life does not belong to Paul but to Christ. In it Paul's own achievements are of no importance, for it is Christ who lives in him.

There is no room for any attempts of his own to make himself good and righteous, and so to justify himself. Indeed, such an attempt would be impossible, unnecessary and ungodly. Impossible because God owes no one anything, and no one can put God in his debt; unnecessary because God has already accepted us; and ungodly because it would be ungrateful not to accept what Christ has done for us.

 ## STUDY SUGGESTIONS

Word study

1   What is the difference in meaning between the words 'by' and 'through' in 'not … by the works … but through faith' (v. 16), and 'by grace you have been saved through faith' (Ephesians 2.8)?

Review of content

2   **(a)** What did the visitors from Jerusalem say to the people in Antioch?

   (b) What risk did the Antioch Christians run, if they listened to the visitors?

3   How was it possible for the difference in teaching to arise in spite of Paul's earlier agreement with the Jerusalem apostles?

4   What had Peter's attitude been before the visitors arrived, and how did their arrival affect him'?

5   The visitors from Jerusalem made two mistakes. What were these mistakes?

6   **(a)** What did Paul mean when he said that works of law do not justify us before God?

   (b) What did he mean when he said that if justification were through the law, then Christ 'died for nothing'?

7   In what way did Peter and Paul agree, and in what way did they not agree?

Bible study

8   What connection, if any, is to be found between the prophet Elijah's words to the Israelites in 1 Kings 18.21 and the words of Paul in Galatians 2.11–16? What do the words imply in each case?

9   What connection is there between Galatians 2.12; Mark 14.66–72 and Acts 4.5–13? What do these three passages tell us about Peter's character?

Discussion and application

10 Paul saw that the demands of the visitors would split the Church, leading to Gentiles being regarded as second-class Christians. What are some of the differences which split the Church today? Do any Christians in your country or in your church regard others as 'second-class Christians'? If so, for what reasons?

11 It is really unthinkable to have different Communion services for different people. But today some churches ban members of some other churches from participating in Holy Communion with them. Do you think this is right? Give your reasons.

12 Paul was not attacking Peter but was urging him to act according to his beliefs. Some people suggest that in the dispute between Paul and his opponents, Peter was trying to keep the peace by walking a middle path. How can we decide when it is right to compromise in a dispute? What do Paul's words in Galatians 1.10 teach us on the subject?

13 In this passage we see only Paul's side of his disagreement with Peter. What do you think Peter might have said in answer to Paul's accusations?

 Special note B

Faith according to Paul

Everyone who has read the New Testament must be aware that 'faith' is one of its key words. Christians have thought and written much about faith, and examined it from every possible angle. But the New Testament writers and their readers knew the word 'faith' only as it was used in ordinary everyday language. They did not make the distinction between the way in which we speak about 'faith' in a religious sense, and the way in which we use the word when we are not talking about our Christian faith.

The most striking difference is that when we discuss faith in a religious sense, we are usually talking about *our* faith, so we are really talking about ourselves; but when we refer to faith in a secular sense, we are talking first and foremost about someone else. When I say, 'I have faith in so-and-so', I do not mean to say that I have some quality called 'faith', but that the other person is someone whom I can trust. If a man says he has faith in his wife, he means that she can be trusted. And if we say we have faith in someone who has to carry out a difficult job, we mean that we believe that person can be trusted to carry out the job properly. It is the same with the verb, 'to believe': if I say that I believe someone, I mean that in my experience that person can be trusted to speak the truth. In all those cases we are speaking, not so much about ourselves, as about some other person.

There is no reason why it should be different when we speak about faith in God. We may have been taught to think of faith as a religious virtue, which we have, or do not have, as the case may be. But the New Testament writers knew the word 'faith' only in its ordinary meaning. Although they had been thinking deeply about faith, they were writing for people who knew only its everyday meaning. So, when they wrote about faith in God, they wanted to stress that God could be trusted.

This is true in English, but it is even clearer in Greek. For where we speak on the one hand of the 'faith' or 'trust' of the person who believes, and on the other hand of the 'trustworthiness' or 'honesty' or 'faithfulness' of the person who is believed, the Greeks had only one word for both sides of the relationship. The one word *pistis* means not only 'faith' or 'trust', but also 'reliability', 'faithfulness', 'trustworthiness', 'honesty', or an 'oath'.

And, just as in English we may say, 'the love of God', which can mean either the love which God has for us, or the love which we have for God, so Paul often wrote *pistis Christou*, 'the faith of Christ', by which he could mean either 'the faithfulness of Christ', or 'faith in Christ'. The usual translation is 'faith in Christ'. But Paul was not concerned with translation. To him *pistis* was neither 'faith' nor 'faithfulness': the same word included both the faithfulness of Jesus and the faith of the believer. The two belong together. We can distinguish between them in our minds, but we must not separate them, and Paul certainly did not separate them. Faith, like love, is a two-way process.

So, when Paul spoke of faith, he wanted to emphasize that God, in Jesus Christ, can be trusted absolutely. He was aware that faith demands a decision on our side. We have to take God on trust. We do not see God, and we sometimes find it difficult to see his care for us in our lives and in the life of the world. There is a paradox here: we can only discover that God can be trusted, if we begin by trusting him. Just as the proverb says, 'the proof of the pudding is in the eating', so the 'proof' of God is in trusting him. Yet there is a good reason for trusting him. The reason is Jesus Christ. That God, in Jesus Christ, shared our life, with its joys and sorrows, that he shared our death, even the appalling death on the cross (Philippians 2.8), that he took on himself the responsibility for our sins (Galatians 1.4; 1 Corinthians 15.3), should be more than sufficient reason to trust him. Faith is necessary for our salvation; but it is not our contribution to our salvation, for it depends entirely on God's faithfulness.

Galatians 3.1–5

The Galatians' earlier experience

 Summary

Paul reminds the Galatians how they became Christians, and asks whether they want to exchange the Spirit for the 'flesh'.

 Notes

3.1. Bewitched: The Galatians seem to have come under a spell. Paul uses this word to stress the unexpectedness and seriousness of the 'about-turn' of the Galatian Christians.

Publicly exhibited This translation is not quite accurate, and could be misleading. The Greek verb means:

1 'to write beforehand', 'to predict' (Romans 15.4); or

2 'to make known through a written proclamation', 'to proclaim publicly'.

Paul was asking, 'Has someone put a spell on you, in spite of the clear explanation you have had of the crucifixion of Christ?' (JB).

3.2. The only thing: This indicates that Paul is drawing the Galatian Christians to the most essential reference point for resolving the issue caused by the troublemakers. All else then becomes unimportant and will clutter up the issue.

Receive the Spirit This is the first time the word 'Spirit' appears in the letter. Paul refers to the reception of the Spirit probably for three reasons.

1 In early Christian understanding, receiving the Spirit means experiencing the 'new birth' or entering into new life with God (Romans 8.9; 1 Corinthians 3.16; 12.13; 2 Corinthians 1.22; Galatians 4.6). The point is that if the Gentile Christians are given new life by God and become full members of God's family by believing the gospel, there is no need to introduce any other requirement to ensure their having this status.

2   The giving of the Spirit is linked to the promise of the new covenant to which the old looked forward (Ezekiel 36.24–30; compare Jeremiah 31.31–34). Indeed, Paul discusses this in Galatians 3.8–14. The point then is that Galatian Christians are experiencing what the Old Testament pointed to. They fall precisely into God's scheme of things. It must be remembered the Old Testament was the one main weapon in the troublemakers' case. But this is now explained as being fulfilled by the hearing of faith and not by performing the works of the law.

3   Paul is also preparing the way for his discussion on Christian behaviour. As we shall see in Galatians 5, this is defined by the Spirit and not the law. All this indicates the significance of referring to the Spirit as the only thing Paul wants to know of the Galatians.

Believing what you heard Paul's Greek words can also mean 'the obedience of faith', that is to say, 'acting on your faith'.

3.3. The flesh: The Hebrew word *basar* and the Greek word *sarx*, both meaning 'flesh', do not mean 'the body' in contrast with the soul, nor does 'flesh' mean 'the material' in contrast with 'the spiritual' (NEB), and certainly not our 'lower nature'. 'Flesh' means human beings as they actually are (see note on Galatians 1.16). It means especially that they are not God, and that they are mortal. The contrast between Spirit and flesh is the contrast between God's work and people's own achievements. In many cases the best translation of *sarx* is 'self' (5.13, 16). The NIV translates correctly: 'After beginning with the Spirit, are you now trying to attain your goal by human effort?'

3.5. Work miracles among you: In the early Church, the work of the Spirit was often accompanied by spectacular manifestations, such as speaking in tongues, 'miraculous' healings, and other 'signs and wonders' – as it still is in some churches today. In 1 Corinthians Paul warns against paying too much attention to such things. They are meaningful and have a place in the life of the Church, but other gifts are also the work of the Spirit, such as, for example, the ability to teach, or to do welfare work without being patronizing, and above all the gift of love, which is the greatest of all (1 Corinthians 12—14). Here, however, Paul makes a special point of mentioning the more spectacular gifts.

 Interpretation

Paul now addresses the Galatians on the contradiction between the gospel of Christ and the teaching of his opponents. He does not give their teaching in detail; the Galatians knew that already. However, we do not know exactly what it was, and we can learn only a little about it from what Paul writes. But this much is clear: they were insisting that in order to earn God's favour, Christians had to obey certain commandments of the Jewish law.

Paul appeals to the Galatians by reminding them of what had happened when they became Christians. He says that he presented the gospel openly and clearly and that they accepted it.

The gospel was preached to them without any strings attached: God's grace is given freely. It was offered freely to the Jews, when Jesus worked among them, and not only to faithful Jews, but also to 'tax-gatherers and other bad characters' (Luke 15.1, NEB), that is to say, not only to those who obeyed the law but also to the disobedient. When Paul preached to the Galatians, he offered it without the obligations of the law. The Galatians had received the Spirit simply by accepting God's free offer.

In contrasting the Spirit and the flesh, Paul is stressing the contrast between God's work for us, and to us, and in us, with any attempts to gain salvation by our own efforts – in the case of the Galatians by depending on certain commandments of the law.

That the Galatians had received the Spirit was shown by the evidence of 'miracles'. There seems to have been a strong charismatic element in the Galatian churches, including miracles of healing; indeed, Paul himself was reputed to heal the sick (see Acts 14.8–10). They could not deny that these things happened among them; and they knew that they had received these gifts because they had believed the gospel, not because they observed any Jewish laws.

These things were evidence that God had accepted them. And all this had come to them as God's free gift, which they only had to accept, and which they had accepted. Now, Paul asks, do you want to throw all this away, and start again with your own efforts? Had all that God had done for them been in vain?

 # STUDY SUGGESTIONS

Word study

1   Which of the following contrasts was Paul referring to as 'flesh' and 'Spirit' in v. 3?

   (a) The body and the soul

   (b) Material things and spiritual things

   (c) Human achievement and God's work

   (d) Our lower nature and our higher aspirations

Review of content

2   How had the gospel first been presented to the Galatians, and how had they responded to it?

3   What evidence had Paul offered that showed the Galatians had received the Holy Spirit as 'God's free gift'?

4   What did Paul fear was now happening to the Galatian Christians?

Bible study

5   What links can you see between Galatians 3.1–5 and Luke 15.1?

Discussion and application

6   In Galatians 3.5, Paul referred to 'miracles' as evidence that the Holy Spirit was at work among the Galatians. What are some other signs or gifts which show that individual Christians or churches have received the Spirit? What signs or gifts of this sort, if any, can you see in the church to which you belong?

7   How would you answer someone who asked: 'How can we believe in the truth of the gospel unless God gives us miracles to prove it?'?

Galatians 3.6–9

The promise came before the law

 Summary

Paul proves from Scripture that justification has always been through faith in God's promise, for 'Abraham believed God, and it was reckoned to him as righteousness', and in Abraham all the nations were to be blessed.

 Notes

3.6. Abraham: The appeal to Abraham is to be expected. He was regarded as the father of the Jewish people and was often regarded by the Jews as the model of a devout and righteous person. Hence, Abraham is the important test case. If Abraham was made righteous not by the works of the law but by faith, Paul would be very close to winning his case.

'Believed God, and it was reckoned to him as righteousness' God had spoken to Abraham, and Abraham had believed him, and that is what counts as righteousness in God's sight. The Genesis text does not mean that God really desires something called 'righteousness', but will accept 'faith' instead. It means that faith is all that God requires: faith is the righteousness which God demands, for it is the right response to his promise. The appeal to Scripture is important as Paul wants to show that what he is teaching is not a novelty but has its basis in it.

3.7. Descendants of Abraham: That is to say, Abraham's people. The Jews often used 'sons of ...' or 'children of ...' for any sort of connection, as in expressions such as 'sons of righteousness'.

3.7, 9. Those who believe are the descendants of Abraham ... those who believed are blessed with Abraham: The two clauses are grouped together here to show the drift and goal of Paul's argument. Paul wants to show that only by faith can one be reckoned as a descendant of Abraham, and not by the works of the law. Furthermore, as God had already promised that nations would be blessed in Abraham, his readers must expect Gentiles to be included in God's plan of redemption.

44

However, this could happen only by faith. Thus, the coming of Gentiles into Abraham's family must be by faith.

3.8. 'All the Gentiles shall be blessed in you': The quotation is from Genesis 12.3, which most modern versions translate as, 'By you all the families of the earth shall bless themselves', meaning that people will say, 'May God bless us as he blessed Abraham' (but the GNB and NIV agree with Paul's interpretation of the Genesis text). In either case, as Paul was saying, the Genesis text means that the calling of Abraham was of universal significance, as well as being of special significance to the Jewish people who regarded themselves as his descendants.

 ## Interpretation

The point of this part of Paul's argument is that he wanted to show that the right relationship between God and his people had always been governed by God's promises and the people's response in faith. When God called Abraham, there was as yet no written law. God spoke, and Abraham believed him (even though what God was promising him seemed unlikely), and that was all there was to it. That was 'righteousness', and that was the right relationship between God and Abraham.

This did not mean that Abraham did not have to obey God. He did. God commanded Abraham, and Abraham acted upon his commands. In a sense we could say that Abraham was obeying 'God's commandments' or even 'God's law'. But the point Paul wants to make is that God's favour to Abraham, and the relationship of faith which grew out of that favour, came first. Abraham's obedience was the outcome of his faith, not the other way round.

So, at the first stage the law played no part at all. Paul's argument is supported by the fact that outside the books of the *torah* (the 'books of Moses') the Old Testament writers rarely refer to any specific commandments of the laws of Moses. God's commandments were regarded as important, and people were expected to carry out God's will. When the prophets accused the people of Israel of having disobeyed God's will, they were probably thinking of specific commandments; but they rarely mentioned them as such. For example, Micah based his criticism of people's conduct on the fact that God 'has told you, O mortal, what is good; and what does the LORD require of you but to do justice, and to love kindness, and to walk humbly with your God?' (Micah 6.8).

The gospel, that is to say, God's promise, came first, and for Abraham and Paul the only possible response was faith. God's promise often meets with unbelief, but the *right* response, the 'righteousness' of Genesis 15.6, is faith.

Furthermore, Paul wanted to show that in that very promise to Abraham, the Gentiles were already envisaged. Interpreting the 'families of the earth' to refer to the nations (i.e. Gentiles), Paul pointed out that it was always God's intent that the Gentiles be blessed along with Abraham. This could be achieved only by faith, as all descendants of Abraham were such by faith.

 # STUDY SUGGESTIONS

Word study

1 What did Paul mean by 'descendants' of Abraham in v. 7?

Review of content

2 (a) What did Paul mean when he said that 'the scripture ... declared the gospel beforehand to Abraham'?

(b) In what way was God's promise to Abraham especially relevant to Paul's argument against his opponents?

3 Genesis 15.6 'does not mean that God really desires something called "righteousness", but will accept "faith" instead'. What does it mean?

Bible study

4 In what way does the teaching of the following passages contradict the teaching of Paul's opponents among the Galatians: Genesis 12.3; Habakkuk 2.4; Romans 4.1–13?

5 Compare the words of the prophet in Micah 6.8 with those of Jesus in Mark 12.28–31. What difference, if any, do you see between the meanings of the two passages?

Discussion and application

6 Some people ask, 'If God counts our believing in him as "righteousness", why do we need to keep the Ten Commandments as well?' How would you answer them?

7 'God's promise came first.' What is the significance of this statement for those who preach the gospel today?

Special note C
Righteousness and justification

These are two key words in Paul's thinking, so we need to look at them carefully. This is especially important because they can easily be misinterpreted, which in turn would lead us to misunderstand what Paul wrote.

1 It is tempting to regard the biblical idea of 'righteousness' as another word for 'justice', but this would be a mistake. Justice means giving everyone his or her due. A 'just' person is someone who carries out all his or her obligations, who treats people as they ought to be treated, who gives to all people what is owing to them, and who allows them to keep what belongs to them. A just society is a society in which all people have their fair share, and are all treated by the same rules. And a just judge, or a just court of justice, is one which punishes the guilty, acquits the innocent, and in some cases rewards the deserving. This idea of justice comes from the Romans, whose laws were in many respects very fair, and have been an example to many nations.

But not all nations thought, or think, as the Romans did, and the Old Testament idea of 'righteousness' is different from the Roman idea of 'justice'. The Old Testament does contain similar ideas of justice. They are present, for example, in the law of the *talio* (meaning 'retaliation'): 'you shall give life for life, eye for eye, tooth for tooth, hand for hand, foot for foot, burn for burn, wound for wound, stripe for stripe' (Exodus 21.13–25). The purpose of this law was to end the ancient custom of blood feud, and also to prevent excessive punishment. In Israel it was forbidden to kill other members of a clan simply because one member had committed a crime. It was also considered wrong to kill a man for stealing a sheep, or to cut off his hand for stealing a loaf. Punishment was not allowed to hurt the offender more than the crime had hurt the victim. But this sort of justice was not called 'righteousness', and *sedaqa*, the Hebrew word which we usually translate by 'righteousness', is never used in connection with punishment. It is actually very difficult to say exactly what *sedaqa* means. We come close to it, if we think of an atmosphere in which the right relationships can flourish. In this sense, the covenantal context cannot be avoided. For Israel her relationship with God is defined principally by the covenant. To be 'righteous' or to possess *sedaqa* means to live within the terms of the covenant. To be 'justified' in this context would mean that a person has been vindicated or given the divine verdict that he or she has lived in faithfulness to the covenant. Furthermore, the appeal to God to act righteously is the call to God to be true to his covenantal promises (Isaiah 42.6–7; 45.8, 13, 19; Micah 7.9).

A Hebrew word that comes nearer to 'justice' is *mishpat*, which is usually translated as 'judgement'. But in *mishpat* the emphasis is on vindicating the innocent and protecting the helpless, rather than on punishing the guilty. Note, for example, how in the case of Solomon's first judgement, nothing is said about any punishment of the guilty woman: all that was needed for a right judgement was that the child should be given to the rightful mother (1 Kings 3.16–28).

2   The Greek word *dikaiosynē*, meaning 'righteousness', also differed from 'justice'. Many Greek people did, indeed, interpret 'righteousness' as 'giving everyone their due', but this interpretation was challenged by others. The philosopher Plato, for example, argued that it could never be 'righteous' to harm people, even if they deserved it. 'Righteousness' was seeking people's true good and, above all, the true good of the community.

3   Paul was a Jew, and when he used the Greek word, he also had the Hebrew idea in mind. 'Righteousness', as he understood it, did not mean that people were good, or honest, or law-abiding, but simply that they were in the right relationship with God. He would assume that this right relationship with God would also make them good, and honest, and fair-minded, and probably law-abiding. But what made them 'righteous' was not their own goodness, it was God's goodness, his grace, which they had received through faith.

4   The words *dikaiōma* and *dikaiōsis*, meaning 'justification', are 'forensic' terms, that is to say, words used in a court of law. Their precise meaning is 'a favourable verdict' by a judge, or by some sort of law court. This is usually interpreted as meaning an acquittal, or a verdict of 'not guilty'. The doctrine of justification, interpreted in these terms, means that, because of the passion and death of Christ, God acquits us of our guilt. We are all guilty before God but, guilty though we are, God acquits us.

This interpretation stresses two important points. It takes our guilt before God seriously. When we stand before God, we are all guilty, for we have offended against his holy law and against his holy love, and the death of Christ was needed to put us right with God. It also stresses that what really matters is God's judgement: if he declares us not guilty, his verdict stands.

However, there are difficulties with this interpretation. We accept that what matters is God's verdict, and that he is free to judge as he chooses. But, we may ask, if we are all guilty of offending against his holy law, how can he declare us 'not guilty'? We are taught that God's judgement is 'true and just' (Psalm 119.1–37: John 8.16; Revelation 19.2); but to declare the guilty 'not guilty' seems to make him an unjust judge. In some sense, it may be said that Paul tries to tackle this thorny issue in Romans 3.21–26. How exactly the logic works itself out is not quite clear. But what is clear is Paul teaches in that passage that God seeks to justify the ungodly without being unjust himself. Again, what is also clear is the connection between this action of God with the 'faith of Christ' (see Special note B) and Christ's offering of himself as an atoning sacrifice.

5 Some scholars who find the above notion troubling appeal to the fact that not all court cases deal with criminal law. They suggest that the words which Paul used were also appropriate for cases of civil law: especially in cases dealing with property, when the court has to decide who the legal owner of a certain property is. In the ancient world this property might be a slave. Now, there is strong evidence that we are slaves of sin, and the devil can show evidence that we have served him, and can claim that we belong to him (see John 8.34; Romans 6.17; Colossians 2.14; Revelation 12.10). But God the Judge decides that we belong to Jesus Christ, who 'bought' us (Mark 10.45; 1 Corinthians 6.20), and set us free (Galatians 4.8–11, see also John 8.36, Romans 6.18, 22; Revelation 1.5). It would be absurd to ask to whom Jesus paid the price. This was not a business transaction. All that the New Testament writers want to stress is that Jesus paid dearly for putting us right with God. This interpretation would bring Paul's teaching on justification in line with his teaching on redemption.

6 Some churches use the word 'justification' in the sense of 'making people righteous'. The Greek words which Paul used cannot mean this. But we may be certain God's work of justification is effective. God does not do things by half, and when Christians have been accepted by him as his own, and in turn have accepted him as their God, they will repent of their wrong ways, and become new people. They still continue to stumble and fall, and in this sense they are still sinners, but they are no longer *slaves* of sin, and this will show in the new and 'godly' lives they lead.

7 In his Letters Paul rarely used the words 'forgive' and 'forgiveness' (only Romans 3.25; 4.7 and, if these Letters are by him, Ephesians 1.7; Colossians 1.14). However, it is important to realize that his teaching implies that God has forgiven us our sins.

Parents who forgive naughty children may still demand that the children should admit their faults, and may even find it necessary to punish them; but in spite of everything, they still love their bad children as much as if they had done no wrong. Similarly God, as a loving Father, forgives our sins, and continues to love us. Whatever we may have done to spoil our relationship with him, his attitude to us remains the same. This is the reason why he set in motion the whole work of our justification and redemption, and sent his Son into the world to live with us and die for us.

Galatians 3.10–14

The curse of the law and its solution

 Summary

Paul uses Scripture to show that:

- All who rely on works of law are under a curse, but
- Christ has redeemed people from the curse of the law, and brought the blessing of Abraham to the Gentiles.

 Notes

3.10. All who rely on works of the law: Paul wrote, 'all who are of works of law', but the NRSV conveys the meaning of the quotation of Deuteronomy 27.26.

Under a curse Since Paul is going to cite Deuteronomy 27.26 next, the 'curse' is best understood in the context of the Deuteronomy passage. In this context, many curses are mentioned and they are to come about when Israel disobeys the law. The central thought is that of a reversal. Not only will the land be blighted, but also Israel will be thrown out of the land. These words also introduce the main theme for discussion in this section. It is about the curse of the law. In a way, Paul has already prepared his readers for this discussion. In the previous section (Galatians 3.6–9), he stressed the blessing that was connected with the promise to Abraham. The curse is the opposite of the blessing and its mention suggests that all is not well with the divine plan to bring in the blessing, as there is now an obstacle. What might have been shocking to Paul's original readers is Paul's claim that all who are of the works of the law are under a curse. Who is Paul referring to? Based on the discussion of 2.16, we may regard them either as people who insisted on some particular Jewish practices as constituting boundary markers or people who believed in following the entirety of the Jewish law. If it is the former, Paul may be arguing that those who insist on making Gentiles conform to Jewish distinctives are against the 'spirit' of the law and are thus under its curse. In this scheme of things, the quotation from Deuteronomy appears to be secondary. If it is the latter, Paul's trend of thought probably ran something like this: the blessing of Abraham was meant to be conveyed to the nations through Israel, the chosen nation. However, Israel fell under the curse of Deuteronomy when it failed to obey the law. This led to the breaking of the old covenant and the resultant exile, which Deuteronomy also predicted (Deuteronomy 28.64–68). If Jews were to continue relying on the works of the law, they would be continuing in this state of affairs, which would be advantageous neither for Israel nor the nations. It seems that the latter is to be preferred as it captures the flow of Paul's thought better and gives importance to the quotation from Deuteronomy. Viewed this way, we can see why Paul goes on to write about how Christ cancelled the curse and channelled the Abrahamic blessing to the Gentiles, ending the stalemate (3.13–14).

3.11. The one who is righteous will live by faith: Paul was either quoting from memory from Habakkuk 2.4 or paraphrasing it, i.e. giving the gist of its meaning. Paul's quotation is translated variously as 'the righteous shall live by faith' (AV, RSV, Moffatt, Phillips, JB, NIV), or, 'he who through faith is righteous shall live' (NEB, GNB). The latter translation accords well with Paul's way of thinking, but the first translation accords better with the Habakkuk text. This is the second scriptural quotation in Paul's argument and it serves to show that it has always been God's intention that the righteous shall live only by faith and not the works of the law. In its context, Habakkuk appears to be addressing a different matter, but what makes it appropriate is the 'crisis context', and such a crisis fitted in with the prediction of Deuteronomy 27. Habakkuk was shown by God that the Babylonians would come to conquer Israel. In this crisis, those who remained true to God would be singled out by their faith/faithfulness. It would be these people who would live. Interpreting this and drawing out the essential lessons, Paul argues that it is faith and not the works of law that will result in life.

3.12. Whoever does the works of the law will live by them: To continue his case that life comes from faith and not the works of the law, Paul quotes Scripture for a third time, from Leviticus 18.5. According to Paul, it sums up the programme of the Jewish law: the doers of the law will live, which is an alternative programme to that of faith: the righteous by faith will live. Paul seems to be thinking that this programme has failed. This may be gathered from the mention of the curse of the law in two verses earlier.

3.13. Christ redeemed us: This is not the Greek word which Paul normally used for 'redeem'. It literally means, 'to buy up', but also carries the sense, 'to deliver at some cost to the deliverer'. Paul clearly did not mean that someone had to be paid or compensated for our delivery, but simply wanted to stress the high personal cost to the Redeemer.

The curse of the law Since the word 'curse' has been mentioned before, it is best to understand the 'curse of the law' in that light. This means that

Paul is referring to the curse that would befall the nation of Israel if she were to disobey the law. This has duly come about and Israel therefore needs redemption from Christ (Messiah). (See also note on Galatians 1.8, 9 and Special note D.)

By becoming a curse for us This is a difficult phrase. However, the quotation (the fourth!) that follows helps us to decipher the meaning. Paul modifies a quotation from Deuteronomy 21.23. In its original context, the passage refers to the exposure of a criminal after he has been executed. That person was deemed cursed. However, in the time of Paul, this passage was often understood by Jews to refer to crucifixion. Hence, Christ might be said to be cursed since he was crucified. Why should God allow this to happen? Paul clarifies this in this verse partially that it is for the Jews (= 'us').

Who hangs on a tree Paul actually wrote, 'on wood', that is to say, 'on a piece of timber'. The Greek word *xylon*, meaning 'wood', could be used for a tree (Revelation 22.2), but was more commonly used for dead wood, such as tree stumps, firewood, wooden beams or ships (or the wooden bars in a xylophone). Here the 'wood' means the cross (as in 1 Peter 2.24).

3.14. In order that in Christ Jesus the blessing of Abraham might come to the Gentiles: This is the second reason why Christ became a curse. It is so that the blessing originally intended by God to come through Abraham to the nations may be made effective. We have now come full circle in Paul's argument. This blessing was impeded by the curse of the law which has to be removed by Christ by his being cursed on our behalf. Now that the impediment is gone, God's original purpose may be fulfilled.

Receive the promise of the Spirit through faith Connecting all the way back to Galatians 3.2, Paul wishes his readers to understand this Abrahamic blessing as identical with the receiving of the Spirit through faith (see comment on Galatians 3.2). At the end of such a protracted argument, we can see another reason why Paul insisted that the 'one thing' is the receiving of the Spirit.

 Interpretation

We are tempted to preface our study of this section with the words: 'Warning: difficulties abound here!' But such difficulties are eased if we bear in mind a few things:

1 Paul has not taken leave of the earlier discussion on the Abrahamic promise and blessing;

2 the Old Testament verses cited are of importance to Paul's case; and

3   Paul sets out to show that those who rely on the works of the law are
    in danger of 'missing the boat'.

Paul begins by writing what appears to be a shocking statement: 'all who
rely on the works of the law are under a curse' (3.10). This is then
supported by an appeal to Deuteronomy 27.26. The curse (or curses)
predicted of Israel, including the exile, would come true if she did not
obey the law. From this it becomes evident to Paul not only that those
who rely on the works of the law are under a curse but also that none can
be justified by the law (Galatians 3.11). He follows this up with a second
quotation from Habakkuk 2.4. This is not arbitrary because what connects the Deuteronomy passage with this passage is the 'crisis context'.
According to Deuteronomy, a crisis would come in the life of the nation
that would threaten her survival, if she did not obey the law. For
Habakkuk, this was looming on the horizon with the anticipated coming
of the Babylonians. But Habakkuk was taught by God that in such a state
of affairs those who would live would do so by their faith/faithfulness.
This crisis may also be known as the exile. The exile was a result of the
breach in the old Mosaic covenant. Paul thus seems to suggest that if the
Jews keep relying on the law, i.e. the Mosaic covenant, it would spell
doom for them. Why? The nation has failed before and terribly. Moreover, that era has ended.

Paul refers to the Old Testament a third time to argue that the
programme of faith is not the programme of the law (Galatians 3.12).
Both programmes offer life. The law's programme is best summed up by
Leviticus 18.5. Life could come only through doing the deeds of the law.
This is in contrast with the programme hinted at in Habakkuk 2.4: a
programme of faith.

But what is this programme of faith? Or more precisely, in what is this
faith to be exercised? Paul now brings up finally the case of Christ. It has
always been implicit but is made explicit now. For the Jewish nation to
proceed to the life that God intended her to have, the curse must be
lifted. According to Paul this was achieved when Christ was crucified.
Appealing to Scripture for the fourth time (Deuteronomy 21.23), Paul
connects Christ's crucifixion with the curse. Christ was cursed not
because of his misdeeds but for the sake of others. The 'us' in Galatians
3.13 most probably refers to the Jews. Christ, i.e. Messiah, died and was
cursed as a representative of the nation. However, what Christ has
achieved is not just for the Jews but also for the Gentiles. His taking away
of the curse made it possible for the Abrahamic blessing to flow to the
Gentiles, which had been God's intention all along. This blessing is
understood as the receiving of the Spirit which comes to a believer by
faith (3.14).

Thus Paul's argument has come full circle and, along the way, he has
shown why the Jews cannot insist on relying on the works of the law (or
the Mosaic covenant). He has also shown how Christ fitted into the
whole divine scheme which began all the way back with Abraham and

continued with Israel, and was now realized in the new era through faith, which is evident in the giving of the Spirit. Arising from Paul's way of discussing these matters, there are two things worthy of note.

The first is that Paul appeals to Scripture frequently here. The reason for this may be that he thought the debate with his opponents was resolvable only through Scripture. This means that it is important for the interpreter to begin with Scripture in any attempt to understand Paul's overall argument in Galatians rather than with general principles. Second, Paul thinks corporately and not individualistically. He was not appealing to 'everyone's' experience but to the experience of the nation of Israel. This is not surprising as the troublemakers were Jews, trying to impose Jewish ways on Gentiles, and probably doing so with the appeal to Scripture. This way of corporate thinking takes into account the dynamic development in the relationship between God and his Jewish people. For Paul, the final phase has come, which connects with the earliest phase, i.e. Abraham. In this phase, Gentiles receive what God has always intended to convey to them through the Abrahamic promise.

Indeed, there are still many loose ends to be tied but we think the general drift of Paul's profound argument here has been made clear. But we should not miss the point that in all this Paul wishes to emphasize that God's faithfulness was shown in the death of Christ on the cross. In Christ, God came down on our side, and became one of us; he took on himself a human life with all its pains, and also with the consequences of our sins. This act on God's part was costly and painful: as we know, it meant the cross. The various New Testament writers emphasize, each in his own way, how costly this was. Mark and Matthew have perhaps shown this most movingly by recording Jesus' cry, 'My God, my God, why have you forsaken me?' (Mark 15.34; Matthew 27.46). Even though the psalm Jesus quoted (Psalm 22) ends in hope, the words show deep anguish. Besides the extreme physical pain, the Son of God also suffered the utter desolation of feeling forsaken by his Father. Paul did not paint such a picture here, but he too was aware of the cost, and showed this by the word he chose for 'redeemed'.

 STUDY SUGGESTIONS

Word study

1 In Galatians 3.13 Paul uses a different word for 'redeem' from the word he normally uses. What is its literal meaning and what was Paul's reason for using it here?

Review of content

2 What might be Paul's reason for referring to the word 'curse' so frequently in this passage?

3 Our whole relationship with God depends on his faithfulness and on our faith. In what way or ways has God shown his faithfulness?

4 **(a)** What did Paul mean when he said that Christ redeemed us from the curse of the law 'by becoming a curse for us' (v. 13)?

 (b) From what do we need to be redeemed?

 (c) What did Paul mean by the special word he used for 'redeemed' in v. 13?

Bible study

5 What does Matthew 27.46 tell us about the 'cost' of our redemption by Jesus on the cross?

Discussion and application

6 Good preachers often 'preach the law', in the sense that they make it clear what obedience to God means in the way we live our lives as Christians. How does Galatians 3.10–14 help them to avoid certain misunderstandings when they preach on this subject?

7 Some people ask, 'If obeying the law does not "justify" us, how do we know what we should do in order to be justified?' How would you answer?

Galatians 3.15–22

The law cannot make the promise void

 ## Summary

Once an agreement has been ratified, it cannot in honesty be altered or cancelled. So the promise of God to Abraham cannot be altered by the law, which was given 430 years later.

 ## Notes

3.15. An example from daily life: Paul now introduces an analogy, an example from ordinary human conduct, to prove something he was saying about God's conduct, and to help the Galatians to understand his meaning more clearly.

A person's will ... no one adds to it or annuls it The word *diathēkē*, here translated by 'will', also means an 'agreement' or 'covenant'. In the dealings between God and human beings the initiative is entirely on God's side, and this is why some translators have used 'will' (as in the NRSV and the NEB). Paul wants to convey that God, once he has given his promise, has not made any changes to it. So it is probably better to think in terms of a covenant or an agreement: 'when two people agree on a matter and sign an agreement, no one can break it or add anything to it' (GNB).

3.16. It does not say, 'And to offsprings', as of many; but it says, 'And to your offspring,' that is, to one person, who is Christ: Paul is referring to the accounts of God's promise to Abraham in the Jewish Scriptures (Genesis 12.7; 13.15: etc.), where the collective noun meaning 'seed', 'semen', or 'offspring' is used for Abraham's descendants. This could mean one individual as well as many. Paul could have believed that the verses in Genesis meant one person only. But knowing what God has done in Christ made him realize that the promise referred not only to the many 'offsprings' who were to be blessed by it, but especially to the one 'Offspring', Jesus Christ, in whom the blessing was fulfilled. But readers who look up the texts in the Old Testament (and in Romans 9.7 and 2 Corinthians 11.22, where Paul also refers to the promise to

Abraham) find that the NRSV and other modern translations do not use the word 'offspring' at all, but the plural 'descendants', and so obscure the point that Paul wanted to make here. Only the NJB uses a collective noun with the same meaning, 'progeny', in both cases.

3.17. Four hundred thirty years: This computation of the period of time between Abraham and the giving of the law on Mt Sinai is similar to the one in Exodus 12.40.

A covenant See note on Galatians 3.15.

3.18. Inheritance: The word 'inheritance' occurs for the first time in the Letter and is fitting here, as it continues the thought of the analogy given in 3.15 and starts the development of a theme – about Christians being the heirs of Abraham and heirs of God – that concludes only at 4.31. The word also harks back to God's promise to Abraham in Genesis 15.7–8; 21.10 (see also Deuteronomy 1.39; 2.12). In the Genesis passages, the 'inheritance' refers to the land Abraham's heirs would one day receive. The concept was later expanded to include spiritual blessings (2 Chronicles 6.27; Psalm 37.9; Isaiah 54.17). In Paul's thought the concept has also been broadened to include the new world that is to come (Galatians 5.21; 1 Corinthians 6.9–10; Colossians 3.24).

3.19. It was added because of transgressions: This can be interpreted in various ways.

1   It could mean that the law became necessary because of people's disobedience: it was not part of the original covenant, but was added because people did not do God's will.

2   It could mean that the law was needed to make people realize that they were sinners: 'It was added in order to show what wrongdoing is' (GNB).

3   Some people think that Paul meant that the law was given in order to make people transgress.

4   The NEB and REB translate, 'it was added to make wrongdoing a legal offence.' This seems the simplest interpretation, and is supported by Galatians 5.23. It would also explain why the law forbids more things than it commands. According to the rabbis the law of Moses commands 248 actions, and forbids 365 actions.

Through angels This is not in the book of Exodus, but was widely believed by Jews.

By a mediator The promise had been given directly to Abraham; the law was given indirectly to Israel through Moses. Moses is the mediator being referred to in this verse.

3.20. A mediator involves more than one party: The Greek text actually reads, 'a mediator is not of one'. What makes it puzzling is that the 'one' is not further defined. Consequently, the statement has been interpreted in many different ways. The most common interpretation begins with the idea that one person can speak and act without an intermediary; but when two groups are involved, they usually need an intermediary. The two groups in this case are the angels who are God's messengers and the people of Israel. The point then is that the status of the law is inferior to the Abrahamic promise because it was given through a mediator. Unlike the law, the promise was spoken directly by God without the need of a mediator.

God is one This statement is actually part of the Jewish creed known as the *Shema*. The words are taken from Deuteronomy 6.4 and are meant to express the fundamental belief of Jews, i.e. there is only one God. As it is used here, the idea is probably that if God is one, his plan is also one. His oneness guarantees the promise to Abraham will not be withdrawn.

3.21. Is the law ... opposed to the promises of God? Arguing so strongly that the law is inferior to the Abrahamic promise runs the risk of making the law opposed to God's promises. Hence, Paul has to make it clear that this is not what he is implying.

If a law had been given to make alive, then righteousness would indeed come through the law The general sense seems clear. The law cannot 'make alive' and thus cannot grant 'righteousness'. But this does not mean the law is evil or against God's plan.

3.22. The scripture has imprisoned all things under the power of sin: Some scholars take 'scripture' to mean the Mosaic law but, more probably, it refers either to the testimony of the whole of the Old Testament or a particular passage that Paul has already introduced in his discussion: this could be Deuteronomy 27.26, cited in Galatians 3.10. What is clear, however, is that 'all things' are being imprisoned under the power of sin. This includes Israel who has been given the law. By saying 'scripture' is the agent behind the imprisonment, Paul may have in mind the law or the Old Testament declaring all people are sinners (see 3.10). Alternatively, Paul may be saying that the law or the Old Testament defined sins, and by so doing made any transgression against God's will to be even more serious. Whatever the case may be, what must not be missed is that this imprisonment is allowed by God for a greater purpose: that all, i.e. Jews and Gentiles, may receive God's promise through 'faith of Jesus Christ' (see Special note B), and not by works of the law.

 Interpretation

This section begins with an analogy. Even among humans, once an agreement has been ratified, it is binding. It may be true that unreliable people sometimes enter into agreements which they will not keep, and sometimes make promises which they will not carry out. But among honest people an agreement is an agreement, and must be honoured; and a promise is a promise, and must be kept. If this is true among humans, how much more will God, who is infinitely more reliable than any human, abide by the covenant which he made with Abraham, and keep the promise which he made to him.

Paul was well aware of the many times when God's covenant with Israel had to be renewed, but he was not concerned with that. His concern was to show that God could be expected to honour the promise he had made to Abraham. In Paul's view, that promise pointed to Christ. The way in which he argued this may seem strange to us, but it is clear what he wanted to convey: that Jesus Christ is the fulfilment of God's promise to Abraham.

God keeps his promises. So the promise which he made to Abraham cannot be annulled by the law, which was given so much later. If God had given a law which would make people acceptable to him and grant them true life, that would mean that God had withdrawn his promise. This could never be, for God is absolutely reliable; and God had never given such a law.

But this leads to the question, 'If the law was not meant to bring about the inheritance of the Abrahamic promise, why was it given at all?' Paul's answer, 'It was added because of transgressions', can be interpreted in four different ways (see note on v. 19). Of those four, the last seems to be the most likely. A law, any law, 'defines transgressions'. Doing what the law forbids, or not doing what the law commands, is a transgression, which can be duly punished by suitable penalties.

However, this framework remains empty, if it is not filled with something more than just obeying the letter of the law. The law contains numerous pointers to that 'something more', but cannot enforce it.

For example, it is important that we should not commit adultery (Exodus 20.14). But if two people are to live a good and happy married life, according to God's will, much more is needed. The love on which a good marriage is built cannot be provided by law. Similarly, we must not kill (Exodus 20.13), but it is not enough for us merely not to murder people. Such instructions as 'if your enemies are hungry, give them bread to eat; and if they are thirsty, give them water to drink' (Proverbs 25.21, and see Romans 12.20) cannot easily be fitted into any law, and cannot be enforced. And even though they are important, in showing us how love works in practice, they cannot give us the love we need (see Matthew 5.44). The list of examples could easily be extended. The verdict must stand: the law as given through Moses defines transgressions, but it cannot 'make alive' (v. 21). It cannot in itself *make* people love God or one another.

So the law is good, but it is not the way by which we gain God's favour. God's favour is his free gift, not a reward for services rendered and it does not come to us 'by legal right' (v. 18, REB). The promise God made to

Abraham, and its fulfilment in Jesus Christ, were given by God in his amazing grace. The Bible writers never ceased to be amazed at God's grace. In the Church we sometimes miss this sense of wonder, though it is expressed in the well-known hymn, 'Amazing grace' (by John Newton who, rather like Paul, had led an ungodly – and even blasphemous – life until by God's grace he was almost literally 'made alive' by being saved, against all the odds, in a shipwreck).

God has already accepted his people. That is all the justification they need. All that he requires of us is that we should accept his grace through faith in Jesus Christ. And that is when our obedience to the law becomes something 'positive', growing out of our love for God and our wish to please him, rather than out of a 'negative' fear of offending him and suffering the consequences.

STUDY SUGGESTIONS

Word study

1 What are some other possible translations of the Greek word which the NRSV translates as a 'will'? Which translation makes its meaning clearest, and why?

2 For each of the following words write a short sentence to show its meaning as used by Paul in this passage: intermediary; transgressions; covenant.

Review of content

3 In vv. 6–8, 18 (and again in v. 29) Paul emphasized that God's promise to Abraham was fulfilled in Jesus Christ. What was it that made Paul recognize and understand that this was true?

4 What is the most probable meaning of Paul's statement that God 'imprisoned all things under the power of sin'?

5 (a) Why did Paul say that if law rather than faith was meant to govern our relationship with God, this would mean that God had withdrawn his promise?

(b) Why did Paul reject such an idea?

Bible study

6 What connection do you see between Paul's arguments in Galatians 3.15–22 and the teaching of Jesus according to Matthew 5.17–48?

Discussion and application

7 Why was the law given at all? How far do you find that the Ten Commandments and any other part of the Mosaic law helps us to live in the right relationship with God? To what extent, if at all, do you find them unhelpful?

8   If God is faithful to his promises, what is his present relationship with the Jewish people? Find out if you can (tactfully!) what the views of Jewish people today are on this subject.

Special note D
The law

One of the problems in discussing the idea of the 'law' is that this word can be used in more than one sense. This was true in Greek and Hebrew just as it is in English.

1   The Greek word which the New Testament writers used for 'law' was *nomos*, which was used in a number of different ways.

(a) The word *nomos* meant every sort of custom hallowed by ancient use or tradition: the manner in which things had always been done. This included also religious custom, the way in which the gods had always been worshipped, and ought to be worshipped.

(b) The word *nomos* also meant the written law, by which justice was administered. But the Greeks did not believe that lawgivers were free to invent and decree laws as they pleased (as some modern lawgivers do). So the laws of the ancient Greek city-states were believed to be based on the first meaning of the word, (a), and to be of divine origin. The law was therefore the standard of conduct, and its authority was absolute. This respect for the law is illustrated beautifully by the conduct of the philosopher Socrates, when he had been condemned to death 'for preaching strange gods'. He was innocent, but he had been convicted according to the law. When he had the opportunity to escape he refused to do so, for he did not wish to act against the law. In the ancient Greek city-states, the law was regarded as the actual 'king', no matter who the rulers were who administered the law.

(c) This changed to some extent in later times, when rulers began to be regarded as divine, so their will was 'law'.

Greek philosophers also extended the meaning of *nomos*, in two directions.

(d) First, they included the moral laws by which everyone ought to live; and because people regarded it as natural that they should do so, they called this the 'natural law'.

(e) Second, they discovered that in the natural world nearly everything happens in a regular manner: if you sow seeds of corn, they will produce corn, not apple trees; the sun rises every morning, and sinks every evening, etc. They called this regularity of natural phenomena the 'laws of nature'.

(f) Jews and Christians chiefly used *nomos* as a translation of the Hebrew word *torah* (see below). Paul normally used it in this sense, but not always.

2 The Hebrew word *torah* means 'guidance', 'teaching', 'instruction'. It could be used for the instruction given by a teacher (Proverbs 4.2), or for the guidance given by God through his prophets (Isaiah 1.10). But it was used most commonly for his commandments, and for those five books which contained his commandments: Genesis, Exodus, Leviticus, Numbers and Deuteronomy.

(a) God had revealed himself as the ruler of his people Israel. The *torah* is an expression of his absolute sovereignty over his people, and it must be obeyed, because the Lord is Israel's heavenly king. God has the good of his people at heart, and his commandments are a gift of his love. Thanks to his *torah*, his people knew how they could walk safely through the difficult paths of life. They could delight in his statutes, for they knew that the psalmist was right in saying: 'Your word is a lamp to my feet and a light to my path' (Psalm 119.105).

(b) There is a very close connection between Moses and the law. Moses was revered in Israel as the lawgiver, and it is thus not surprising that the meaning of *torah* became closely connected with Moses, as evident in the following instances. First, *torah* may be known as the Mosaic law (Joshua 8.32; 23.6; 1 Kings 2.3; 2 Kings 14.6; Ezra 3.2; Daniel 9.11, 13). But as this law was given in the context of the making of the covenant at Mt Sinai, *torah* also takes on, second, the meaning of the Mosaic covenant (Exodus 24.7; 32.46; Sirach 24.23; 2 Esdras 7.45–46; 1 Maccabees 1.57). In this covenant, the Ten Commandments play a very significant role. This being the case, they may also be known as *torah* (Exodus 24.12).

(c) In New Testament times there may be evidence to show that Jewish attitudes to the *torah* had changed slightly. Rabbinic Judaism seems to have stressed two points: it was only in the *torah* that, first, God had revealed himself; and, second, a person could have a relationship with him. This could mean, and often did mean, that the *torah* was put between God and the people in such a way that he could no longer be seen as a living God. Of course, by stressing its authority, the rabbis wanted to make sure that God's will was done. The rabbis knew, and taught, that the *torah* had not created the relationship between God and his people. That was an act of his grace. The *torah* maintained that relationship, and people could remain in fellowship with God only by observing every letter of the *torah*. But such zeal for the *torah* could mean, and sometimes did mean, that God's will was *not* done. That was the case, for example, when attempts were made to stop Jesus from healing on the Sabbath, though God desired that someone should be helped at once (Luke 13.10–17).

We could almost say that the Old Testament prophets had regarded Israel as the family of God, in which the Father had laid down certain rules for the conduct of his family, while the rabbis tended to regard people as slaves of the *torah*. This is perhaps not quite fair, as the rabbis did want to ensure that God's will was done, but they also tended to lose sight of the personal relationship between God and his people.

(d) The Gospels show that Jesus regarded the *torah* as the revealed will of God, but his relationship with the Father was not governed by it. His relationship with God was unique, but this did not mean that he was not obliged to do God's will. On the contrary, God's will meant all the more to him because he was God's Son. And this was the crucial point: Jesus knew that the *torah* was made for people, people were not made for the *torah* (see Mark 2.27). The *torah* shows how people should behave *as a result* of being in a right relationship with God, but it could never take the place of that relationship. Jesus' obedience was the obedience of a mature son.

3 The early Christians had to deal with a new situation. It was not difficult for them to agree that the *torah* was given to Israel, and that Gentiles were not expected to live by all its commandments; that had already been agreed by the rabbis. But problems arose, as we have seen, in communities where there were both Jewish and Gentile Christians; and we have also seen how Paul thought the Church ought to deal with such problems.

But there is still the deeper question of the function of the law, and this is where Paul made his most significant contribution, by showing the churches that the law must serve our relationship with God, not govern it. In this he was guided both by the Old Testament and by the life and teaching of Jesus. Paul too regarded the law as the revealed will of God, but he recognized that the relationship between God and his people had been created by God's undeserved favour. The law had been given later to define the limits within which his family ought to live (see note on Galatians 3.19), and to show how they should behave. The law was God-given and good. But as Jesus had shown it was not God, and in some circumstances God's will for us might override, or even be contrary to, the letter of the written law.

Galatians 3.23—4.7

Slaves and children

 Summary

Paul explains that the law has a temporary role: it acted as a disciplinarian and a guardian before Christ came. This is no longer needed, now that Christ has come. His coming brought about redemption and adoption.

 Notes

3.23. Before faith came: Paul wrote, 'before *the* faith came', meaning 'the faith that has been mentioned', i.e. 'the faith of Jesus Christ' (see Special note B). He might have written, 'before Christ came', without much difference in meaning.

3.24. Our disciplinarian: The Greek word *paidagōgos* means literally 'boy-leader', which the NRSV renders as 'disciplinarian'. In some households at that time, a slave might be employed to escort a boy to and from school so that he would not get into danger or fall into mischief. The role of the *paidagōgos* is essentially positive (protection and guidance) although he was also charged with the responsibility to teach him proper manners and discipline him if necessary. This picture illustrates aptly the good but temporary role of the law.

Until Christ came Paul wants to convey that with faith in Christ the believers have reached a maturity, in which they no longer need a 'disciplinarian' to keep them in order.

We might be justified by faith The goal of being subjected to the discipline of *torah* is to be justified by faith. The implication is that if the Galatian Christians were to follow the teaching of the troublemakers by returning to the works of the law, they would be regressing and not reach the real goal of *torah*.

3.24–26. We … we … you … you: For the Jews among the Galatian Christians the *torah* had been 'disciplinarian', as it had for Paul. It was they whom he included with himself in the pronoun 'we' in these verses, although most of the Gentiles among them, too, had formerly been under the restraint of religious laws and customs. With the change to 'you' in v. 26, Paul was addressing *all* the Galatians, Jews and Gentiles alike. See also the 'we' in 4.3–5 and the 'you' in 4.6–7.

3.27. Baptized into Christ: Most scholars think of this as referring to water baptism in the name of Christ. However, it is possible to regard the phrase as a metaphorical way of speaking of belonging to Christ. A similar example may be found in 1 Corinthians 10.2, where Paul speaks of the Israelites' being baptized into Moses (see also 1 Corinthians 12.13).

Clothed yourselves with Christ This is another metaphorical expression. The picture intended is that of changing clothes. The old life, like old clothes, is stripped away, and the new is donned. The metaphor is widely used by Paul (Romans 13.14; 1 Corinthians 15.49–54; 2 Corinthians 5.3; Colossians 3.10–12).

3.28. There is no longer Jew or Greek, there is no longer slave or free, there is no longer male and female: This powerful statement is related to the earlier verses. Being baptized into Christ and putting on Christ is for the purpose of forming a new community by breaking down boundaries that separate (see Theological essay 1). Paul did not mean that those distinctions no longer existed. There are different nations and cultures, there were slaves, and there are still people whose condition is as bad as that of slaves; and people are either men or women. But whatever our race or nationality or social status or sex, these distinctions do not affect our relationship with Christ – and as Christians ('in Christ') such distinctions should not affect our relationships with each other. The distinctions mentioned here are the most profound within human society: 'Jew or Greek' describes the racial/cultural distinction; 'slave or free', the social/economic distinction; and 'male and female', the sexual/gender distinction.

3.29. Abraham's offspring, heirs according to the promise: This recalls the theme of 3.7 and indicates what sort of trajectory Paul's argument has taken in this chapter.

4.1. No better than slaves: This was true of a minor in Roman times in the matter of property and discipline. He was still under the rule of the father. In making these comparisons Paul was clearly thinking of house slaves in a good family, rather than the gangs of slaves who worked on the estates of large landowners, or those who worked in the mines under appalling conditions, or as galley slaves. House slaves were regarded as part of the family, although they did differ from the children. Under Roman law all prisoners of war, before being sold into slavery, underwent a ceremony in which they were deprived of their personality, so henceforth they were regarded, not as people, but as things. They could legally be ill-treated, sold, or killed. Though they were part of the family, they could be discarded, if they were no longer wanted, so their position was never secure. Jewish law, however, regarded slaves as human beings and directed, among other things, that slaves must not be thrown out if they wanted to stay with the family they had served (Exodus 21.5–6).

4.2. Until the date set by the father: When the father thought that the time was ripe for the heir to take his rightful place, the 'disciplinarian' would no longer be needed.

4.3. The elemental spirits of the world: This is a term derived from Greek philosophy, which can also be translated as 'elemental principles' (NIV, NJB) or 'ruling spirits' (GNB). In any case, Paul was referring to the powers or 'gods' of the Galatians' former religion, and particularly to the sun, moon and planets, which were regarded as mighty 'gods', both among the Greeks and in local cults of that region (see note on Galatians 4.8).

4.4. Born of woman, born under the law: Paul stresses that Jesus was born under exactly the same conditions as all human beings with the phrase 'born of a woman'. 'Born under the law' describes his Jewish identity. The Jewishness of Jesus Christ is mentioned because the history of God and the Jewish people cannot be set aside as unimportant for our understanding of God's plan and purpose for the world.

4.5. To redeem: means 'to purchase', 'to buy'; the word could be used for any purchase, but was used especially:

1 for ransoming a prisoner of war; and

2 for buying a slave with the purpose of setting him free.

This statement is addressed to the Jews and the word 'redeem' alludes also to the great redemption from Egypt. Just as the nation of old must be redeemed from the bondage of Egypt, so also must the present Israel be redeemed from the bondage (or curse) of the law.

Adoption as children The word 'adoption' appears only once in Galatians and, in the New Testament, it is found only in Letters attributed to Paul (Romans 8.15, 23; 9.4; Ephesians 1.5). In the Roman society of Paul's day, the 'redemption' of a slave was sometimes followed by adoption. Adoption was taken very seriously; the children of household slaves were often adopted as children of the family, and it was believed that an adopted person actually *became* the son or daughter of the adopting parents. However, Paul may have been strongly influenced by the Exodus event (Romans 9.4). Israel was redeemed from Egypt to enter a covenantal relationship with God, in which God became Father of the nation (Hosea 11.1). In the same manner, believers are redeemed from the 'elemental spirits of the world' to be made children of God.

4.6. God has sent the Spirit of his Son into our hearts, crying, 'Abba! Father!': This experience of adoption is possible only because of the Spirit in believers' hearts. The word 'Abba' is not Greek but Aramaic. It is found here in a Greek discourse because it has become an established element of Christian prayer and piety. Christians called God 'Abba' because this was the characteristic word used by Jesus to address God (Mark 14.36).

4.7. If a child, then also an heir: This is not clearly defined. Paul simply meant that, being God's children, we receive all that he had promised to Abraham.

 ## Interpretation

At first sight this passage appears confusing, for Paul is using two different pictures, which he seems to be mixing up. He first speaks of children, who are in a position similar to that of slaves, until they grow up; and then he speaks of the redemption of a slave. But he had good reasons for using the two different pictures, and in fact he did not mix them up.

The Jews were very proud of being children of Abraham (see John 8.33, 39), and heirs to God's promises, and therefore God's children. Paul admits this but he argues that they were nevertheless in the same position as slaves, for they were kept under control by the law (see Galatians 2.4), which acted as their 'disciplinarian'. This does not mean that the law was a means of oppression. On the contrary, the law is holy and good (see Romans 7.12). Children need to be disciplined; so God's children needed the law. But the training of children is not an end in itself. The purpose of all training and education is to produce free and responsible adults. So it is with the law. It was not an end in itself, but was given with the purpose of producing free and responsible adult believers. Christ is the end of the law (see Romans 10.4), not as if he made the law worthless, but because he brought about the emancipation of his people. He came, not to abolish the law and the prophets, but to fulfil them (Matthew 5.17; see also Romans 3.31). The freedom which Christ gives was the aim of the law.

The Gentiles on the other hand, before they heard the gospel message, 'were enslaved to the elemental spirits'. Their religion meant that they too were in bondage, to powers or principles of the material universe which were not God (see Galatians 4.8). The practice of religion, any religion, usually means observing certain rules. The Latin word *religio*, 'religion', means a 'bind', and the word expresses very well that religion binds people by limiting their freedom. That was the position of the Galatians before they heard the gospel: they were kept in subjection by their religion. But Christ has redeemed them, set them free, and made them God's children by adoption.

So, Paul argues, whatever may be the differences between Jews and Gentiles, the coming of Christ has had the same effect on both. He has emancipated both Jews and Gentiles and, in relation to Christ, 'there is no longer Jew or Greek, there is no longer slave or free, there is no longer male and female'. How seriously he took this is shown by the fact that he wrote, 'we were enslaved to the elemental spirits of the world.' Unlike the Gentile Galatians, he had never served 'elemental spirits', but he had been subject to the material constraints of the Mosaic law, so that any difference between himself and the Galatians was irrelevant. God had sent his Son to redeem both 'those who were under the law', and those who had served other gods.

The statement that 'all of you are one in Christ Jesus' was of great importance, for at that time the distinctions between people were taken very seriously. We have already noted the segregation between Jews and Gentiles, advocated by the Jewish visitors to Antioch. The Greeks divided the human race into Greeks and 'barbarians', and on another occasion Paul insisted that the gospel concerned both Greeks and 'barbarians' equally (Romans 1.14). According to Luke, Paul taught that God 'from one ancestor … made all nations' (Acts 17.26).

The difference between free people and slaves was regarded by many as fundamental. The Greek philosopher Aristotle had argued that a slave was merely an animate piece of property, and *by nature* different from a free person. Moreover, we have already seen (note on Galatians 4.1) that Roman law provided for a ceremony by which slaves were deprived of their personality. Jewish law, indeed, regarded slaves as people, but in Paul's day even a Jew might have been surprised at Paul's advice to Philemon: 'Receive (Onesimus) back for good no longer as a slave, but as more than a slave: as a dear brother' (Philemon 16, REB).

The difference between men and women is, of course, a natural one. But here too Paul maintains that they are equal in their relationship with Christ. It is unavoidable that this verse should be quoted frequently today in discussion between those churches in which men and women can serve equally in the ordained ministry, and those which have an exclusively male ministry. Some people ask whether Paul himself realized the implications of his words. From 1 Corinthians 14.34–36 it seems that he did not, but there are some problems with these verses. They interrupt Paul's argument, and may refer to something about which we know nothing (perhaps some specific women, perhaps 'prophetesses' who preached strange teachings?). On the other hand, we do know the names of some women whom Paul counted among his collaborators: Lydia (Acts 16.14–15), Prisca (Priscilla, Acts 18.2; Romans 16.3; 1 Corinthians 16.19), Phoebe (Romans 16.1), perhaps also Mary, Julia, Tryphaena, Tryphosa (Romans 16.6, 12, 15), and Junia, who was prominent among the apostles (Romans 16.7, although NIV has Junias, i.e. a male name, instead). But we do not know exactly in what functions they collaborated with him.

Important though the issues are which are raised by Galatians 3.28, we must not lose sight of the purpose for which Paul wrote this verse. He was trying to show that God's children, men and women, free and slave, Jews and Gentiles of every nation, are *one* family, governed by mutual *love*. In 3.5 he had mentioned some 'charismatic' gifts as evidence of the

Spirit. Here, he digs deeper: the great gift of the Spirit is the love by which we enter into that intimate relationship with God which makes us cry, 'Abba, Father' (4.7).

 STUDY SUGGESTIONS

Word study

1 What is the precise meaning of the word 'redeemed' (4.5), and for what was it especially used?

2 What do you understand by the word 'slavery'?

Review of content

3 What was the position of slaves in a good household in New Testament times, and what was the essential difference between a slave and a child?

4 What did Paul mean by the statement that 'the law was our disciplinarian ... But now that faith has come, we are no longer subject to a disciplinarian' (3.24–25)?

5 In what way did Paul mean that our redemption by Jesus resembles the custom of adopting slaves as children of the family?

6 What did Paul mean by 'elemental spirits of the world' in 4.3, and in what way were both Jews and Gentiles 'slaves'?

Bible study

7 In what way does the teaching of Paul in Galatians 3.23—4.7 reflect the teaching of Jesus in John 8.31–38?

Discussion and application

8 Many people today use Paul's statement that 'in Christ ... there is no longer male and female' to support their belief that women as well as men should be ordained as ministers or priests. How far do you think this was what Paul – or his hearers – had in mind? What is the practice of your own church in this matter? What is your opinion on the subject, and why?

9 What was the chief difference between Jews and Gentiles in Paul's time? What, if anything, can (a) churches and (b) individual Christians do today to break down barriers between people of different nationalities, cultures and races, either within the Church or in the community as a whole?

Theological essay 1
Justification and the inclusive community

MARK L. Y. CHAN

Introduction: The controversy over justification in Galatians

The life of faith for the Christian is about being reconciled to God and transformed in one's relationship with people. For sin not only separates us from the holy God, it distorts the way we relate to one another as well. The signs of this distortion are plain for all to see. Just think of the untold lives lost through wars and ruined in sectarian violence. Or consider the exploitation of the weak by the unscrupulous, and the manipulation of the unsuspecting by those with evil intentions.

When sinners are cut off from God, they invariably find themselves alienated from each other. Correspondingly, when sinners are redeemed and reconciled to God, there are significant positive changes in the way they regard other people and relate to them. To be spiritually reconnected to God is to be transformed in our social relationships.

In place of the distorted and often destructive way in which people are treated, we find Christians treating others in a manner that conforms to what God desires for human relationships. Instead of looking down on others because they are not like us, or taking advantage of the vulnerable, those who follow Christ will respect the dignity of all people and work to safeguard their interests. Such a life-affirming and unselfish stance towards others must characterize the life of the Church.

The correlation between being justified before God and life in Christian community is a theme that Paul picks up in his spirited letter to the Galatians. Some missionaries had apparently gone to the church at Galatia and preached a message requiring the largely Gentile Christians there to adopt circumcision and Jewish dietary practices in addition to their faith in Jesus.

Judging from Paul's characterization of this teaching as a 'different gospel' (1.6–7), we may surmise that these agitators or 'Judaizers' were insisting that people had to accept their teaching if they were to be saved. Paul rejects this emphatically. Not only were they placing ethnic restrictions on God's gracious generosity (2.11–14; 4.17), they were making life difficult for the Galatians (4.29; cf. 5.11) and destroying the gospel that he had preached. It was in the context of his handling of this pastoral situation that Paul developed his teaching on justification by faith.

At the heart of Paul's argument with the Judaizers is the issue of how a person is 'justified' before God. The word 'justified' (from the Greek verb *dikaioō*) is one of a few related words that Paul employs in his letter to

71

describe how a person is accepted before God. The verb 'to justify' is related to the adjective 'just' (*dikaios*) and the noun 'justice' (*dikaiosyne*). Many scholars translate the latter as 'righteous' and 'righteousness' respectively, to bring out the correlation between being justified before God and standing in a right relationship with God. To be justified is to be righteous before God.

Paul reminds his readers that it is through faith in Christ alone that they are reckoned and rendered as righteous before God. He says this to counter the demand of the Judaizers that the Galatians must join the covenantal lineage of Abraham by observing the law if they are to be justified. And the sign of that transfer of allegiance to the Jewish faith and community is circumcision. In commending this, the Judaizers were simply reiterating the process by which Gentile proselytes were initiated into Judaism.

Against this Paul argues that it is through faith in Jesus Christ alone that the covenantal promises made to Abraham are available to all, whether Jews or Gentiles. Just as Abraham was counted righteous before God on account of his faith (3.6), so Paul argues that all who trust in Christ are counted as righteous or justified. All who believe, he asserts, 'are the descendants of Abraham' (3.7). The covenantal promises given to Abraham are realized in Christ, and Christians, by virtue of their union with Christ *the* offspring of Abraham (3.16), partake of the blessings promised to Abraham (3.26–27).

The Christian faith, centred on Jesus Christ, is not a deviation from the faith of the Old Testament but a continuation and fulfilment of it. When Paul says that Christ became a curse for us so that 'the blessing of Abraham might come to the Gentiles' (3.13–14), he may well be echoing the Lord's promise to Abraham that from his 'offspring shall all the nations of the earth gain blessings for themselves' (Genesis 22.18). The enlarging of God's covenant with Israel to include the Gentiles is part and parcel of the historical outworking of the divine redemptive plan. To insist that the Gentile Galatians undergo circumcision and take on board the other religious regulations of Judaism is in Paul's mind a travesty of the gospel.

Paul is at pains to emphasize that justification is by faith because to get it wrong here would lead to a heightening of tensions between the various groups in the church, particularly between Jewish and Gentile believers. Everyone is saved and inducted into the body of Christ in the same way. Paul says of the Galatians: 'in Christ Jesus you are all children of God through faith' (3.26), who together address God as 'Abba! Father!' (4.6). The apostle is concerned that the social form of the church be consistent with this fundamental reality. Since all alike are justified through faith in Christ, there is no room for the kind of hierarchical discrimination that elevates one group over another. Regardless of one's ethnic identity, economic status, or gender, all are loved, forgiven and accepted in Christ. The experience of salvation in Christ impacts the way believers understand themselves and relate to each other within the Church. Justification by faith has definite ecclesial consequences.

The new inclusive community of the justified

The gospel is a great leveller. In Christ, 'there is no longer Jew or Greek, there is no longer slave or free, there is no longer male and female' (3.28). In saying this, Paul is not doing away with racial and cultural differences. He himself sustains ethnic differences in 1 Corinthians 7. Jews and Gentiles retain their ethnic identities while slaves work alongside the free, even though individuals from both classes are connected by faith in Christ and worship alongside each other in the early churches. Obviously, people do not stop being male and female after believing in Jesus.

What it does mean is that one's identity is not determined ultimately by what race or tribe one is from; nor is it dependent on one's economic wealth or one's gender. Rather, the Christian's identity is defined finally by his or her relationship with Christ. To be sure, followers of Jesus are inescapably rooted in specific social and cultural contexts, and they gladly embrace and celebrate their God-given ethnic identity. The Church of Christ is undeniably multi-ethnic, and it comprises men and women from all social and economic strata.

Yet over and above the traits and differences that mark Christians out is their common allegiance to Christ and the common basis of their entrance into the covenantal community. This oneness of God's people under the Lord Jesus is a new reality brought about by the historical unfolding of God's redemptive plan. From the standpoint of New Testament theology, the life, death and resurrection of Christ constitute the dawn of a new chapter in God's eschatological plan for the world, a plan that will culminate with the second coming of Christ. All who are justified in Christ have been set free 'from the present age' (1.3), as Paul reminds the Galatians. They are now a 'new creation' (6.15), and as the 'Israel of God' (6.16), they are partakers of the covenantal promises of Abraham. And this new covenantal community of God's reconciled people is distinguished by an inclusiveness that transcends cultural differences. Paul elaborates on this in Ephesians: Christ has smashed the dividing wall between Jews and Gentiles, abolished 'the law with its commandments and ordinances', and created in Christ 'one new humanity in place of the two' (Ephesians 2.14–15).

Equality and unity of all believers in Christ is at the very heart of the gospel. The gospel removes those dividing walls that separate people on the basis of race, economic standing and gender. To regard Gentile believers as somehow second-class because they are not Jews is in Paul's view a violation of the gospel. Similarly, any discrimination based on social class or gender superiority is contrary to the truth of the gospel.

Unfortunately, even in churches today we continue to find racial prejudice at work, where some people are regarded as inferior on the basis of the colour of their skin. Living in a predominantly Chinese society in South-East Asia, one is made aware of the subtle (and sometimes not so subtle) discrimination that regards some non-Chinese races as somehow less trustworthy, unmotivated or prone to laziness, given to promiscuity, etc. Such cultural biases and stereotyping are sadly present in our churches as well. We see this for instance in the way certain congregational policies are put in place to ensure that leadership will always go to those from the dominant racial group, while those who are not 'our kind of people' are excluded from positions of power and influence.

It does not take long to move from a demeaning attitude to a denigration of another ethnic group, which in turn leads to an outright 'demonization' that escalates into destructive violence. Ethnic tensions and communal conflicts give birth to open warfare, as carnage and atrocities follow from the radicalization of identity politics. One needs look no further than the recent history of sectarian violence in Sri Lanka, the bloodbaths in Rwanda between the Hutus and the Tutsis, and the conflicts in the Balkans between the Croats and the Serbs. In such situations of tribal violence, Christians are often as guilty as other perpetrators, for they have, tragically, allowed their tribal allegiance to take precedence over their identity in Christ.

Separation of people along ethnic lines is often tied to the kind of one-upmanship that is pegged to one's socio-economic status. In a highly materialistic society, a person's worth is often measured by the amount of his or her possessions. The wealthy are given preferential treatment while the poor are at best ignored and at worst oppressed. Sadly, we find the values of our society often reflected in the way leaders are selected in the Christian community.

In many South-East Asian churches, particularly among the Chinese, it is not uncommon to find leadership positions occupied by people of means, usually business owners and professionals. While many of them are spiritually mature and appropriately gifted, the observation nevertheless remains valid: very often a person's standing in church appears to correspond to his or her standing in society. How is it that there is consistently a lack of qualified spiritual leaders among those who are lower down on the economic ladder? That there is 'no longer slave or free' in Christ should remind the Church today that whether one is rich or poor, acceptance before God is decided solely on whether one is justified by faith in Christ.

That same Christ-centred inclusiveness should be evident in the way male and female relate in church as well. Women had a lower religious status in first-century Judaism. They were excluded from observing certain 'special days, and months, and seasons, and years' (4.10) during menstruation. In asserting that there is 'no longer male and female' in Christ, Paul in effect raises the status of women in the male-dominated culture of his day. Commentators suggest that he may have in mind the sentiment expressed by the synagogue prayer in which the worshipper thanks the Lord for not making him a Gentile, a slave or a woman when he wrote Galatians 3.28. By way of contrast, Paul argues that the gospel has no room for the marginalization or subjugation of women.

In different ways, women today continue to be disadvantaged. This manifests itself for instance in employment practices where invisible barriers ('glass ceilings') are erected to prevent women from getting the top jobs in a company, even when they are eminently qualified. Once again, what goes on in the world is often repeated in the Church as well. Through a variety of policy decisions, women are in many instances effectively excluded from key leadership positions in the Church simply on the basis of their gender. If a Gentile can exercise leadership alongside a Jew, and if a slave can freely do the same as a citizen, there is no reason why a woman cannot exercise her gift of leadership in the Church.

Not all discriminatory practices against women are benign; some are deadly. In certain societies, female infants are killed at birth for no other crime than being born girls and not boys. According to the World Health Organization, from 100 to 140 million girls and women in the world are estimated to have undergone female genital mutilation for non-medical reasons, with approximately three million girls at risk of being subjected to the same procedure each year. Such is the cruelty of this practice that it has been internationally recognized as a violation of human rights. Equally abhorrent is the practice of 'honour killing', whereby men in the family murder female members deemed to have brought dishonour upon the family. What constitutes 'dishonour' can range from a refusal to enter into an arranged marriage, to unsanctioned sexual behaviour, to rape or adultery. There is an average of about 12 such honour killings in the United Kingdom every year.

The examples canvassed above are only some of the myriad ways in which people are discriminated against and excluded from fellowship. Beyond the spheres of ethnicity, economics and gender are other forms of discrimination, e.g. against the elderly, against young people, those with physical disabilities, etc. All this indicates the distortions to human life that have been brought about by human sin and alienation. But this is not just a reality that is found in the world and has nothing to do with the Church. On the contrary, we maintain that what goes on in the Church is not unconnected with what God intends for human society.

Through Christ, God has begun the redemptive process of reversing the fragmenting and dehumanizing effects of sin on human life. This is nothing less than the actualization of the kingdom of God on earth, which will be completed only at the second coming. Meanwhile, the Church as the new covenantal people of God is to be a sign and a prototype of life under the kingly rule of Christ. To the extent the Church embraces in the here and now all people regardless of their race, economic status and gender, to that extent she bears witness to the powerful reality of redemption in Christ.

Conclusion: The searching word and the transforming Spirit

To be justified in Christ is to behave in a manner that is Christ-like, which is manifested in the way Christians exemplify a welcoming and inclusive attitude towards other people. But does inclusiveness in the Church mean that anyone is accepted into the community indiscriminately? Some have argued, for instance, on the basis of Paul's assertion in Galatians 3.28, that the Church cannot exclude people who are practising homosexuals since, supposedly, there is not to be any form of discrimination in the body of Christ. Or is there?

Paul's strongly worded condemnation of those who preached another gospel would already suggest that inclusiveness for him is not the same as absolute tolerance. Furthermore, his warnings against gratifying 'the desires of the flesh' (5.16) or 'the works of the flesh' (5.19) indicate that inclusiveness for him is no justification for licence. There remains a distinction between what is of the Spirit of God and what is of human fleshly sinfulness. Paul appeals to the word of the gospel that has been entrusted to him as the basis for distinguishing between what is of God and thus consistent with the truth, and what is a deviation from the truth.

Justification by faith points to (a) the judicial standing of the sinner who is declared righteous before God on account of his faith in Christ, and (b) the moral and behavioural transformation of the sinner by the Holy Spirit. Believers not only stand righteous before God, they also live and behave in a manner that demonstrates that they are indeed righteous as God is righteous. In the language of traditional theology, *justification* and *sanctification* go hand in hand. Despite his strong assertion that justification is by faith and not through keeping the law, Paul nevertheless exhorts the Galatians to moral living in 5.13—6.18. He reminds them not to use the freedom that they have in Christ 'as an opportunity for self-indulgence' but to 'enslave' themselves to each other in love because the whole law is fulfilled in the command to love one's neighbour as oneself (5.13–14).

And as we have argued, Christians show themselves to be transformed in Christ when they treat people with dignity and embrace them into the community of faith. Such an 'other-centred' orientation runs counter to the ways in which we instinctively look after ourselves and protect our own interests, often at the expense of others. Such is the entrenched self-absorption of the human heart that only through the supernatural work of God's Spirit in believers will the Church mirror the gracious acceptance of Christ and be the kind of inclusive community that Galatians 3.28 speaks about. It takes moral courage to go against the grain of our society in refusing to measure people by the yardstick of ethnicity, wealth or gender. Such a countercultural way of life is possible only through the transforming power of the Spirit, which is an inseparable part of being justified by grace through faith.

Galatians 4.8–20

Paul's concern for the Galatians

 Summary

Showing great concern for the spiritual welfare of the Galatians, Paul appeals to them to remember how they became Christians. He does this so that they may not be deceived by the flattery of his opponents.

 Notes

4.8. By nature are not gods: Paul does not deny the existence the 'gods' of the Gentiles, but asserts that they are not the one true God. Religions were not 'invented' because people wanted to indulge their imagination. In most religions people try to keep on good terms with realities over which they have no power. In many religions people worship the sun because of its power to give warmth and light, to make things grow, but also to cause droughts and famines. Mother earth feeds her children with grains and fruit. Clouds give refreshing and life-giving rain, but also bring frightening thunderstorms and terrible floods. Other forces are more subtle but equally strong, such as, for example, the sexual urge, which exercises tremendous power over people. All these powers or material 'principles' seem to be capricious. They can work for good or for evil, and people feel it is important to keep them friendly or, if they are hostile, to pacify them and to make them friendly. As many of these powers or 'gods' are connected with the year of nature, the calendar plays a large part in many religions, which makes the observance of the stars and planets an important matter: the proper seasons must be observed, and the proper ceremonies must be performed, otherwise, so people believe, terrible things might happen. When some natural disaster strikes, such as an earthquake, or a dry summer leading to a poor harvest and famine, or a plague of locusts, or an epidemic among people or cattle, people always wonder what they have done wrong: has some ceremony been forgotten, or performed wrongly? Religious observances are often festive and cheerful, but an element of fear plays an important part.

4.9. To be known by God: Paul was writing in Greek, but he was a Jew (2 Corinthians 11.22; Philippians 3.5). In Hebrew 'to know' also means 'to love'. It is often used for 'making love', or 'having sexual intercourse', but can also be used for many different sorts of love: the emphasis is on the closeness and intimacy of the love. Hence, 'to be known by God' means to be loved intimately by God.

4.10. Special days, and months, and seasons, and years: This seems to show that Paul's opponents laid great stress on the observance of the Jewish calendar. Judaism differs from many religions in that its annual festivals, which were originally connected with the seasons of sowing and harvest, have become days to remember and relive *historic* events, i.e. God's saving acts in history. God's salvation had freed Israel from the idea that religious observance can influence nature.

These festivals are observed at the proper time, and in the proper form, but they celebrate the freedom which God gives. However, in Paul's day there were some Jewish sects in which the seasons had again become the masters, and astrology played a large part, with ideas about the good or bad influence of time and chance, and of the planets, on human affairs.

4.12. You have done me no wrong: Paul does not feel that he has been personally insulted by their conduct even now.

4.13. Because of a physical infirmity: Paul's words mean literally 'through weakness of the flesh', but we have no way of knowing what his ailment or disability was. We only know that it must have been something unpleasant to see, so that people might have wanted to shun him. The 'thorn given me in the flesh' (2 Corinthians 12.7) may have been the same thing.

4.14. You did not ... despise me: Paul actually expressed himself more strongly: 'You did not spit on me.' Spitting was in ancient times a strong show of contempt. There is also evidence to show that ancient people spat at a diseased person in order to prevent the disease from afflicting them.

An angel of God The Greek word *angelos* means a 'messenger'. It is used for a human messenger in Luke 7.24; 9.52; James 2.25, but in the New Testament it usually means a heavenly messenger (e.g. in Luke 1.11, Romans 8.38; Revelation 1.1; etc.).

4.15. You would have torn out your eyes: Some interpreters think that this hints at the nature of Paul's ailment. But it is picture-language, meaning that they would have done anything for him. In ancient times the eyes were considered the most precious organs.

4.19. Little children: This translation is perhaps too literal. Paul did not mean that the Galatians were only little children in the faith, but used this word as a term of endearment, to show that they were dear to him. Earlier in his letter he had stressed that they were no longer little children (3.23—4.7).

Pain of childbirth Paul uses a very graphic image to speak of the relationship between the Galatian Christians and himself. Leading them to the new life and freedom that is in Christ was like giving birth: an often slow and painful process.

Christ is formed in you This is the end result of the 'birthing' process: that the Galatian Christians might be like Christ. This has a bearing on the critical issues the Letter is addressing. Becoming like Christ will mean experiencing fully the life of freedom from bondage to the law or the elemental spirits of the universe.

 ## Interpretation

The Galatians had once been 'in bondage' to powers and principles which were not God. But they had heard the gospel, and had come to know God, or rather, they had learned that God knew them, that is to say, loved them. Since they had become God's children, enjoying the freedom of his children, Paul could not understand how they could possibly wish to return to a condition of slavery. By observing 'special days, and months, and seasons, and years' the Galatians were reverting to ways which were very similar to their former practices. They had, in fact, not become more Jewish, but less so. Paul had no objection to setting certain days apart for worship and prayer (Romans 14.5–6), but he was strongly opposed to people doing this in order to pacify God as if God needed to be pacified.

Paul now appeals to the Galatians to become as he is, and accept the same freedom by which he lives, for he has become as they are. He had shown this freedom in the way in which he lived as a Jew, when he was among Jews: but to the Gentiles, who were outside the law, he became as a Gentile (1 Corinthians 9.19–23). In other words, he adapted himself to the people among whom he worked. For many people this is one of the most difficult things they have to do, and perhaps especially for those in the Christian ministry. When people arrive in a new environment, they often come across customs which are different from those they have been used to, even including differences in the way people live their Christian lives. This means they have to decide which of their old customs they may rightly abandon, and which new customs they should adopt, always examining their own consciences, but also remembering that they do not have to earn God's favour by religious observances. This was a problem early Christians had to face all the time. They had to adapt themselves to the customs of the people among whom they worked, without becoming unfaithful to their Master, Jesus.

Paul saw that ministers of the gospel must stand alongside their people. You can only proclaim the forgiveness of sins if you are yourself a sinner who has been forgiven, and if your people know this. You can only truly comfort people in their grief, if you feel the same pain which they feel. You can only guide people properly, if you stand where they stand, so that you can walk together with them. And you cannot really stand beside people, if you show, or pretend, all the time that you are different.

This is one side of the matter. The other side is that the people so guided must walk with their guide. He is by their side, but if they refuse to walk with him, they will either stay where they are and get no further, or they will go astray. So Paul urges the Galatians to walk with him.

In the next few verses Paul reminds the Galatians of his ministry among them. He remembers that time with gratitude, and he has no quarrel with them. But he is wondering whether their affection for him has changed because he has told them the truth.

Paul warns the Galatians against being deceived by the flattery of his opponents, who had probably told the Galatians that they could become 'superior' Christians by following their rules. He also points out that 'strict' preachers often seek their own glory. People derive a lot of satisfaction from telling other people what to do, and are often honoured for it. We can see this clearly in the way in which the leaders of some 'strict' sects enjoy the power which they have over their followers, and in the honour in which their followers hold them. There was the famous example of Jim Jones, who founded a new sect and organized them in a community in Guyana. When he told his followers that they had no place in the present world, and that they ought to kill themselves and their children, this was exactly what most of them did: they killed their children and committed suicide. This was an extreme case, but it illustrates the power and hold which religious leaders can have over their followers.

But Paul was not really interested in his opponents. He was interested in his 'little children' (v. 14) and anxious to see them develop as true Christians. He wished he could be with them again, and able to soften the harsh tone of his letter by showing his love for them. As things were, he simply did not know how best to speak to them.

 ## STUDY SUGGESTIONS

Word study

1 What is the full meaning of the word 'know' as used by Paul in 4.8–9 to describe the relationship between God and the Galatians?

Review of content

2 (a) For what chief reasons have 'special days and months and seasons and years' been regarded as important in many religions?

(b) For what other reason do some religions, and especially Judaism, relate their worship and festivals to 'times and seasons'?

3 What had been the relationship between Paul and the Galatians when he first visited them, and in what way had it changed?

4 What did Paul suspect were the real motives of his opponents in their dealings with the Galatians?

Bible study

5 Which verse from this passage did Paul express more fully in 1 Corinthians 9.19–23?

Discussion and application

6 'Friends … become as I am, for I also have become as you are.' In what situations today is it especially important for Christian ministers and missionaries to 'become as' those to whom they minister? What are some of the steps they need to take in order to do so?

7 The 'Christian year', with its seasons of Advent, Christmas, Lent, Easter, Ascension and Pentecost (and usually a Harvest Festival) evolved in northern countries. What relations do these 'seasons' of religious observance bear to the seasons of nature? What difficulties, if any, does this cause for churches with different seasons and climates?

Galatians 4.21–31

Two sons and two covenants

 Summary

Paul allegorizes the story of Hagar and Sarah to speak of two covenants. All who are not 'of faith' belong to Hagar the slave, who is also the 'present Jerusalem'. Those who have faith belong to the 'Jerusalem that is above', and are thus free.

 Notes

4.21. You who desire to be subject to the law, will you not listen to the law?: Paul was using the word 'law' in two different meanings. The first time he meant the commandments of the law, the second time the 'books of the law', which we call the 'books of Moses'.

4.22. One by a slave woman and the other by a free woman: The story of Abraham's two sons is told in Genesis 16, 17 and 21.

4.23. According to the flesh: that is to say, in the human way.

Through the promise Sarah had already passed the age at which women ordinarily cease to conceive children, but God had promised that she would bear a son, and he keeps his promises. Paul takes this to mean that all God's promises would be inherited by Sarah's son and his heirs.

4.24. This is an allegory: The Greek word which gave rise to the English word 'allegory' basically means 'to say something else'. It is used for a story or picture-language in which each character or image stands for some idea or quality. The basic assumption is that a text can sometimes contain hidden or deeper meaning. Hence, Paul did not mean that Sarah and Hagar had not been real people. He was using the story of the two women to emphasize a deeper spiritual truth, believing that the text of Genesis 16, 17 and 21 contains a meaning more profound than that which a simple reading of it is able to give.

These women are two covenants The 'covenant' is fundamental to Israel's understanding of her relationship with God and her calling in this world. The two covenants referred to by Paul are the covenant made at Sinai and the new covenant, which was believed to supersede the former (Jeremiah 31.31).

Hagar, from Mount Sinai Paul does something astonishing when he equates the covenant at Mt Sinai with Hagar. Mt Sinai was the place where Moses received the law (Exodus 19), and the law defined fundamentally how the nation of Israel was to worship God and conduct their lives. But Israel also understood herself as the descendants of Isaac, the son of Sarah, and not of Ishmael, the son of Hagar. In this sense, Jews would never connect Mt Sinai or the present Jerusalem with Hagar. It has been suggested by some scholars that this astonishing exegetical move was Paul's attempt to reverse his opponents' exegesis. The theory runs something like this: according to the troublemakers, Gentile Christians may be regarded as the children of Abraham only if they were reckoned according to the line of Ishmael (the son of Hagar), and not Isaac. Paul counters that all who are 'not of faith' – including the Jews – belonged to Ishmael, and those of faith – including the Gentiles – to Sarah! Paul's warrant for so doing is not exactly clear. It could be that by word-play Hagar and Sinai might be connected geographically, as the Arabic word *hagar* might refer to Mt Sinai; but much doubt has been cast on this. Or it could be that Paul was thinking of 'schemes': both the birth of Ishmael (Hagar's son) and the effort to obtain life with God through the law belong to the category of 'human schemes' or schemes that involved principally human initiative and action.

4.25. Hagar is Mount Sinai in Arabia: It is not certain whether the word 'Hagar' is in the original text. If it is not, the text will then read 'Sinai is a mountain in Arabia' (NJB). This makes the reading rather mundane as it appears to offer only geographical information although it has been suggested that the intent of this is to point out that Mt Sinai is outside the land of promise.

The present Jerusalem ... is in slavery with her children This is a difficult expression. The usual interpretation is that Paul was referring to Judaism, but in his view the Jews were not slaves, though they were equally restricted by the law, like children still under a 'custodian' (3.24; 4.1–2). Other interpreters think Paul may have meant the church in Jerusalem, but he had already made clear that he had no quarrel with that church (2.1–10). Whatever the case may be, what Paul says here is difficult for Jews as they regard Jerusalem as the special chosen city of God and the symbol for the people and nation.

4.26. Jerusalem above: that is to say, the heavenly city of God, of which the Christians are citizens (Philippians 3.20). This means Paul has not abandoned the idea that Jerusalem is the symbol for God's people. However, he speaks of the 'Jerusalem from above'. Many Jews did in Paul's day expect a new Jerusalem from above to replace the current earthly Jerusalem (Psalm 87.3; Isaiah 54; 2 Baruch 4.2–6; 4 Ezra 7.26;

13.36). Hence, Paul has not abandoned his Jewish heritage but is indicating that the new has come, i.e. the fulfilment of their expectations, inspired by prophecies, and they should not cling to the old. In this regard, Paul's thought is similar to some other New Testament writers (Hebrews 11.10, 14–16; 12.22; 13.14; Revelation 3.12; 21.1–3).

She is our mother Paul seems to have thought of the Christians as citizens of the heavenly city, temporarily living on earth. 'Jerusalem above' was the 'mother city', and the churches were 'settlements' on earth.

4.27. For it is written: Paul cites from Isaiah 54.1. If we bear in mind the context, we will see how appropriate the quotation is. Through the prophet, God promised that one day Jerusalem would be rebuilt with a glory unsurpassed (Isaiah 54.11–12). Her condition of barrenness would end, leading to fertility. In short, Paul is saying that what Isaiah foresaw has now come to pass.

4.28. Isaac: was Abraham's son by Sarah.

4.29. Persecuted the child: This is a rather strong interpretation of Genesis 21.9, which merely states that Ishmael was making fun of Isaac, or perhaps mocking (the NRSV translation of the Genesis verse, 'playing with her son Isaac' is too weak).

4.30. Drive out the slave and her child: The quotation from Genesis 21.10, which contained Sarah's order, is now applied to the situation of the churches in Galatia. The troublemakers who were imposing their enslaving views must be resisted and told to leave.

 ## Interpretation

In spite of the difficulties some of Paul's statements may pose for modern interpreters – and also Paul's contemporaries – the flow of his argument and the purpose of the passage is clear.

Paul wanted to illustrate the contrast between slaves of the law and God's free people by another example from the Old Testament. He was firmly convinced that the 'Jerusalem above' is free, and she is our 'mother', and that Christians are citizens of heaven (see Philippians 3.20). They live on earth, but they carry the passport of the heavenly city. The Jerusalem above is the mother city of Christians. The same idea is expressed somewhat differently in Revelation 20.9 and 21.2, 10, and may have been familiar among early Christians. The writer to the Hebrews describes the faithful people of the Old Testament – especially the patriarchs – as pilgrims on the way to their heavenly homeland. This suggests a similar idea (Hebrews 11.13–16).

It is quite possible that Paul could be responding to the brand of interpretation that the troublemakers brought with them. Jewish identity as being shaped around Abraham is a concept that was frequently found then. Quite possibly, these troublemakers might have taught that the only way that it was possible for the Gentile Christians of Galatia to be treated as children of Abraham was for them (a) to observe the law and (b) to be reckoned according to the line of Ishmael, Hagar's son, and not Isaac. In a totally unexpected way, Paul argued that the reverse was true. All those who relied on the law (i.e. being connected with Mt Sinai and the present Jerusalem) were reckoned according to the slave woman, Hagar. Those who had faith were connected to the Jerusalem from above, the free city, and were reckoned according to Isaac, the son of Sarah.

Thus the two women who were connected with Abraham were used as an allegory to speak about two covenants. Their story is found in Scripture, in the book of Genesis. Paul looked beyond the surface text to see the plan that has been unfolded in Christ. From the vantage point of this divine plan, he saw a pattern connecting Hagar, Mt Sinai and the present Jerusalem. They all spoke of the old, of human effort and schemes, and represented slavery. Conversely, Paul saw a connection between Sarah, faith and the Jerusalem from above. These represented the new – and has been prophesied as coming to replace the old – faith in divine power and promise, and freedom.

The whole allegory, then, is about the incompatibility of the old and the new. The old stood for slavery and the new stood for freedom. The Galatian Christians belonged to the new, and were thus called to freedom. They must not let the enslaving views of the troublemakers shackle them. Instead, they should stand firm in their freedom by resisting such teaching, and insisting that it should stop. If it became necessary, they should also be prepared to tell these teachers to leave.

 STUDY SUGGESTIONS

Word study

1   What is an 'allegory'?

Review of content

2   What did Paul mean when he spoke in this context of 'slaves', and exhorted the Galatians not to 'submit again to a yoke of slavery' (5.1)?

3   Paul used the story of Abraham's wife Sarah, and his slave-girl Hagar, and their sons Isaac and Ishmael as an 'allegory'. In that allegory, what did Ishmael and Isaac respectively stand for?

4   What did Paul mean when he said that 'the Jerusalem above … is our mother'?

Bible study

5   In what way can Philippians 3.20 and Revelation 20.9 add to our understanding of this passage'?

Discussion and application

6   'Christians live on earth, but they carry the passport of the heavenly city.' How would you explain this statement to someone wishing for information about the Christian Church?

7   Is your church congregation or area linked to a 'mother church'? If so, what is the relationship with the mother church and what are the practical advantages or disadvantages, in your opinion?

8   How far do you think it is helpful to think of the Church as a whole as our 'spiritual mother'? Give your reasons.

Galatians 5.1–15

Christian freedom

 Summary

Since Christ has set the Galatians free, they must not accept again a yoke of slavery. True righteousness comes through the Spirit, by faith working through love.

 Notes

5.2. If you let yourselves be circumcised, Christ will be of no benefit to you: For the first time in the Letter we are given a clear indication what the concrete issue was circumcision. This was already hinted at in 2.3 (see note). Paul states strongly that if the Gentile Christians were to submit to circumcision so as to assure themselves that they belong to God (or Abraham's family), it could only mean that Christ would be of no benefit to them.

5.3. He is obliged to obey the entire law: This had evidently not been made clear by Paul's opponents. There is evidence that some Jews of Paul's day would have shared the same viewpoint.

5.4. Have cut yourselves off from Christ: Not only would Christ not benefit the Gentile Christians if they were to submit themselves to circumcision; they would also be cut off from Christ. This constitutes the strongest warning that Paul can ever give, and is reinforced by the next clause: 'you have fallen away from grace.' This is so because it is to set people free that Christ has come (5.1). To reject this freedom and to return to the works of the law would mean severing yourself from what Christ has achieved. If this achievement is a result of God's grace, it can only logically mean that to deviate from it is to depart from the sphere of grace.

5.5. Spirit ... faith ... hope of righteousness: All the important terms of Paul's case are brought together here. In Paul's case, the Spirit's work (3.2–5) and faith in what God has provided in Christ Jesus (2.19–20; 3.6–18) are paramount in the understanding of how one might be righteous with God. Righteousness, i.e. a righteous verdict of God that may be appropriated now by faith and with the Spirit as the guarantee, remains ultimately a hope still. The hope is that the verdict of God on the day of judgement will be positive.

5.6. Faith working through love: Paul clearly indicates that faith is not passive. Since it is connected to the hope of the righteous verdict that will be pronounced on God's Day of Judgement, it is active in deeds. These deeds are defined principally by love. All this is what 'faith working through love' means.

The Greek language, which is very rich, has different words for various sorts of love: *erōs* for passionate love, and especially for the love between a man and a woman; *storgē* for love within the family, e.g. between parents and children or brothers and sisters; and *philia* for the love between friends, and generally between people who like each other.

Jews and Christians, however, preferred to use another word, *agapē*, which was rarely used by other people. The Greek translators of the Old Testament probably started this. We do not know whether they chose this word deliberately, but it did have certain advantages. Most sorts of love are either spontaneous, or grow naturally. They are also selective, and therefore limited in scope. Men usually feel passionate about some women (or preferably one woman) but not others, and women feel passionate about some men (preferably one man) but not others. The members of a family do not choose to love each other, they just do love them, and though they may sometimes quarrel violently, this does not mean that they cease to love one another. And we cannot help liking some people, and not liking others.

The Christian love, *agapē*, on the other hand, embraces all those who come our way. *Agapē* includes love for people whom we do not like, and even for our 'enemies' (Matthew 5.44). Of course it is better to 'love one another with mutual affection' (Romans 12.10); but even if we cannot like some people, we can still love them with *agapē*. *Agapē* can be tender and affectionate, and even passionate (the word occurs frequently in the Greek version of the Song of Solomon). But even when it is not, we can still seek the true good of both friends and enemies, of the people we like, and those we do not like.

5.7. You were running well: The Greek word was used especially for what we should now call track events in the stadium. The Galatians had a good chance 'to win the prize'.

5.9. A little yeast leavens the whole batch of dough: As Jesus himself pointed out (Mark 8.15), even a small amount of yeast will spread through a large amount of dough. In the same way, for the Galatians to accept the one rule of circumcision as necessary for their justification will make them once again subject to the whole of the law, and poison and destroy their whole relationship with Christ.

5.11. If I am still preaching circumcision: Paul's opponents may have said that Paul himself believed that circumcision was necessary and sometimes preached accordingly, but had not told the Galatians. Paul counters this by asking, 'Why am I still being persecuted?'

The offence of the cross has been removed The Greek word used for the NRSV 'offence' is *skandalon*, and actually means a 'stumbling block'. It is often used to refer to something that causes opposition or revulsion. In this case, it is the cross. The holding up of the cross as God's demonstration of his grace and love, and the way to righteousness, constitutes a stumbling block to many people, including Paul's opponents. Therefore if Paul preached circumcision, it could only mean that he was removing the 'stumbling block' of the cross from his message.

5.12. Castrate: The Greek word means to 'cut off', and was used specifically for castration. This may perhaps be the crudest statement made by Paul in all his Letters. It indicates how frustrated Paul is with the disruptive teaching of the troublemakers (on this further, see the chapter on 'Reading Galatians and Philippians together').

5.13. Not … self-indulgence, but … love: The manner in which Paul's opponents misused the Mosaic law created a divisive concern for the ego or the self. Paul contrasts this with the true freedom created by Christ's law of love.

5.14. The law is summed up in a single command: The Greek *pleroō* actually means 'to fulfil' instead of 'to sum up'. The idea here is that all the commandments and requirements of the law are fulfilled in the command to love. This shows that although Paul may have emphasized freedom, it does not mean he stands for lawlessness. The freedom in Christ must result in the fulfilling of the law through loving one's neighbour (see Theological essay 2).

 ## Interpretation

Paul now begins to explain what Christian freedom is like, stressing that it is the gift of God, so that nothing we do, or allow others to do to us, can add anything to it. However, for Gentiles to allow themselves to be circumcised, as his opponents had evidently urged the Galatians to do, was not only unnecessary, but would be the wrong thing altogether. In itself circumcision is neither an advantage nor a disadvantage for our salvation (v. 6). However, if we try to use it as a means to gain salvation we show that we think that Christ is not enough, and so separate ourselves from him (v. 2). Paul was not saying that a circumcised person cannot be saved; he had himself been circumcised (Philippians 3.5, and see note on Galatians 2.3). But circumcision can add nothing to what we have received in Christ.

Paul sees circumcision, and with it the whole law and all attempts to justify ourselves, as denying the sufficiency of God's grace. He did not deny that faith should be active. Faith is God working in us, and the Christian life must be lived (v. 6). By the gift of God's grace and through faith, we have been set free to do his will, and this freedom is the basis of Christian living. Paul's great objection to the teaching of his opponents was that their insistence on the letter of the law, as a means of justification, actually offended against the law and threatened Christian love, which is God's will.

God's will is that we should love our neighbour as ourselves (v. 14). But we cannot do this if we direct all our efforts towards making ourselves good, trying to earn God's favour and gain a front seat for ourselves in heaven. If we do good to other people in order to become better people ourselves or to earn God's favour, then we are not really loving them, for we are doing it for our own benefit and satisfaction, not for their good. Love means that we have other people's interest at heart, rather than our own.

This love is made possible by God's grace. Once we believe and know that Christ has redeemed us, and that we do not need to worry about adding anything to that, then we are free to love, and can begin to care for others.

God's grace is not confined to the Church: we often find *agapē* among people of other religions or no religion, who have been touched by God's goodness without knowing it. But those who have learned about God's grace, and yet try to justify themselves, put true love out of their reach.

Jesus and the Pharisees agreed, and Jews and Christians still agree, that love for God and our neighbour is the chief commandment of the law (Leviticus 19.18; Deuteronomy 6.5; Luke 10.27). Paul followed his Master in this, but in this passage he stresses the love for our neighbour, and does not even mention the love for God. Perhaps his opponents talked much about loving God, but did not see that loving God cannot be separated from loving people. In any case Paul's chief concern was to put an end to the strife and lack of love which were making the Galatian Christians 'devour one another'.

'Religious' people are often inclined to separate the love of God from the love of people. But the biblical teaching is that they must go together. Not long ago, there were great tensions between Christians and Muslims in Indonesia. However, when a great tsunami struck the city of Bandar Aceh in Indonesia in 2004, many Christians from all over the world rallied together to give aid to the city, even though it was predominantly Muslim. As Jesus has taught, whatever we do for anyone who needs us, we do it for him (Matthew 25.31–40).

God does indeed reward deeds of love (though not by 'giving us rewards'). But if the chief motive for what we do is the hope of reward, there can be no love. A religion of law is a work of the 'flesh', for it is concerned with self. In spite of their stress on the letter of the law, Paul's opponents were offending against its chief commandment, which is the commandment of love.

? STUDY SUGGESTIONS

Word study

1 In what chief way does the meaning of the word *agapē* differ from that of other Greek words for 'love'? How does this make it especially useful for describing Christian love for one's neighbour?

Review of content

2 In what way does attempting to justify ourselves before God conflict with our relationship of love for him and for other people?

3 If 'neither circumcision nor uncircumcision counts for anything' (v. 6), why was it wrong for the Galatians to allow themselves to be circumcised?

4 In what way does the attempt to gain salvation by obeying the letter of the law actually offend against the law?

Bible study

5 (a) What is the chief difference between the teaching of Jesus according to Mark 12.8–31 and Matthew 22.34–40 and Paul's teaching in Galatians 5.14?

(b) In what way might the teaching of Jesus in Matthew 25.31–40 help to explain that difference?

Discussion and application

6 What different sorts of love are distinguished in the language of your country or culture, and what words are used to describe them? Is there a word similar in meaning to the meaning of *agapē* as used by writers in the New Testament? If not, how do people describe that sort of love in your language?

7 'God's grace is not confined to the Church; we often find *agapē* among people of other religions or no religion.' Give some examples of *agapē* that you have yourself experienced from people of other religions. What reason do you think they would have given, if asked, for loving others in that way?

8 Christians are sometimes accused of running schools and hospitals and development schemes, not because they love people but because they want to persuade them to become Christians. How would you answer such criticism? How does it compare with what Paul was saying about his opponents in Galatians 4.16–18?

Theological essay 2
Freedom and obligation

SAMUEL TSANG

Introduction

Freedom and obligation are two essential elements of the gospel message. In political language, freedom is often seen as being free to do whatever one wants, and obligation as a kind of restriction to freedom. However, the opposition is only apparent. This study will show that they are actually two mutually dependent elements of the gospel.

Many Christians glean the concepts of 'freedom' and 'obligation' from Galatians 5—6. However, the whole letter can be read in this way, provided the reader is informed of its background. Little is written about the power dynamics of the forces external to the text. Most studies of Galatians focus on the Galatian readers. This essay will focus on the story of Paul as a diaspora Jew, Paul was not so romanized as to discard his Jewish identity. He preached his message from a Jewish perspective without being ethnocentric. He applied the concepts of 'freedom' and 'obligation' to all people.

The Galatian message is worth pondering in the light of the political climate of the twenty-first century. The message of freedom and obligation is significant to all, but I will apply it to two particular groups of people: those who live as migrants in a new land and those who have lived under colonization. In both situations, powerful forces can coerce the weak to conform to a different identity – just as it was in Paul's day. Paul's Gentile mission is a model of the ethics of freedom and obligation. His message speaks to all who either live as migrants or have been oppressed.

Freedom and obligation for migrants

Migrants frequently face the pressure of cultural adjustments. This turmoil can extend to the second and third generations. Many migrants find themselves competing with the indigenous population for living space and territory. So the migrants form their own subculture with its own rules. Some of these rules arise out of the experience of alienation. Such a subculture, in turn, creates boundaries to ensure that its members do not lose their common cultural identity. This being the case, the adherence to cultural identity often evolves into ethnocentricity, which ultimately results in a form of racism.

As an Asian-American biblical scholar teaching in a Chinese-speaking seminary in America, I am particularly intrigued by the theme of cultural identity within Paul's thought. For many of us, the 'motherland', though at times a distant location and concept, still carries a powerful sway in our cultural and emotional makeup. Paul also expressed his cultural and emotional connection with the 'motherland'. Yet, Paul preached a gospel without restriction of ethnicity, rituals and land. As a diaspora Jew, Paul formulated his ideas of freedom and obligation from a transcultural gospel. I believe Paul's ministry in Galatia can become a model for migrants and those who engage in cross-cultural ministry.

As Galatians indicates, some of the habits and hang-ups of traditionalism are ethnically related. Typically, such habits are framed in terms of the Jewish law. Thus, national and ethnic issues of identity cannot be completely separated from issues of salvation. After all, the Jewish law is the marker of salvation for the Jews. However, Paul's theological conclusion points to a gospel independent of ethnicity.

Paul was a colonized Jew. The Gentiles now ruled the Jews. There was mutual distrust between Jews and Gentiles. The Jews' reasons were ceremonial and religious, while the Romans' were political and tax-related. Discrimination between ethnic groups was rampant. The Romans saw those who could not speak Greek or Latin as inferior beings. Jews saw Gentiles as sinners and uncircumcised (2.15).

The ethnic dimension of Paul's Gentile mission was definitely a concern for both Paul and his agitators. Paul's mission confronted the problem of ethnic–religious boundary lines. The agitators (whether Jewish or Gentile) forced a certain interpretation of the Jewish law on to the Galatians. In the new era of Jesus and the Spirit, Paul rejected this interpretation of Christianity (4.4; 5.18). The boundary between peoples is redrawn in Christ. This, however, does not mean that Paul had abandoned his Jewish culture completely, nor that he demanded that his audience cast off their cultural identity. Rather, Paul demolished the cultural barriers people set up to keep the Christians from living out true salvation.

Paul made sure certain cultural lines were permanently obliterated. An initiative such as taking a collection for the Jews in Jerusalem in Galatians 2.10 pointed the way forward. The apostle of the Gentiles cited the decision made by the Jerusalem leaders, so that Gentile money was no longer impure. The Jerusalem poor gladly accepted this new mode of operation. Freedom from the law means that Jews can now have free fellowship with Gentiles, without obsession with ceremonial purity. The Gentiles should be trusting towards their Jewish brothers and sisters in the Church, and go the extra mile in serving them. Thus, Paul's churches must express salvation through mutual service. The Jews should no longer cling to their tradition. Instead, they were obligated to exercise freedom to accept Gentile fellowship. The Gentiles were obligated to trust freely the Jews for a greater unity under one head, Christ.

What are, then, the obligations for the believers? For Paul, there is, first, an obligation to reach out in the spirit of humility. Paul exhorted the Galatians to 'do good to *all* people' in 6.10 and not only to people of the household of faith. If justification came freely, then a growing Gentile church had no right to look down on their poorer and smaller Jerusalem counterpart or alienate their Jerusalem brothers just because of cultural differences. By example, Paul evangelized the Gentiles (2.8). His missionary action accords well with 3.28.

Another obligation for the believers is to abandon any former honour (reinforced by rituals). It is no accident that the new covenant is a landless covenant. In the ideology of the Old Testament, land, ritual and seed were all national symbols of former honour. Now 'land' has lost its former significance with the arrival of the 'Jerusalem from above' (4.25–26). Ritual has been disregarded with the arrival of the Spirit (3.2–5). Seed has been fulfilled in the universal salvation from the One Seed, Jesus Christ (3.16).

Through the Pauline lens of the gospel, we can now turn to specific examples of modern social honour and value systems. I will explain using the Asian-American church as a case study. In my culture, personal honour comes in the avoidance of shame. This leads to the need to 'save face'. When placed against the truth of the gospel, 'saving face' must always take a distant second place to the truth. If one were to transpose the Pauline context with the modern Asian church, 'saving face' is then essentially equivalent to the 'law'. The avoidance of confronting untruths in the name of 'saving face' has caused many church leaders to develop an attitude of indifference. They often avoid shaming themselves or others by taking the path of least resistance. In a 'face-dominated' culture, maintenance is valued over progress. Progress always produces resistance, both in Paul's day and in ours. This is a form of cultural bondage, which Christians must re-examine and uproot.

Another way the cultural bondage exhibits itself in Asian culture is in the unquestioning deference to the elderly. Mixed with this unremitting, age-based hierarchy is ranking and classification based on languages. Since many of the elderly members speak only the language of origin, the leadership naturally belongs to those fluent in the mother tongue. The preferred language becomes a powerful qualification for leadership in the diaspora community. The language phenomenon demonstrates the longing of the diaspora for a replication of 'motherland'. In fact, it has become a hard and fast rule for many Asian-American churches (e.g. Chinese, Korean) to reserve their senior leadership for the older generation who speak the mother tongue. The best leaders are overlooked because of artificial obstacles set up in memorial to the motherland. These obstacles have diluted the next generation of Christian leadership so severely that the Los Angeles Times, a secular newspaper, printed an article in 2007 about the Asian-American 'religious leadership vacuum'. Such a tradition has in fact prevented the diaspora church from following Jesus' great commission and reaching people of all groups and cultural backgrounds. Regrettably, because of a vested interest in their own cultural system, few leaders are willing to invest in the next generation, the members of which do not speak the mother tongue. For these entrenched leaders, the 'law' is their rigid and convoluted cultural system, part of which stands in opposition to the gospel.

In the light of the discussion above, Christians in migrant churches should learn to yield their identity with the motherland to their much more important identity with the 'Jerusalem from above'. Paul's Gentile churches had to resist cultural trends. In whatever circumstances he found himself, Paul tried to universalize the gospel thoroughly by focusing on the universal Fatherhood of God. Paul raised local leaders as much as possible, and did not claim superiority as a Jewish forebear of the Christian faith.

Freedom and obligation for the formerly colonized

The Galatian gospel also speaks to those who live in former colonies but are now operating in a global environment. Although many former colonial subjects have become empowered, they have not forgotten the injustices and injuries inflicted by the colonizers. Another pitfall for those previously oppressed is a tendency to adopt a pattern of oppression upon their chosen subjects.

Set against the background of imperial Rome, Paul's introduction of the idea of a new age points to a better way for reconciliation between the oppressed and the oppressors. Both the prologue and epilogue of Galatians discuss in detail the old and the new age (1.3; 6.15). The idea of 'age' is very common in Jewish theology. For many Jews, the present age was a struggle against the forces of evil while waiting for the coming age. The coming age was a time when the elect would be delivered from the evils of this life and would enjoy peace. With the new messianic age, Paul clarified the equality between Jews and Gentiles. They are both the new creation (6.15). The colonial subjects are no longer bound by hatred toward their colonizers, but they are to express love for all people. Paul not only forgave but also reached out to all people.

In every Letter Paul writes, the ideal of 'peace' is always preceded by 'grace'. If grace is a central message of Paul's gospel, peace must be the by-product (1.3). Paul's theology has little to do with peace as a feeling or the absence of war but everything to do with the Hebrew ideal of *shalom*. For Paul, 'peace' is a relational term that comes as a result of knowing God's grace and living by the Spirit (5.22–23). Peace can be expressed directly through forgiveness and reconciliation between peoples.

In contrast, Paul's agitators did not behave the same way. While we can read the agitators as either Gentiles who loved to follow Jewish laws or Jewish Christian missionaries who tried to impose the law, these agitators used the law of the colonized Jews to 'oppress' the Gentiles. This is not abnormal in the light of a typical colonial situation, when the oppressed turn around and use their cultural–religious bias to oppress others.

The law became the agitators' instrument to restrict the freedom of the Gentiles (5.1). They might have even abused the story of Abraham (4.21–31) to say that those who were not circumcised were children of the slave woman Hagar. Consequently, Abraham's covenant became an instrument of oppression rather than freedom.

There is a subtle parallel between the Galatian social situation and that of many former colonies in the modern period. The original missionary movement was inadvertently associated with colonial powers of the West. Ironically, in recent years, the rapid growth of Christian churches has shifted the arena of Christianity from the West into the 'Two-Thirds World'. Those who experience the blessing of church growth may gloat over the Western churches. Many 'Two-Thirds World' Christian organizations are initiating a reverse missionary movement to the West. The formerly colonized have now gained a new power through the work of the gospel. While there is much potential in these well-intentioned movements, the end result could be problematic if they are not founded on humility and love. The newly empowered believers must remember that their present status is based on inclusion within the universal family of God the Father.

In Galatians 4.6, Paul's usage of the Aramaic word, 'Abba', had long been understood and contextualized within the early Gentile church. The concept of universal fatherhood is already implied in 1.1–2, as Paul used the word 'Father' almost like a title or a name. However, by adding 'our' to 'Father' in 1.4, he explicitly reminded his audience of the uniqueness of a personal God who ruled over both Jewish and Gentile believers. God was 'our' and not 'my' Father. The paternal language functions to bring out the theme of the collective election of both Gentiles and Jews (3.28). In 4.6 Paul spoke as if the Aramaic expression was familiar to his Gentile audience. This was used, probably, in their normal worship. The lack of explanation shows that this unique aspect of the gospel – of Jewish origin – had been completely universalized even among Gentile churches. Cultures and ethnicities could change, but the gospel with its teaching of the universal Fatherhood of God should remain the same. More importantly, the Spirit enabled this recognition of fatherhood (4.6), which in turn produced the fruit of the Spirit in the Church (5.22–25).

For the newly empowered people, who were previously colonized, there are freedom and obligations that come through the gospel. First, they have gained freedom to be called children of Abraham with all other heirs of God's promises (2.7; 4.31). They are given the right to be the children of God (4.6) and thus are equals with brothers and sisters from the old colonial nation. The universalizing message supersedes cultural boundary lines. Second, based on Paul's teaching on the fruit of the Spirit, they also have the freedom and the obligation to love (5.22–23). Because they are freed from hatred towards their former oppressors, they now acquire a new power to love. Even though believers are not justified by love but by faith, the true expression of justification is love (5.22). Third and most importantly, they have the freedom from their past which was bound by the flesh (5.19–21). Anyone seeking to move into growing the Church through mission must not make the same mistakes as the agitators, whose cultural baggage still weighed heavily on their gospel preaching. Much care is needed to effectively serve a community that has been formerly colonized.

For the formerly colonized, culture exerts overwhelming influences in forming identity. Paul fought hard against such influences when they contradicted the true gospel. Paul often stood in critical dialogue with his own tradition and culture. In so doing, he avoided some of the mistakes his agitators had made and at the same time built a Christianity that penetrated every part of his known world.

Given the Pauline principles mentioned above, we will address their applications within the Asian-American community. The identity of many Christians in the Chinese community is still tied up with colonial memories. The terms people use to label individuals associated with their former enemies reveal much about their ties with the past. Many Asian immigrants, even after years of residing in the host country, still label the locals as 'foreigners'. Such labels are innocently used without censure because the entire Chinese immigrant community has long accepted these terms within their ethnic psyche. The labelling of a Caucasian person as *wai guo ran* ('foreigner' in Mandarin) is common-place in everyday conversation. I rarely hear migrants calling themselves 'foreigners' in a host country. This whole idea of 'foreigner' has to do with the foreign invasions of Asia in the colonial period. The vocabulary of the Chinese people reflects their collective memory of an earlier time – a time filled with bitterness. Yet, the gospel in 3.28 implies that this kind of labelling – an association with the 'old age' – should be eradicated because Christ's new age has come. Paul's gospel emphasizes the need to replace past bitterness with forgiveness and love.

Another label which conveys an even greater sense of animosity comes from those who dwell in their motherland. Many Chinese living in Asia call foreigners 'foreign ghosts'. Such names are given partly due to hatred of colonial oppressors and partly due to their light skin colour (i.e. 'ghost' white). These terms of contempt are not only used by most non-Christians but also by many Christians. Such vehement contempt should have been negated by the love command associated with the fruit of the Spirit (5.22). If words express values, the Christians will do well to adopt a new set of vocabulary that is more mission-minded and kingdom-minded.

With regard to the above examples, there is a greater reality at hand. Those Christians who dwell with negative cultural values are defining themselves according to a historical tragedy. Part of their cultural identity is closely tied to that bitter ethos. Such an ethos is a bondage resulting from one's refusal to break with the past and is an obstacle to freedom.

True freedom comes from fully living in the new Christian identity by actively resisting cultural identities that oppose the gospel. Only when this freedom is experienced can Christians fulfil their obligations.

Conclusion

The message in Galatia still speaks vividly to today's world. No matter where we find ourselves, we need to embrace the Christian identity, as expounded by Paul, which comprises both freedom and obligation. For those migrants who experience alienation, Paul's gospel encourages believers to take up social responsibility by contributing to their surroundings. The very cultural lines that perpetuate the migrant's alienation are now annulled. The new-found impetus to pursue a positive role in society stems from freedom from one's cultural bondage. For those who were formerly colonized, Paul's gospel provides healing which frees them from hatred and bitterness. In their new-found identity in the gospel, they will slowly learn to embrace those who come from the oppressor groups. The past injuries will be gradually eclipsed by new relationships characterized by forgiveness and love, as believers undertake their obligations earnestly. Although we no longer live in the midst of the doctrinal struggles of the Galatians, the freedom and obligation message will always be effective, relevant and powerful for people of all races, at all times and in all circumstances.

Galatians 5.16–26

Works of the flesh and fruit of the Spirit

 Summary

Paul contrasts the works of the flesh with the fruit of the Spirit.

 Notes

5.16. Live by the Spirit: The Greek literally reads 'walk by the Spirit'. However, as Jews often used the Hebrew word 'walk' to mean 'conduct', NRSV is correct to translate it as 'live by the Spirit'. What should not be missed is that the Spirit plays a fundamental role in Paul's understanding of ethics. Probably the Spirit is referred to here more as resource than norm, i.e. the Spirit provides the strength and the wisdom to practise God-given principles, especially the command to love, rather than offering us rules and regulations to stick by.

The flesh 'Flesh' does not mean our 'lower nature' (NEB which has been revised to 'unspiritual nature' in REB). Just 'human nature' (GNB) comes closer to what Paul meant, and 'self' is probably the best translation (see note on Galatians 3.3).

5.17. These are opposed to each other: With this verse Paul describes the reason for many human predicaments and failures. There is a 'war' going on inwardly since 'flesh' and Spirit are always in opposition. Christians have to learn to subdue the 'flesh' and submit to the Spirit.

To prevent you from doing what you want This is a difficult phrase. Paul may mean that the opposing influences of the Spirit and the 'flesh' create a conflict within every Christian: our self-will tries to stop us from obeying the Spirit, but the Spirit counteracts our self-will. However, this interpretation is not certain.

5.18. Led by the Spirit: This is an interesting description of the Christian's relationship with the Spirit. It is used probably because Paul was thinking of the Exodus pattern. Humankind was in bondage until set free by Christ (Galatians 3—4). Once set free, they would be led on a journey by the Spirit towards their ultimate home.

Not subject to the law This may give support to the suggestion made above. The Greek actually reads 'not under law'. This can mean 'not being under the bondage of the law' (3.23) or 'not being subject to the law'. Of course, Paul may mean both.

5.19. The works of the flesh are obvious: This introduces a catalogue of vices such as we often find in ancient writings. These lists were traditional, so we need not think that Paul's opponents indulged in all of them. However, he may have included some because of what his opponents taught or did, and 'strife' and 'dissensions' clearly describe what was happening among the Galatians (v. 15).

Fornication The Greek word meant sexual intercourse with a prostitute, but was used generally for all sexual intercourse between people who were not married. The early Church regarded the lifelong relationship between one man and one woman as supremely important (see Mark 10.11-12; Matthew 5.31-32). Paul regarded any offence against this relationship as very serious, because it offended, not only against a rule, but against love.

Impurity The Greek word could mean anything that was dirty. Paul meant careless sexual relationships.

Licentiousness The Greek word means 'unruly conduct'.

5.20. Idolatry: i.e. the worship of images: but Jews used it for the worship of other gods than the God of Israel.

Sorcery i.e. the use of witchcraft, spells or potions.

Enmities are the hostilities between people.

Strife is the quarrelling which results from such enmity.

Jealousy The Greek word *zēlos* could mean 'jealousy', but it usually means 'zeal', especially 'excessive zeal'. This must be what Paul meant, as jealousy is covered by the word 'envy' in v. 21.

Anger The Greek word can mean any sort of feeling or emotion, but strong feelings often lead to anger, and this must be what Paul meant.

Quarrels This translation is questionable. The Greek word was used for infighting about positions of honour. 'Selfish ambition(s)' (NEB, REB, NIV) is better.

Dissensions and **factions** were two faults against which the Galatians had to be warned.

5.21. Drunkenness and **carousing:** were rare in ancient Israel, and the Gospels contain only one warning against them (Luke 21.34). The Greek word translated 'carousing' meant a festival in honour of the god Bacchus, but was also used for wild drinking parties.

The kingdom of God This phrase, so common in the Gospels, was rarely used by Paul. When he did use it, he usually connected it with the conduct of the Christian life. In this he followed the practice of the rabbis, who stressed that God is King now, and connected the kingdom of God with obedience to God. In this text Paul may have wanted to stress that citizens of the Jerusalem above (4.26), where God is King, ought to live and act as citizens of his kingdom.

5.22. Fruit of the Spirit: What is contrasted with the works of the flesh (5.19) is the fruit of the Spirit. Notice two things. First, the term 'fruit' is used deliberately to convey the notions of effect, growth and gift, i.e. through the Spirit's work in a person's life he matures spiritually, and produces spontaneously the qualities that are pleasing to God. Second, the term is singular. Paul usually uses the singular (Romans 7.4; 1 Corinthians 9.7; Colossians 1.6, 10) and therefore we must not press too much meaning out of this. However, it is just possible that Paul may be stressing that these qualities are not to be separated but should be understood as the nine facets of the one Spirit-led life.

Love, joy Love comes first, as being the 'incentive' (see Philippians 2.1–2) for the other qualities which characterize life in the Spirit, with joy (the Greek word denotes great joy) second only to the love which inspires it.

Peace is not merely the absence of strife. Though Paul was writing in Greek, he would also have thought of the Hebrew word *shalom* (see note on Galatians 1.3).

Patience The Greek word has a variety of meanings: patience to wait a long time, long-suffering to tolerate other people's faults, endurance to bear suffering, and perseverance to carry out a difficult task.

Kindness The Greek word suggests 'usefulness', but was generally used for 'kindness', with the idea that kindness is practical and helpful.

Generosity The Greek word is a very general term, and is usually translated as 'goodness' (AV, NIV, NJB). When 'goodness' is expressed as concrete deeds for others, the notion of 'benefaction' or 'generosity' results. This explains the NRSV translation of the word as 'generosity'.

Faithfulness The Greek word *pistis* includes both sides of a relationship of trust; so it means both 'faith' and 'faithfulness'. See Special note B.

5.23. Gentleness: Paul's conduct makes it clear that he did not mean softness. The Gospels show that Jesus too, gentle though he was, was not soft (Matthew 12.34; 23.13, etc.).

Self-control See Proverbs 16.32 for a good commentary on what this means.

There is no law against such things This seems to confirm our interpretation of Galatians 3.19 above.

5.24. Crucified the flesh: The use of this metaphor or picture-language is astonishing in the first-century world, as crucifixion was never viewed positively. This would have come across as crude humour. Paul's positive use of it is due to the important meaning of Jesus' crucifixion to Christians. Thus Paul writes that belonging to Christ means also having our 'flesh' crucified so that it cannot exercise its baneful influence (vv. 19–21) over us.

5.25. Live by the Spirit … guided by the Spirit: The Greek word translated by the NRSV as 'guided' more properly means 'kept in step' (NIV). True life with the Spirit is life in harmony with his directions and leading, i.e. keeping in step with him and not falling behind or outrunning him.

 ## Interpretation

It may seem at first as if Paul is here contradicting himself. Throughout this letter he has been arguing that Christians are set free from bondage to the law, and now he is himself laying down what seems like laws, telling people what to do, and what not to do. But Paul never suggested that freedom from the law meant that we need not obey God. On the contrary, by redeeming God's people Christ has set them free to obey God's call to love, and there is no law against love. So the law is no longer needed to keep us in bondage, though it does still serve as a guide.

Without Christ, people are 'in the flesh' and, separated from God, they tend to be chiefly interested in themselves. The fourth-century theologian Augustine of Hippo once aptly defined sin as 'the heart turned in on itself'.

This does not always show itself in vices. Some very religious people are interested only in their own salvation and nothing else, so that though they behave in a religious way and obey all the rules of the Church, they are still in the flesh. The law, however, can deal only with those 'works of the flesh' which are actually vices, and try to prevent people from committing them.

It is absurd for people whom Christ has redeemed still to go on doing 'the works of the flesh', but Paul knew very well that even though Christians are led by the Spirit, they are still tempted by works of the flesh. Just as the Israelites in the wilderness sometimes yearned for the 'fleshpots' of Egypt, forgetting that in Egypt they had been slaves (Exodus 16.3), so Christians are tempted by sin, forgetting that sin means slavery (see John 8.34). And we fall for temptation again and again. So Paul urges the Galatians not to succumb to the works of the flesh, but to accept and enjoy the fruit of the Spirit.

The list of vices is not meant to be complete. Like similar lists it contains only selected examples. Most of them seem to have been chosen at random, but the middle ones are connected with the troubles in Galatia. By giving specific examples, Paul has avoided the trap, into which many preachers fall, of being so vague that no one applies the words to themselves.

Enmity, strife, excessive zeal, selfish ambition, anger, and party spirit threatened the life of the churches in Galatia. There is nothing wrong with zeal for a good cause, but our zeal must be positive, and we must not treat people who disagree with us as enemies to be vanquished. Organizing ourselves in groups or parties is often necessary, and may be the best means of achieving necessary social, political or religious change. But it becomes harmful if we put the interests of our own party or group before all else. In Revelation 2.2–7 the church at Ephesus is praised for its 'zeal' for the truth, but is also criticized for its lack of love. And dissension between rival Christian groups can seriously damage the 'health' of the Church today, especially in countries where Christians are a small minority among strong traditional or other religions.

In one of the earliest Christian writings outside the New Testament, a letter written towards the end of the first century to the church at Corinth, Clement, a bishop of Rome, warns the Corinthians against a 'revival of that wicked and ungodly *zēlos*, by which, indeed, death came into the world' (1 Clement 3.8). He uses the word *zēlos* in a wide sense, covering excessive zeal, rivalry and envy (see note on Galatians 5.20), and points to examples in the Old Testament of noble people suffering through the zeal or the envy of others. Clement continues:

> Let us take the sublime examples of our own generation. Through excessive zeal and envy the greatest and most righteous 'pillars' were persecuted, and battled to the death. Let us set before our eyes the good apostles. Owing to wicked zeal Peter suffered, not once or twice but many times, and thus bore witness and went to the glorious place which was his due. Owing to zeal and strife Paul gained the prize of endurance. (1 Clement 5.1–5)

He then refers to other victims of persecution, and ends this section of his letter with the general observation, 'Excessive zeal and strife have destroyed great cities and uprooted mighty nations' (1 Clement 6.4). The passage is unclear, because it refers to things which Clement obviously expected the Corinthians to know about, but which we do not know. However, it seems clear that at a time of persecution probably under Nero in AD 64, some 'Christians' were prepared to betray to the authorities fellow Christians of whom they disapproved. The later history of the Church also shows many sad examples of excessive zeal leading to strife among Christians, often causing the deaths of innocent people.

Paul contrasts the works of the flesh with the 'fruit of the Spirit'. He speaks of 'fruit' in the singular, because what the Spirit gives is not a number of different things, but a new life, characterized by certain qualities and full of joy, in which the chief aim is 'to glorify God, and fully to enjoy him for ever'.

However, life in the Spirit is not an easy option. It is given to us, so it is not the result of hard work, but it calls for much hard work, and often suffering too. Love often meets with hostility. As Christians in a largely secular or non-Christian world we may suffer scorn from unbelievers, or persecution by the state. And proclaiming the gospel requires a lot of patience, for we may not see the results until the next life. Those who live by the Spirit follow a crucified Lord.

Paul knew also that the fruit of the Spirit does not come automatically. The new life must be accepted and practised: so, 'if we live by the Spirit, let us also be guided by the Spirit' (v. 25).

❓ STUDY SUGGESTIONS

Word study

1 In Galatians 5.19–23 Paul lists the 'works of the flesh' and the 'fruit of the Spirit'. What is the chief difference in meaning between 'works' and 'fruit', and why did Paul use 'works' for the flesh and 'fruit' for the Spirit?

2 What is the usual meaning of the Greek word *zēlos*, and what is its full meaning as used by Paul in this Letter?

Review of content

3 (a) In what way may it seem as if Paul is contradicting himself in the passage?

(b) How would you explain that Paul is not in fact contradicting himself here?

4 What did Paul do to ensure that the Galatians would apply his words about 'works of the flesh' to themselves?

5 For what reason did Paul put love and joy first among the features of life in the Spirit?

Bible study

6 In which verse or verses of this passage does Paul's teaching reflect the teaching of Jesus according to (a) Matthew 11.29–30 and (b) Mark 10.21?

Discussion and application

7 Clement of Rome described how excessive zeal can lead to strife among Christians (1 Clement 5.1–5). In what way, if any, do churches in your country, or individual Christians of your acquaintance, show excessive zeal? How can we distinguish between concern or 'zeal' for truth, and lack of love?

8 What sort of behaviour would you find in:

(a) a congregation characterized by works of the flesh; and

(b) a congregation characterized by the fruit of the Spirit?

9 Which one of the 'vices' listed by Paul in this passage do you think is the greatest danger to the Church today, and why is it so?

Galatians 6.1–10

Law of Christ

 Summary

Paul counsels his readers to bear each other's burdens and show love to all, so as to fulfil the law of Christ.

 Notes

6.1. Received the Spirit: that is to say, led by the Spirit. This is true of every Christian: Paul was not thinking of some special sort of person.

Restore The Greek word simply means 'repair' (in Matthew 4.21 it is used for mending fishing nets), but it was also used for restoring relationships, making peace between people.

6.2. Bear one another's burdens: This is picture-language to express the concept of mutuality, i.e. all members have responsibility for each other's welfare. The Greek word for 'burden' literally means 'weight', and is often used to speak of burdens of an oppressive type (Matthew 20.12; Acts 15.28; 1 Thessalonians 2.7; Revelation 2.24).

Law of Christ That Paul in all his negative statements against the law is not promoting lawlessness is made clear again in this verse. 'Law' can be understood positively since it is now related to Christ. But what the 'law of Christ' is Paul does not make clear. What is however clear from the verse is that it is connected with the bearing of each other's burdens. Three main lines of interpretation of what this 'law' is are found in scholarly writings. The first is that it refers to Jesus' teaching about loving one another (Matthew 22.36–40; John 13.34). The second is that it refers to any teaching of Christ (Matthew 28.20; John 15.12). The third is that the Jewish law is the 'law of Christ' in so far as it is understood and adaptively performed in relation to who Christ is, and what he has done and taught. What Paul wrote earlier in Galatians 5.14 may be helpful here. There he states it is the love command that *fulfils* the Jewish law, whereas here he states that it is bearing one another's burdens that *fulfils* Christ's law. A clear pattern appears: love or loving action fulfils law (Jewish or Christ). If this pattern is intentional we may reasonably conclude that the 'law of Christ' is the Jewish law understood and adapted in relation to the person, teaching and achievement of Christ, and it is fundamentally about showing love.

6.3. Those who are nothing think they are something: This refers to arrogance or conceit. The connection with v. 2 may be that it is conceit that will prevent Christians from bearing each other's burdens.

6.4. All must test their own work: Honest self-appraisal is held out here as a cure for the tendency to be conceited.

A cause of pride Taking pride in one's achievements is not forbidden by Paul. This is to be measured not against another person, so as to feel superior to him or her, but against oneself for the purpose of recognizing and measuring growth.

6.5. All must carry their own loads: This does not contradict what is mentioned in v. 2 for two reasons. The first is that a different Greek word is used. This word is often used to refer to 'inescapable and everyday responsibilities', i.e. responsibilities that all humans will have. The second is that Paul's teaching on mutuality does not negate the importance of individual responsibility.

6.6. All good things: that is, shelter, food and other necessities of life. Compare the words of Jesus in sending out the Twelve to heal and preach (Matthew 10.9–11; Luke 10.5–8).

6.7. God is not mocked: that is to say, God cannot be cheated (JB) or deceived. The Greek verb means 'to mock', 'to treat with contempt', but the words which follow show what Paul meant. Whatever people sow, that they will also reap. If you sow rice, you will not harvest corn.

6.10. The family of faith: i.e. the Church.

 ## Interpretation

This passage follows naturally from what Paul had said before. People who are controlled by the 'flesh' and perform its works are constantly finding fault with each other. This makes it possible for them to look down on others, and to be proud that they are not like other people. If they are religious, they may even thank God that they are not like other people (see Luke 18.11). Such people think that they are something, and do not realize that they are nothing.

The 'law of Christ' is different. He wants people to bear each other's burdens. Generally speaking, this means he wants us to stand by people in their difficulties. Martin Luther once said: 'To love does not mean ... to wish someone else well, but to bear someone else's burdens, that is, to bear what is burdensome to you and what you would rather not bear.' One of the most difficult burdens to bear is the burden of people's sins, which Paul could be thinking of specifically when he wrote Galatians 6.2. However, Christ did not segregate himself from sinners. In fact, he was a friend of sinners (Matthew 11.19; Luke 15.1).

It may seem strange that Paul here speaks of the 'law of Christ', after having said so clearly that Christ has freed his people from the law. But free people are not lawless. In fact, people who are freed by the Lord Jesus understand the primary intent of God's laws, which are summed up in his teaching about love. This basic principle will help them understand the will of the living Lord, and the applicability to particular situations of different laws that are enacted for the smooth functioning and benefit of society.

So it is not our business to criticize others, but rather to help them bear the burden of their problems, their sins, and their shame. But it is our business to criticize our own actions. This is what Paul meant when he wrote 'all must carry their own loads'. In other words, everyone is responsible for his own actions.

Paul now moves to another point. Within the Church certain people have specific tasks, such as teaching and preaching. This may take up a lot of time and energy, and leave them little time to earn their living. Other members, who do earn money, must be ready to share their resources with those who cannot. The early Church had no paid clergy or ministry. Paul himself always tried to earn his living by working at his trade of tentmaking (1 Corinthians 4.12), but he makes it clear that those who devote their lives to the ministry of the gospel ought to have their needs provided for.

Paul ends this passage by urging the Galatians not to get tired of doing what is right. Even if we serve people for love, and are not working for any reward other than that of knowing that we are doing God's will, we can sometimes become disheartened. But it will encourage us to know that 'we will reap at harvest time', that is to say, our work of love will bear fruit.

Working for the good of all people, 'and especially to those of the family of faith' may sound like a sort of collective selfishness: look after your own people first. But to be fair, it would have been wrong for the small and poor early Church to go in for wide-ranging welfare work, while expecting people outside the Church to care for starving members of its own congregations. It would have been equally wrong for members individually to undertake all sorts of 'good works', but to take no notice of the needs of fellow Christians. Their communion at the Lord's Table also meant a community in which, when one suffered, all suffered (1 Corinthians 12.26).

It is very noticeable that the tone of Paul's writing has changed in the course of this letter. After the fiery beginning, and another outburst of anger in the middle (3.1–3), he ends by being quite tender. He really did care for his 'little children'.

 STUDY SUGGESTIONS

Word study

1 In what way does Paul's use of the word 'law' in Galatians 6.2 differ from his use of it in other parts of this Letter?

2 What was the 'load' (6.5) which Paul said each person must bear for him or herself?

Review of content

3 What was Paul's particular concern in 6.1–5, and how does it relate to his teaching in 3.23—4.7?

4 (a) In v. 2 Paul said: 'Bear one another's burdens.' In v. 5 he said: 'All must carry their own loads.' Does this mean he was contradicting himself? If not, how should we reconcile the two statements?

(b) In what ways can we 'bear one another's burdens', and in what circumstances do we have to 'carry our own loads'?

Bible study

5 Which verses in this passage reflect the teaching of Jesus in **(a)** Matthew 7.1–5 and **(b)** Luke 18.9–14?

Discussion and application

6 What are some of the ways in which vv. 1–5 apply to the practice of the Christian life?

7 What are some of the temptations to which 'religious' people are particularly subject?

8 What does v. 10 mean:

(a) for the life of the Church itself, and

(b) for the work of the Church in the world?

9 What are the advantages and disadvantages of Christian ministers being paid by:

(a) the central authorities of the churches or denominations to which they belong;

(b) the individual congregations which they serve; or

(c) earning their own living?

10 In what ways, if any, do the ministers or other members of your church 'restore' those who trespass? In what ways do they 'bear one another's burdens'? What more, if anything, could they do?

Galatians 6.11–18

Conclusion

 Summary

Paul repeats some of his earlier warnings and teachings, and makes a final appeal to the Galatians to eliminate the problem that is afflicting them.

 Notes

6.11. Large letters: This may possibly imply that Paul had a physical infirmity. This could be a problem either with his eyes or with his hand. More probably, the letters were large because Paul wanted to be emphatic. This applies not to the whole Letter but the concluding section, or part of it.

In my own hand Paul usually employed secretaries to write his letters. The Letter to the Romans was written by Tertius (Romans 16.22), 1 Corinthians 1.1 contains greetings from Sosthenes, and 2 Corinthians and Philippians from Timothy, so it seems reasonable to think that Sosthenes and Timothy acted as Paul's secretaries. Similarly, it seems that either Silvanus or Timothy wrote the Letters to the Thessalonians for him. No second writer is mentioned in the Letter to the Galatians, so Paul may have written this letter entirely by his own hand, but it also seems possible that he wrote only the final greetings himself.

6.12. That they may not be persecuted for the cross of Christ: Paul refers here to what he thinks is the motivation of the Jewish Christians in persuading the Galatian Christians to be circumcised. The larger Jewish community (i.e. non-Christian Jews) would have viewed the Jewish Christians' effort to reach out to the Gentiles as threatening the Jewish heritage or watering down certain Jewish traditions. Indeed, their belief in the cross of Christ would already have led to the suspicion that they were treating the Jewish law with too much latitude. All this could then lead to reprisals. But if these Jewish Christians could succeed in toning down their theology of the cross and persuade the Gentile Christians to be circumcised, i.e. to follow fully Jewish ways, such reprisals would be pre-empted.

6.13. Do not themselves obey the law: Paul may have meant that even the most religious person is not free from sin. This would be true, but it is more likely that he meant that his opponents stressed *only some* of the commandments of the law.

They may boast about your flesh that is, take pride in their achievement in getting Gentile Christians circumcised ('flesh').

6.14. The world has been crucified to me, and I to the world: Paul here emphasizes that the only thing which Christians can boast of is the cross of Christ, which sets us free to 'crucify the flesh' (5.24) and live by the Spirit (see notes on Galatians 5.16–17). Again, we can see how central the crucifixion of Christ is for Paul's theology.

6.15. A new creation is everything: Paul here summarizes the heart of his argument. It is not about being circumcised or remaining uncircumcised. Instead, what ultimately counts is a 'new creation'. This term points to God's promise to remake the world, where sin, futility and death will be no more (Romans 8.18–27; 1 Corinthians 15.50–58). This involves also the 'remaking' of humankind through Christ and the Spirit (2 Corinthians 5.17; Galatians 3.2–5; 5.5–6) so that they may befit that new world. In this world, ethnic identity and ritual markers will be valueless.

6.16. This rule: The Greek word is *kanōn*, from which the English word 'canon' is derived. It refers to a standard by which things are measured. The 'canon' referred to here is the one already mentioned in the earlier verse.

The Israel of God This means the whole people of God. Paul was not thinking of a 'new Israel' as distinguished from the 'old Israel', but of God's Israel being extended to include all the nations (see Romans 11.17–18; Revelation 7.1–14).

6.17. The marks of Jesus: The Greek word *stigma* means (a) a 'stab' or a 'sting'; (b) a 'brand' (to indicate who owned an animal); or (c) a 'tattoo'. As Paul would have shared the Jewish objection to tattooing (Leviticus 19.28), this meaning appears to be excluded. It is just possible that Paul shared with some Christian mystics, including St Francis of Assisi, the rare phenomenon of having in his hands the *stigmata* of Jesus, the marks of the nails of the cross. But most scholars believe that Paul was here referring to the wounds that he had suffered during his ministry. However, it was sometimes said that people who belonged to the God of Israel carried his 'mark', the 'mark' in this case being picture-language (Exodus 13.16; Isaiah 44.5; Ezekiel 9.4), so it is possible that Paul may have been referring to his baptism, which 'marked' him as belonging to Christ.

Interpretation

Paul ends his letter by repeating and stressing some of the points he has made earlier, and adds what he suspects to be the motives of his opponents. One motive is the desire that 'they may boast about your flesh' (6.13): they want to be able to boast that they have managed to convert the Galatians properly, by making them carry the outward sign of belonging to Israel: i.e. circumcision.

Another possible motive was the hope that, by remaining outwardly as Jewish as possible, 'they may not be persecuted for the cross of Christ'. At the time when Paul wrote, Christians were regarded as belonging to a Jewish sect. The Jewish faith was a *religio licita*, a legally permitted religion. Indeed, Julius Caesar, the first Roman emperor (died 44 BC) had granted the Jews special privileges. As long as Christians were regarded as converts to Judaism, they enjoyed the same privileges. Paul may have guessed that the Christians might lose those privileges as soon as the authorities learned to distinguish between Jews and Christians. Clearly, if all Christians were circumcised, it would be much more difficult for outsiders to see the difference between them and the Jews. Furthermore, any potential reprisals from the larger non-Christian Jewish community would be pre-empted if it could be demonstrated that Gentiles were being circumcised and taught to adopt fully Jewish ways.

But Paul had already made it clear, not only that circumcision was pointless for a Gentile, but also that insistence on circumcision was a denial that the cross of Christ was sufficient for salvation. So if Paul's gospel carried the risk of persecution, it would be persecution for the cross of Christ. In fact, this is precisely what began to happen a few years later. Paul himself is believed to have been a victim of the first large-scale persecution (in Rome in AD 64).

The fact that Paul's opponents observed only parts of the law may be linked to the way in which the law was a burden to a Gentile. To a Jew living in a Jewish environment, the law ought not to be a burden, but a 'light to his path' (Psalm 119.105), and one of the Jewish festivals is aptly called *simhat torah*, the 'joy of the law'. But in a different environment the law does become a burden, and when that happens, people try to get away with as little obedience as possible. Even the most legalistic Christians do not insist on every commandment of the law.

Over against the boasts of his opponents, Paul cannot put up any claims for himself. He is not his own man, for he belongs to his Master Christ. But although we do not know what is precisely meant by 'the marks of Jesus', it is surely relevant that a *stigma* also means a brand of ownership.

The Letter ends without any personal greetings to or from individuals. Some interpreters regard this as a sign of coldness. But, true to his rather variable temperament, after its reproachful, even angry, beginning, Paul's tone became much warmer and gentler in the course of this letter. His reason for not adding any personal greetings may have been that he did not want to single out any one person for special attention: the Galatian Christians were all his brothers and sisters. And surely he could not have sent any more cordial greeting than 'the grace of our Lord Jesus Christ'.

 STUDY SUGGESTIONS

Word study

1 What did Paul mean by 'the Israel of God' (6.16)?

2 **(a)** What are three possible meanings of the Greek word *stigma*, which is translated as a 'mark' in v. 17?

   (b) What are the possible meanings of Paul's statement that he bore on his body 'the marks of Jesus'?

Review of content

3 'I am writing in my own hand' (v. 11). Why was it important that Paul should write part of the letter himself, rather than leave it all to a secretary?

4 What may have been the motives of Paul's opponents in trying to persuade the Galatians to 'rely on works of the law'?

5 In what way might circumcision have shielded the early Christians from persecution?

Bible study

6 In Galatians 6.4 Paul said 'all must test their own work', and here in 6.16 he wishes 'peace' for 'all who walk by this rule'. What connection, if any, do you see between the 'work' and the 'rule' Paul was talking about in Galatians 6 and the 'works' described in James 1.22–25 and 2.26?

Discussion and application

7 What is likely to happen when people regard the law as a 'burden'? Give examples from your own experience.

8 Some people suggest that baptism has become for Christians what circumcision is for the Jews. How far do you think that this is true? In what way does the Church's teaching on baptism relate to Paul's statement in 6.15 that 'neither circumcision nor uncircumcision is anything, but a new creation is everything'?

9 How far, if at all, do Christians in your country today think of the Church, or themselves within it, as 'the Israel of God'?

Philippians

Introduction

The writer and his letter

1 Why did Paul write this letter?

Paul wrote to the Philippians chiefly to maintain and strengthen the friendship which began when he first visited Philippi. This he did by tackling some issues the Philippian Christians were facing and also thanking them for the gift sent to him.

Philippi was an important city in Macedonia, in the north of Greece, and Paul visited it in about AD 52 (see Map). We read in Acts 16.11–40 how he first preached to a small group beside the river, and then built up the Christian congregation there until he had to leave because of violent demonstrations against his teaching. He paid two more visits, probably in AD 57 and 58 (Acts 20.1 and 20.6). During this time the congregation had been growing. They knew that they owed their existence as a congregation to Paul, and they kept in touch with him by letters. When he needed help for poor Jews in Judea, they sent him money. When he himself was in prison, they sent him a gift. There was real friendship between Paul and the Christians at Philippi, as we see from Philippians 1.7; 2.12 and 4.1.

No one knows in which city Paul was in prison when he wrote this letter. Some think that it was in Ephesus or Caesarea, but more probably he wrote from Rome (see note on Philippians 1.13). He had gone to Jerusalem to take the contribution from Gentile Christians to Jewish Christians, but again there were clashes on account of his teaching, and he was arrested (Acts 21.17–39). He hoped to get a fair trial by appealing to Caesar, and so he was sent to Rome and was in prison there from AD 60–2. So far as we know he was never brought to trial. According to a tradition he died in AD 64.

Paul had other special reasons for writing. For example, he wanted to encourage the Philippians, who knew that he was still in prison and were beginning to lose heart. They realized that he might be condemned to death. So he wrote to tell them that, although he was suffering the pain of imprisonment, and indeed might soon be killed, the prison was an excellent place from which to preach the gospel (1.12–14), and so he was full of joy (1.18).

Paul needed also to tell the Philippians about one of their own members, Epaphroditus. They had sent Epaphroditus with a gift for Paul, and to comfort him, but while he was with Paul Epaphroditus fell ill and nearly died. News of his illness had reached Philippi and the congregation was becoming anxious. So, as soon as Epaphroditus had recovered, Paul sent him back to Philippi with his thanks and with this letter (2.25–30).

A third special reason for Paul's writing was the urgent need for unity in the congregation. He wrote in order to bring divided people together again (2.1–4). He had heard of members being divided for various reasons:

1 There seem to have been Jews in Philippi who were persuading one section of the congregation to forget the 'new way' which Paul had preached and to keep the traditional Jewish regulations (3.2–11).

2 Others were claiming to have developed further in the Christian life than they really had, and were thinking of themselves as 'superior' (3.12–16).

3 There was division because two leading members of the congregation, both of them women, could not work happily together (4.2–3).

2 Why should we read this letter?

We read it because it is an opportunity of opening ourselves to the same living Spirit who moved Paul to write it and who led him to live as he lived. This is, of course, true of the other New Testament books. But there are special reasons for choosing to read this Letter to the Philippians.

1 We live at a time when very many Christians are suffering for their faith, as Paul suffered. The plight of the Chaldean Christians in Iraq has recently come to light but countless numbers of unnamed Christians of every continent have also suffered for their commitment to Jesus Christ. The Letter we are studying was written by a Christian who was in prison because of his beliefs to Christians who were also suffering for their beliefs. It has much to teach the Church today.

2 We read this Letter because of the urgent need today for unity among Christians, in order that the Church may effectively preach peace and reconciliation to a divided world. Why should the world which needs to be united take seriously a Church which is itself disunited? So this Letter is of special importance.

3 We read it because we, like Paul, are uncertain about our future, the future of our country and the future of humankind. Unlike Paul, we are often anxious and afraid. So we are strengthened by reading of Paul's confidence that, whatever may happen, God has the future under his control.

4 Many people read this Letter because it is a very good introduction to Paul's other Letters. It contains in a short space many of the important ideas which we find in his other Letters, and 40 or 50 of the most important words.

But we read it above all in order to place ourselves alongside those who first read it, and to expose ourselves to the love and the authority of the same Lord. This is the chief purpose of all Bible study.

Philippians 1.1–2

Greeting

 Summary

Describing themselves as servants of Christ, Paul and Timothy greet the Christians and their leaders at Philippi by conveying to them the grace and peace of God.

 Notes

1.1. Timothy: Paul mentions Timothy in v. 1 because Timothy was with him at the time, and because Timothy was well known to the Christians of Philippi (see notes on Philippians 2.19–22). Timothy did not take any share in writing the letter.

Servants of Christ Jesus The Greek word *doulos* is translated 'servant' in the NRSV, but it is the ordinary word for 'slave'. In the days when Paul wrote, it was the custom for all households to have one or more slaves. But why did Paul call himself and Timothy 'Christ's slaves'? There are two possible reasons for this. First, the equivalent term in the Old Testament is often used for someone whom God has specially commissioned (Numbers 12.7–8; Psalm 89.20). Hence, Paul may have wanted to identify himself with such people. Second, Paul hopes to set the tone of the Letter. The term 'slave' speaks of service and giving up one's rights. Paul believes that such a message is important for the Christians at Philippi. Indeed, in 2.5–11 Paul will speak about how Christ became a slave for the sake of humankind. Of course, the two mentioned reasons are not mutually exclusive. The important thing to note here is that the Master is identified and he is none other than Jesus Christ himself.

To all the saints in Christ Jesus The word 'saint' usually has a different meaning today from the meaning it had for Paul. The Greek word is *hagios* which is often translated 'holy'. It does not here mean 'very good people' but people who are 'set aside' or 'dedicated'. For this reason it may be better to translate it 'God's chosen people'. The words 'saints-in-Christ-Jesus' should be taken together to mean 'those who are in fellowship with Christ Jesus and have been set apart by God for a special purpose'. See also note on Philippians 4.10.

Who are in Philippi Philippi (refer to Map for location) was originally built in the early fourth century BC by the Thracians who lived in the north of Greece. It became famous when Philip, King of Macedon and the father of Alexander the Great, refounded it in 356 BC and gave it his name. It was important to him because of its goldmines, and because the great main road from the East to Western Europe passed through it. It became a colony of the Roman Empire in 31 BC, which brought it many privileges. Not surprisingly, the Philippians were proud of this status. Great buildings were erected and great effort was expended to show the city's loyalty to the Roman Empire. The population in Philippi was very mixed. There were Thracians (the original inhabitants), Greeks, Romans (many of whom were retired soldiers), and people from many different parts of the Roman Empire. There was also a handful of Jews. Consequently there were many different religions and gods in Philippi. The emperor was also worshipped as a kind of god. It was in this sort of a city, among so many different races and religions, that the tiny group of Christians met.

With the bishops and deacons At the time when Paul was writing, the Greek word *episkopos* (translated 'bishop' here) was used for any 'overseer'. The Greek word *diakonos* ('deacon') was used for any helper or servant. So Paul was sending his greetings to those members of the congregation who looked after the arrangements for church services and the money that was given. Later on the Christian Church grew in numbers and was more fully organized. The words were then used in a different way. *Episkopos* became used for the person who had authority to preside at Holy Communion, was responsible for the congregation, and protected it in time of persecution. *Diakonos* was used to describe the person who assisted him in this work. The Greek word itself means 'one who serves'. Paul used it to refer to Christ himself (Romans 15.8), to himself (1 Corinthians 3.5), and to his assistants in the work of evangelism such as Timothy (1 Thessalonians 3.2).

1.2. Grace and peace: This verse may be treated as a kind of prayer: 'May you experience God's grace', i.e. 'may you discover for yourselves that God treats you better than you deserve' (see note on Philippians 1.29). 'May you be given that peace by which God brings you into fellowship with himself and with other people.' Although this is a prayer, it is also a greeting, or rather a mixture of two greetings. The ordinary Greek greeting was *'Charis!'* ('Grace!'), and the ordinary Jewish greeting was, and still is, *'Shalom!'* ('Peace!'). See also Special notes A and I.

God our Father and the Lord Jesus Christ Jesus Christ taught us to call God 'our Father' (Matthew 6.9). The notion of God as father is also found frequently in the Old Testament (Psalm 103.13; Isaiah 63.16; 64.8). But all this does not mean that God is to be understood as male rather than female. God transcends gender as we understand it. In a 'gendered' language, a 'gender' is used for God mainly to avoid calling God 'it', since God is someone with whom we can have a loving relationship. This problem does not exist for languages that are not gendered.

 ## Interpretation

Right at the start, Paul was showing his friendship with the Philippians rather than his authority over them. In most of his letters he reminded his readers of the authority which God had given him to speak and work in his name. He often described himself as an 'apostle' (Romans 1.1). The case is different with this letter. Before he wrote anything else he made it clear to his readers that he was writing as a friend.

Paul used the name of Jesus Christ three times in these two verses to remind the Philippians that living 'in Christ' was the great experience which he and they shared. Paul was a Jew, and since childhood had believed in God. But God had come into the world in Jesus Christ, and since that event the fullest life was a life lived in Christ (see note on Philippians 4.10).

In showing his friendship, Paul described himself and Timothy as slaves. Although the ordinary meaning of the term may be abhorrent to many people, it is actually transformed by the phrase 'of Christ Jesus' in the following way:

1   Christians are slaves *to Christ*, but not to other men and women. Nor are they a slave to traditions or to their own habits. This is made clear in Romans 6.22: 'But now that you have been freed from sin and enslaved to God, the advantage you get is sanctification. The end is eternal life.'

2   They are *owned* by Christ. The owner bought his slaves and then possessed them just as he possessed his home. In 1 Corinthians 6.19–20 Paul says, 'You are not your own: you are bought with a price' (by Christ).

3   Therefore they are *obedient* to this one master, Christ, and to no one else. But Christians are unlike slaves of those days because they are free to obey or disobey.

4   This special slave master gave *protection* and safety. When the great Bishop Polycarp was arrested by Roman soldiers in AD 156, he was told that he could be set free if he would speak against Christ. He said, 'I have been the slave of Christ for 86 years and he has never treated me unfairly. How can I blaspheme against my King who has kept me safe?'

Later in the Letter, Paul would have much to say about Christians serving one another (2.1–4) and about Christ himself being a *doulos* or slave (2.5–11).

Paul called his readers saints. The meaning of this term has gone through quite an evolution in the history of the Church. For Paul, 'saints' were people who had been *set apart* or consecrated by God for a special purpose. Saints who are 'in Christ Jesus' have been dedicated to do what he wants to be done. They were ordinary people, but God had given them special work to do. Later on the word 'saint' came to be used in a different way. It began to mean extraordinary people, i.e. those whom others regarded as living unusually Christ-like lives. So on All Saints' Day Christians praise God for such people of the past. It is of course important that we should take note of these great Christians and thank God for them. But it is precarious to use the same word for them as we use for the people whom Paul called 'saints' in this verse. The danger is that we, the ordinary but committed Christians of today, will be disheartened because we are admiring the lives of extraordinary Christians and feeling we can never be like them. If this happens, there is a further danger: that we shall forget what God expects from us and what we are capable of becoming.

Christians need to accept the title of 'saint' so that they may remember God has set them apart for a purpose and given them a commission. But they also know that this 'being different' does not mean that they are superior to other people. 'Saints' have to be in the world and yet not of it. It is not always easy to find a balance between the two.

The 'saints' or 'Christians' to whom Paul was writing were probably meeting in someone's house. (Perhaps they needed two houses to meet in, because the numbers had grown too big for one house.) We can imagine the following as taking place. It is Sunday and they have gathered from different parts of the city to celebrate the presence of the risen Jesus Christ. It is a mixed congregation, containing both Jews and Gentiles. The service begins with prayers and readings, and then the leader breaks the bread and pours the wine, and the members share the life of God, and are strengthened to go out to serve him in the world. But before they do so, someone says, 'Paul has sent us a letter and I will read it to you!'

Paul called the leaders of the church at Philippi 'bishops' and 'deacons'. The terms as they are used today have gone through quite a change. Instead of having a few *episkopoi* (overseers or bishops) for one church as it was in Paul's time, one *episkopos* is often responsible today for a group of congregations, and has become more and more a *governor*. Most Christians agree that some people must be given the authority to lead the Church. But they do not all agree as to what sort of authority God wants his church leaders to have, or what sort of work they should do. This is one important reason why churches find it difficult to unite. Some say that the only sort of *episkopos* that God intends is the leader of a single congregation. Others say that it is God's will that an *episkopos* should be responsible for a group of congregations. However, in all churches he has important decisions to take, especially decisions concerning the declaring of the true Christian teaching in the face of false teaching. But in some churches he takes most of these decisions on his own, while in others he acts in consultation with other leaders. Some churches expect their 'bishops' or leaders to be involved in political affairs on behalf of the church; other churches do not want them to do this.

We cannot settle this problem (concerning the sort of authority that God wants church leaders to have) simply by referring to this verse or any other New Testament verses. To be sure, the biblical evidence is important but dialogue between different groups of Christians, with the living Spirit of God guiding them, is also important.

The work of a deacon changed as the needs of the Church changed, and today different churches use the word 'deacon' to mean different things. But its meaning of 'the one who serves' has remained, following the example of Christ (Mark 10.45).

In his greeting Paul used two words – 'grace' and 'peace' – which were commonly used by those who were not Christians, so that it became customary for Christians to use them in a new way. In the same way, church leaders in non-Christian countries today often try to make use of old, non-Christian words and customs, rather than invent new ones. Someone who is translating the Bible into the language of a newly converted tribe or people often tries to use the word for God which that tribe already uses, unless of course it will lead to entirely wrong ideas about God.

 ## STUDY SUGGESTIONS

Word study

1 The Greek word *doulos* is translated 'servant' here, but it is the ordinary word for 'slave'. Which do you think it is better to use in a Bible translation? Give reasons for your answer.

2 What word does your church usually use for 'God'? Is it:

   (a) a word also used by non-Christians, or

   (b) was it imported from outside?

   What are the advantages and disadvantages of (a) and (b)?

Review of content

3 What were the advantages of being a slave at the time when Paul wrote?

4 What are the two most important truths about a 'saint'?

5 What did the words 'bishop' and 'deacon' mean at the time when Paul was writing?

Bible study

6 What is the chief difference between the beginning of this Letter and the beginning of the Letter to the Galatians (Galatians 1.1–3)?

7 Read Isaiah 49.14–15; 66.12–13; Hosea 11.1–3. Do you think that, in the light of such verses, God should be called 'Mother' as well as 'Father'? Give reasons for your answer.

Discussion and application

8 'Saints have to be in the world, and yet not of it. It is not always easy to find a balance between the two.'

   (a) Which of the two do you think Christians tend to be in your church?

   (b) In your church do you revere any local 'saints' of the past, or none at all, or those traditionally revered by all Christians?

9 (a) What title or titles do you give your church leaders?

   (b) How important are these titles?

Philippians 1.3–8

Thanksgiving for partnership

 Summary

Paul mentions that he thanks God for the partnership of the Philippian Christians in the work of the gospel and prays for them constantly. He is confident God's work in them will not be wasted. Paul also mentions he yearns for them.

 Notes

1.3. My God: These may seem to be the words of a greedy or selfish person, as if he was saying, 'God is mine, not yours.' But what Paul meant was that in the loneliness of the prison he had a companion: God himself. God was his, not someone whom his ancestors had worshipped long ago. God was someone who was around him and to whom he himself had become a willing slave, and with whom he had a special relationship. The writers of the Psalms used the same language: 'The LORD is *my* shepherd' (Psalm 23.1); 'O God, thou art my God; early will I seek thee' (Psalm 63.1, AV).

1.4. Joy: This constitutes a prominent theme in the Letter (Philippians 1.18, 25; 2.2, 17, 18, 28, 29; 3.1; 4.1, 10). Used in Scripture, the word conveys an attitude or an orientation in life rather than a feeling. It is based on God's goodness and assured promises and, hence, it is not dependent on outward circumstances. Indeed, in Old Testament prophecies it is a characteristic of the age to come (see especially Isaiah 12.3, 6; 25.9; 41.16; 49.13; 51.3; 52.8; 55.12; 61.7). Refer to Theological essay 4 for further treatment of this theme.

All of you See also vv. 7, 8. It is clear that 'all of you' are important words because Paul uses them four times in these few verses. He was writing to *all* the members of this small congregation, the uneducated as well as the well-educated, those who had opposed him and those who had agreed with him, those whom it was difficult to like and those whom it was easy to like. He wrote 'all of you' in order to help them to see themselves as one body, and to prevent division among them.

1.5. Your sharing: The Greek word is *koinōnia*, and it is best translated as 'partnership' (NIV, NJB). Paul was writing this letter partly because the Philippian Christians needed deeper 'partnership' among themselves. So it is not surprising that he used this Greek word six times. But this 'partnership' (or 'fellowship') was also something which he valued very highly for himself. He was in prison and was separated from other Christians, and the Philippians supported him and were his 'partners' (see Special note E).

The gospel Seven times in this letter Paul wrote about the 'good news' or the 'gospel'. (These are translations of the Greek word *euangelion*.) The word is used in different ways by Christians of the first century:

- The message *that Jesus preached* (Mark 1.14–15).

- The preaching *about* Jesus, in which his followers declared that he died and rose again. Paul's work was to defend this 'good news' and declare its truth (1.7).

- A book in which was written the story of Jesus. So we speak of 'St Mark's Gospel'.

- The whole *work* of preaching and travelling and caring for congregations which Paul did in obedience to God. This is how Paul usually used the word in this letter, e.g. 4.15: 'in the early days of the gospel, when I left Macedonia'.

Two other points are to be noted. The word has its roots in Isaiah, where it is used in the context of God's promise to rescue his people from exile and defeat the forces of evil (see e.g. Isaiah 52.7; 61.1). Furthermore, it was used in the context of official Roman propaganda. The empire used the word for the birthday and accession of the emperor, and proclaimed these events to be good news for the whole world. Bearing in mind Philippi's pride in being a Roman colony, the use of the term by the early Christians amounted to being a counter to what she held dear. They were claiming in effect that it was only in Jesus Christ that the true good news might be found and not in Caesar or the empire.

1.6. The one who began a good work among you will bring it to completion: The 'good work' here refers to the work of God in saving the Philippian Christians through the proclamation of the gospel and bringing them together as a church. This work is a process that needs completion and it is possible because of God's grace and commitment to his people. The completion envisaged here is probably the full spiritual maturity the Christians are to attain and the full salvation that they will one day experience.

Day of Jesus Christ Paul often spoke and wrote about this 'day' and called it by different names: 'the day of the Lord' (1 Corinthians 5.5); 'that day' (2 Thessalonians 1.10); 'the Day' (1 Corinthians 3.13). What is this 'day of Jesus Christ'? It is the time when God will complete the work which he began with the creation. This will take place at the second coming of Jesus Christ.

1.7. You hold me in your heart: The Greek original is not clear here. The phrase may mean 'I hold you in my heart' (AV, NIV, NJB) or 'you hold me in your heart' (NEB, NRSV). Taking into account the thought-flow, the first meaning is preferable.

All of you share in God's grace with me The Philippians and Paul were both privileged to receive God's grace. Both they and he knew that although they were suffering, God was giving them gifts which were more than they deserved. This is always the main thought in the word 'grace'. See the note on Philippians 1.29 and also Special note A. The translation 'you are all partakers of my grace' (AV) has misled many readers.

Defence and confirmation The terms are to be understood in a forensic way, i.e. Paul is engaged in putting his case before a Roman magistrate, the outcome of which is still not clear. According to Paul, this activity also involves the Philippian Christians, as they are his partners in the work of the gospel.

1.8. Compassion of Christ Jesus: The Greek word behind 'compassion' here is *splanchna*. It was used originally to refer to the intestines. However, since ancient people understood the seat of emotions to be found there, it also has the meaning of 'affectionate love'. Paul links this with Christ Jesus in that it is because of and through him that it is possible for such deep affection to be shown to the Philippian Christians.

 ## Interpretation

In this section Paul was telling his friends at Philippi something about himself and his thoughts about them. He said four things:

1   I am praying for you (vv. 3–4);

2   I am thanking God for you, especially for your generosity (vv. 3, 5);

3   I am like you, because we have both been generously treated by God (v. 7); and

4   I am longing to see you (v. 8).

We notice first the *joy* which Paul showed in writing this. When we remember that he was writing from prison it seems wonderful that he could write with such thankfulness and joy. We may feel that if we ourselves had been in Paul's place we might have been more likely to express our anxiety concerning the future, or concerning the health of

Epaphroditus. What made Paul able to write in the way that he did? Many verses in this Letter provide the answer. Take 1.5–6 as an example. In these verses we are told Paul could be joyful because of the Philippian Christians' unwavering partnership in the work of the gospel, which led to a genuine concern for Paul. Furthermore, Paul knew that such a state of affairs was not temporary as God's work in them would not go to waste.

We notice again that Paul, who was their leader in the Church, wrote as a friend to other friends: 'I long for all of you' (v. 8). Somehow he was able to join the *authority* (which he believed God had given him) with this *friendliness*. Those who received his Letter would, as a result, be happy to consider seriously what he wrote. Their attitude to Paul would be very different from our attitude as we read a notice on a school notice-board, or look at advertisements placed on the roadside by someone who wishes us to buy his cigarettes. It would also be different from the attitude of people who stand listening to a military governor making announcements on the radio.

Paul was confident of their spiritual progress. God, in his love, made himself known to the men and women of Philippi, and they loved him in return and so the church there was begun. This is the 'beginning' which God brought about (using Paul to do it). But God had not left the Philippians alone: he would continue to work in and around them, so that they might increase in their love to him and to each other. So Paul wrote 1.6, first, in order to give encouragement to the Philippians; and we see from 1.28, 29 how much they needed it. He was showing them that God would not neglect them. Second, he wrote in order to remind them that Christians should be developing and growing in their devotion to God.

These are words that many people still need today.

1   They are applicable to any group of Christians working in Christ's name today. The chaplain of a Christian hospital in Pakistan once wrote:

> Often in a hospital like ours we are just the first link in leading someone to Christ. We will never know when or where the next link may be forged. We are certain that God will provide the link. Or sometimes someone comes who has heard the gospel elsewhere and we have the privilege of being used as a further link. At other times we are allowed the joy of being the last link before a person's baptism ... So we are not worried, or burdened, or insisting on knowing how our work will turn out.

2   They are also words for individual Christians. First, they show that we cannot complete our own lives as Christians. Someone who had a very good watch said, 'From time to time it needs mending. But it can't do it for itself, and I can't do it. I have to take it to the maker.' So Christians take themselves to their Maker.

Second, a Christian knows that she must be as patient with herself as God is. The completing will take a long time. Changes will be needed and will not be easy to accept. It is like the story of a crab's life. A crab has to grow a great many different shells over its body before it is fully grown. As the crab's body grows, so that the hard shell is too small to hold the body, the crab throws the shell off and grows a larger one. Its growing process is a long one.

It is not the job of Christians to complete God's work in the world. Their work is to prepare themselves and others; but the completion, the end, is in God's hands.

This completion is assured and is linked with the second coming of Christ.

Living life with regard to this day brings much encouragement and spiritual benefit.

1 Those who expect this day are strengthened in their difficulties and pains. They are like people making a long journey on foot. These travellers are tired as they follow a road through a long, hot valley. But they know that there will come a time in the evening when they reach the village on the mountainside. From there, they can look back, down the road where they had been so hot and tired.

We already know that God is in control. Jesus taught us this when he spoke of God as a 'King' (Matthew 5.35; 17.25–27; 18.23). We also know – if we understand this word 'day' – that nothing can ever prevent God from finishing what he has planned to do.

2 Those who expect this day are also aware that this world is not permanent. They are like a man who lived in a part of Ethiopia where earthquakes often happen. He said he was always aware that life was not permanent and that he had to take seriously the words of Jesus: 'do not worry about tomorrow' (Matthew 6.34). He had to discover how to live now, not how he could live next year. When will this 'day' come? The truth is that we do not know the time (Mark 13.32). What is important is that we should live every day in readiness for it. If we live like this we have confidence (in God): we act with responsibility (towards God).

Special note E
Koinōnia

The Greek word *koinōnia* is very rich in meaning. It occurs 19 times in the New Testament and 13 of these are found in Paul's Letters. As there is no one English word which can be used to capture its meaning fully (except perhaps the new word 'togetherness', or 'commonality'), it is best to use the Greek word itself in our clarification of its meaning. What does it mean to say that a group of Christians can have *koinōnia?*

1   It means that each of them has *koinōnia with God* through Christ. This is the thought in Philippians 2.1 and in 3.10.

2   As a result, they have *koinōnia with each other.* This is what Paul was saying in 1.5, and in 1.7, 21; 4.14 and 4.15. It is important to understand that the *koinōnia* which Christians enjoy with each other is a result of having roots. The 'roots' are the *koinōnia* which each has with God. We can see why one must follow from the other. When each Christian knows that he is accepted by the loving God just as he is, then he is able to accept other Christians just as they are. So there is *koinōnia* among them. They can trust each other. They can allow each other to hold different opinions. They can speak freely with each other. They can forgive each other. But someone who does not believe that he is accepted into fellowship with God is unable to accept others in this way.

Note that sometimes the 'roots' and the 'result' are thought of together. The 'communion of the Holy Spirit' (2 Corinthians 13.14) means 'communion with God the Holy Spirit' *and also* 'the communion with other Christians which the Holy Spirit has created'. So in the Holy Communion service (the Holy *Koinōnia*) each Christian has communion with God *and also* communion with his fellow worshippers.

3   When Christians share work, they have a special opportunity to experience *koinōnia,* like two partners who own a shop and work in it. They have *koinōnia* if they hate the same sins (2 Corinthians 6.14; 1 Timothy 5.22). In Philippians 1.5 Paul reminded the Philippians that he and they had been sharing work for ten years, ever since they met in Philippi (Acts 16.12). In 1.7 he said, 'When I appear in the dock to vouch for the truth of the gospel, you all share in the privilege that is mine' (NEB).

In one town Methodists, Roman Catholics and Anglicans (who knew that they all had fellowship with God through Jesus Christ) joined in the work of visiting every house in the town. In this way, their *koinōnia* was increased.

In the same way, *koinōnia* is strong when the members of a group share suffering or danger. The players in a Salvation Army band in Nairobi were once playing hymns and preaching in a district where there were no Christians at that time. The crowd tried to make the band go away as soon as possible by throwing tins at them and shouting and singing. At the end of the evening a member of the band said, 'We may not have been given any converts. Who knows? But we have certainly been given fellowship among ourselves!'

4   Their *koinōnia* is shown when each *shares in a practical way* what each possesses (see Philippians 4.15). In Romans 15.26 the funds that some Christians sent to the poor were actually called *the koinōnia.*

So today Christians of one country show their *koinōnia* with those of another country by each contributing to the needs of the others. A West African priest came to work for a time in an English town, and after he had left a member of the congregation said, 'We have been giving to the church in Africa for many years. Now we are receiving. This West African has lived among us a life of such joy that he has given us something we shall never forget.'

5 *Koinōnia* exists even *when members are separated. Koinōnia* among Christians does not die when some of the Christians die: we may call this the 'communion of the saints'. It was the same truth that made a Japanese student in America able to be at peace during the whole of his three-year course although he was separated from his wife and family. He said, 'We are all united in Christ.'

6 It is *koinōnia* among Christians which (more than anything else) draws non-Christians into the Church, and into a belief in God's love. An Indian lecturer in a Christian College was a Muslim when he first went to England. Through his work he met a group of Christian students. As a result of the fellowship, love and honesty that existed between them he began to take the gospel seriously, and later became a Christian himself.

STUDY SUGGESTIONS

Word study

1 **(a)** What is the difference between *koinōnia* and friendliness?

(b) How is *koinōnia* translated in another language which you know? What is its literal meaning?

Review of content

2 What made Paul able to write with joy although he was in prison?

3 **(a)** How many times in vv. 3–8 did Paul use the phrase 'all of you'?

(b) Why did he repeat it?

4 What did Paul mean by the 'completion' of God's work (v. 6)? What did he *not* mean?

Bible study

5 Say whether *koinōnia* ('fellowship', 'partnership') refers to:

(a) fellowship with God, or

(b) fellowship with one another, or

(c) a sign of fellowship, in each of the following verses:

(i) Acts 2.42; (ii) Romans 15:26; (iii) 1 Corinthians 10.16; (iv) 2 Corinthians 9.13; (v) Galatians 2.9; (vi) 1 John 1.6.

6 What is the day of Jesus Christ called in each of the following verses?

(a) Romans 2.16; (b) 1 Corinthians 1.8; (c) Ephesians 4.30; (d) 1 Thessalonians 5.2; (e) 1 Thessalonians 5.4; (f) 2 Thessalonians 2.2.

Discussion and application

7 (a) What event or events have most helped members of your congregation to experience 'partnership' together during the past year?

(b) What effect does such *koinōnia* have on other people?

(c) What links, if any, has your congregation with other congregations or with Christians outside your country?

8 What would you reply to someone who said: 'Christians talk a lot about "fellowship". But many other groups of people, both religious and non-religious, have fellowship with each other that is equally strong and effective'? Do you think that Christians can learn about fellowship from other groups? In what ways do members of your own church chiefly have fellowship with each other?

9 (a) How often do preachers preach about 'the day' and about Jesus' second coming? If often, why? If not often, why?

(b) What do they say about it? How far is it good news?

(c) Are people confusing the 'day of Jesus' with the day which could occur if nuclear weapons or climate change destroy the earth? What could you say to people who do confuse the two?

10 Paul seems to have been both the Philippians' friend and a person in authority over them. How far is it possible for someone in authority over you to be your friend?

Philippians 1.9–11

Paul's prayer for them

 Summary

Paul prays for them that they may excel in love, discernment and righteousness.

 Notes

1.9. My prayer: The word used for 'prayer' is studied under Philippians 4.6.

Your love may overflow more and more It was important that Christians at Philippi should more and more love each other so that they might be a united congregation. We shall see (e.g. in 2.2, 14) that there was division and complaining in the congregation.

With knowledge The love that should overflow must be defined by or tempered with 'knowledge' and 'full insight'. Paul uses a very interesting Greek word for 'knowledge': *epignōsis*. In Paul's Letters this word refers to the true knowledge of God revealed in and through Christ. This means Christian love is exercised in the context of a true knowledge of who God is, what his will is and what his plan for this world is, from the standpoint of what Christ has done.

Full insight The Greek term for 'insight' (*aisthēsis*) refers to moral understanding and discernment. The term is frequently found in the Greek translation of the book of Proverbs and the discourses of moral philosophers in Paul's time. However, it occurs only once in the New Testament. The 'full insight' here refers then to the ability to make wise moral judgements in the midst of many differing or difficult choices.

1.10. Determine what is best: The word here translated 'best' means the things that are 'most important in life'. So Paul was telling his readers to make choices in the way they lived, and not always to accept the old ways. They were to ask, 'What matters more than anything else in our congregation?'

Pure and blameless 'Blameless' does not here mean 'perfect'; it means 'not causing other people to stumble'. What Paul meant was this: 'Remember that by your behaviour you either attract people to follow Christ or you make it difficult for them to do so.'

1.11. Harvest of righteousness: The Greek is literally 'fruit of righteousness' (AV, NIV, NJB). The phrase may be understood in different ways:

1 the righteousness which is the fruit (Hebrews 12.11; James 3.18);

2 the fruit coming as a result of righteousness, referring to godly virtues; or

3 the righteous fruit.

Many scholars take option 2 although options 2 and 3 are very close in meaning.

For the glory and praise of God Why did Paul want the congregation at Philippi to 'grow in loving'? It was in order that God might be praised and loved. That is what Christians are for. For 'glory' see note on Philippians 4.20.

 Interpretation

As Paul thought about the Christians at Philippi, he longed for them to become a stronger and a better congregation. They needed, for instance, to be more understanding in the way they looked after each other. But he did not condemn or criticize them: he prayed for them, and then told them (in this passage) what his prayer had been about. In this prayer he summed up the important qualities he wished for his friends in Philippi.

Paul's prayer for them should lead us to reflect on our prayers for others. To start off, let us consider what we should ask for. In all praying it is good to share everything with God, so naturally we share our hopes and fears for other people with him. But praying for others is not telling God what they need. He knows what they most need. Our praying for them becomes: 'Lord, accept my love for them and give them whatever is best for them. Your will be done.'

Who can we pray for? It is probably easier to pray for members of our own family or our own nation, or for people we like. But as we become mature we see that we must offer prayer for everyone who is in need. This is difficult because there are so many people in need that we have to choose for whom especially we shall pray. One man uses a daily newspaper to show him some of the people who need to be prayed for. Many Christians keep a notebook and under each day of the month they list the names of those for whom they will pray that day.

The important phrase in Paul's request for his friends is 'overflow more and more'. This speaks of growth or increase. Our lives are full of 'increases'. Parents may hope for an increase in the number of their children. Workers may hope for an increase in wages. Students hope for an increase in their understanding of a subject. Paul says here, 'This is the place where increase is most needed – in loving!' The congregation that increases its income but not its care for strangers or its understanding of the Bible is a poor congregation.

One of the Christian virtues that should increase is love. This translates the Greek word *agapē* (which we find also in Philippians 1.16; 2.1 and 2.2). We see from 1 Corinthians 13.4–7 some ways in which we can tell that someone has *agapē*: she willingly accepts the trouble that other people give her ('patient', v. 4); she does what she can to meet other people's needs ('kind', v. 4); she is happy when other people have some good thing that she herself does not have ('not envious', v. 4); she draws attention to the goodness and achievements of other people ('not boastful', v. 4); she listens to other people's opinions carefully ('not arrogant', v. 5); she does her best to know what other people's feelings are ('not rude', v. 5); she can see the Spirit of God at work in others ('does not insist on its own way', v. 5); she can accept what others give her, including criticism ('not irritable', v. 5); she can forgive those who have injured her ('not resentful', v. 5); she suffers pain when others do wrong ('does not rejoice in wrongdoing', v. 6); she is happy when others do right ('rejoices in the truth', v. 6); she goes on loving under all circumstances ('bears ... all things', v. 7).

The meaning of the word *agapē* is different from that of three other Greek words also translated 'love', with which it is often confused: *erōs* (love between a man and a woman), *philia* (friendship between people who like the same things), and *storgē* (love between members of the same family). Perfect *agapē* has only been seen in the life of Jesus. So 1 Corinthians 13 is really Paul's description of the way Jesus treated other people. If we 'love', it is because the Spirit of Jesus has been given to us. 'We love because he first loved us' (1 John 4.19). New Testament writers use the same word for God's love for us, for our love for him, for our love for one another, and for our love for ourselves.

If we really 'love' a person we take the trouble to discover and understand ('discern') what that person most needs. If a beggar comes to the house we may give him money and food, with good intentions. But our love is without knowledge and understanding if it leads the beggar to remain a beggar, or prevents him from finding work and from gaining respect for himself. When parents love their children with understanding they treat them in such a way that the children grow in responsibility and independence.

In the same vein, every nation needs to ask the following question: 'Which is more important, a few big factories that increase our overseas trade but employ few people, or a large number of small industries so that many are employed?'

STUDY SUGGESTIONS

Word study

1 How has the word 'love' (v. 9) been translated into another language which you know? What is the full meaning of that word? How good a translation is it?

2 What is the meaning of 'full insight' as used by Paul here? How was it used by others in Paul's day?

Review of content

3 For what reason did Paul pray that the Philippians should 'grow in loving'?

4 What did Paul mean when he told the Philippians to 'determine what is best'?

Bible study

5 Say in each of the following passages:

(a) who Jesus was praying for; and

(b) what he was asking God to do.

(i) Luke 22.32; **(ii)** Luke 23.34; **(iii)** John 14.8–16; **(iv)** John 17.9–11; **(v)** John 17.20.

Discussion and application

6 Compare your own prayers for other people with Paul's prayer for the Philippians in vv. 9–11. When you yourself pray to God for your friends, what do you ask him for?

7 Why is it important that Christians should love 'with knowledge and full insight'?

8 A student once said: 'God's love (*agapē*) for us is so great that it includes every other sort of loving.' Do you agree? Give your reasons.

9 What is it that chiefly enables people to 'grow' in loving?

Philippians 1.12–18

God makes use of opposition

 Summary

Paul wants his readers to know that his imprisonment did not hinder the work of the gospel but actually advanced it. This was so, even if some 'proclaimed Christ' in order to hurt Paul. In all this Paul rejoices because Christ has been preached.

 Notes

1.12. Beloved: The Greek word is *adelphoi*, meaning 'brothers'; but this does not exclude the female members. New Testament writers used this word to convey the idea that the Church is like a family. It indicates also the kind of fellowship that existed among Christians between leaders and led, employers and employed, masters and slaves, Jews and non-Jews, because each served the same Lord. So they could speak freely to one another.

What has happened These words refer to the pain of imprisonment which Paul was suffering.

1.13. It has become known throughout the whole imperial guard: This verse is important because in it we see how marvellously God 'used' or 'redeemed' Paul's imprisonment. But readers may also ask, 'Which guard was it?' This question has bearing on the identification of the place where Paul wrote the Letter. What did Paul mean by the 'imperial guard'? The Greek word is *praitōrion*, which is based on the Latin term *praetorium*. This term refers most probably to special troops – known as the praetorian guard – rather than a building. The primary duty of these troops was to defend the emperor or to protect his interests. The point made is that God has used Paul's imprisonment to put him in a strategic place to bear witness to the gospel.

Regarding the place of composition of Paul's letter, the following are the options.

1   It is likely that he wrote it from Rome in AD 62, because:

(a) We think of Rome rather than any other city when we read of 'the whole praetorian guard' and (in 4.22) 'those of the emperor's household'.

(b) We know from Acts 28.30–31 that Paul was imprisoned for at least two years in Rome.

(c) Paul needed help in prison (from Timothy and Epaphroditus), and Rome was a place where he would need help, because the church there was small and weak.

2   But some scholars think that Paul wrote from Ephesus between AD 54 and 57. They say:

(a) Paul said in Philippians 1.1 that Timothy was with him, and according to Acts 19.22 it was at Ephesus that Timothy was with Paul.

(b) Paul could have been referring to Roman guards in Ephesus when he wrote Philippians 1.13 and 4.22.

(c) During Paul's two years' imprisonment messengers made at least four journeys between Philippi and Paul's prison. If he was in prison in Ephesus there was plenty of time in which they could make these journeys, because Ephesus is near Philippi. But Rome is 1,200 km by sea from Philippi, and it is not certain if there was enough time for such journeys to take place.

3   Others believe that Paul wrote from Caesarea (in AD 59), mainly because we know from Acts 23.35 and 24.27 that Paul was imprisoned there.

From these various answers which scholars give to the question of the place of the Letter's composition, we see that no one is sure what the true answer is. Usually we are better able to interpret a letter if we know where the writer was when he wrote it. But in the case of the Letter to the Philippians the way we interpret it does not depend at all on our knowing where it was written.

1.14. Having been made confident ... by my imprisonment: This is another instance of 'good' coming out of a bad event. More Christians were encouraged and emboldened to proclaim the gospel because of Paul's imprisonment.

1.15. Some proclaim Christ from envy and rivalry: The situation that is envisaged here is the manoeuvring to ensure a positive or negative outcome, which often took place during a pre-trial detention. Apparently, there were some Christians who were hoping that the verdict on Paul would be negative. Who were these people? They were not preachers of false beliefs. They were not the same as those to whom Paul referred in Galatians 3.1, who were persuading others to return to the old Jewish way of thinking about God. If they had been, Paul would have written about them in the same way: 'Who has bewitched you?' As it was, Paul could 'rejoice' that they were preaching (v. 18). Probably they were leading members of the church in Rome, who had been there before Paul first arrived and who were unhappy that he was now being treated as more important than they were. So although they preached a Christian message ('Christ is proclaimed', v. 18), they were envious of Paul. They regarded him more as a rival than as a partner (v. 15). As a result, instead of *koinōnia* or togetherness there was a split between them and Paul ('selfish ambition', v. 17), and this was painful to him ('increase my suffering', v. 17). Clement of Rome wrote to the church at Corinth in AD 96 and commented that it was *envy and contention* from opponents that brought about the persecution of some apostles in Rome (1 Clement 5.2–5).

1.18. Rejoice: Paul states that his reaction to all this is to rejoice because the gospel has been advanced, even though he was slandered in the process. A joyful person does not depend on success or popularity or possessions or any other outward circumstances, although he may sometimes have them. If he cannot rejoice unless things are going well, then he has not yet learnt how to 'rejoice in the Lord'. On the meaning of joy see Theological essay 4.

 Interpretation

It must have been hard for the Philippians to bear that Paul, their founder, was in prison, and to be without news of him. So Paul wrote to tell them his news. Above all he assured them that the gospel was being preached. This is the chief message of the whole section of vv. 12–26. God was using Paul's imprisonment, he said, in two ways. First, those who were not Christians had had to take notice of the gospel (see v. 13). The soldiers who were guarding Paul probably asked, 'Who are these Christians? Why is this man in prison? Who is this Jesus whom Paul serves? What makes him go to prison for Jesus' sake?' And Paul the prisoner was free to tell them. Second, the news that the gospel was being preached in this way was encouraging other Christians to proclaim the gospel (v. 14). Hence, what Paul did was to share with his readers his firm belief that good can come out of bad events, and even in very difficult circumstances Christians can continue to serve Christ, and can tell the world about him (v. 18), because they are strengthened by God's power.

Concerning Paul's suffering, we may note:

1 Although men and women suffer imprisonment for different reasons (e.g. some are political prisoners, others criminals, others 'prisoners of conscience'), there is suffering which all prisoners share and which Paul shared. Being a great Christian leader did not prevent Paul's sufferings from being real.

2   Paul was in prison because of his belief in Jesus. As we read this, there are many who are tortured because of what they believe. The suffering of the Chaldean Christians in Iraq is a recent example. Paul did not suffer more than other Christians, but he represents all who have endured suffering for the sake of Christ.

3   Although Paul's sufferings were as real as those of other prisoners, he received strength from outside himself (like many Christians since). For example, the Philippians supported him by their fellowship (1.7) and, even more, he was strengthened by knowing that God would one day triumph over all evil (3.21). This is the reason why he could say that God was actually using his suffering.

God is Creator and Re-creator. This being the case, he can use what seems to be useless. There are many examples of this. In God's world what some people regard as 'rubbish' can become compost, and milk that some housewives would throw away as 'sour' can become cheese. Paul's imprisonment in Philippi became the time when the jailer and his family were baptized (see Acts 16.16–34). It was this sort of event that led Paul to write, 'whenever I am weak, then I am strong' (2 Corinthians 12.10). The worst thing that has ever been done by human beings was the killing of Jesus, yet under God's supervision it became the best thing that ever happened (Acts 4.11).

Samuel Ajayi Crowther, the first Nigerian church leader, went from Freetown to Lagos in 1850, and prepared to travel and preach over a wide area. Owing to war, he could not move from the coast for 18 months. Instead of complaining of 'disaster', he used the opportunity to translate large parts of the Bible into Yoruba.

A hundred years later, a Christian nurse in North India was murdered by a young man who had a complaint against the hospital where she worked. Her funeral was a time for such joyful thanksgiving for her life that Hindu friends began to take the gospel seriously for the first time.

In all these events we cannot say that God 'sent' the pain or the suffering or the disappointment. What God did was to 'redeem' it, i.e. turn it into an opportunity for good. There does not seem to be any situation, however bad, which God cannot 'redeem'.

Paul's being imprisoned for the gospel encouraged many Christians to proclaim it. Unfortunately, this was done with mixed motives. There was a group that did it out of envy and rivalry. This can also happen between Christians today. Church workers do sometimes envy or fear or dislike one another. It happens because they are sinful human beings. It may also be because they come from different backgrounds with different customs, and for other reasons. As Paul said, 'we have this treasure in clay jars' (2 Corinthians 4.7). Paul himself was of course not without his faults. Sometimes, he was not an easy person to work with (see 2 Corinthians 2.1–4; Galatians 2.11–14). But, as Paul showed in v. 18, we should not resign from Christian work merely because we find other Christians difficult, or because we disapprove of their way of doing their work. The Church must make known the gospel by word and deed, and this does not happen unless members are allowing other members to do it in the way those others think best.

 STUDY SUGGESTIONS

Word study

1   For each of the following three words, write a sentence to show its meaning, and also the difference between its meaning and the meaning of each of the other two: partisanship, partnership, participation.

Review of content

2   What did Paul mean when he said that 'some proclaim Christ from envy and rivalry' (v. 15)?

3   In what ways had Paul's imprisonment 'helped to spread the gospel' (v. 12)?

Bible study

4   What sort of suffering did Paul experience, according to each of the following verses?

   (a) Philippians 1.7;   **(b)** 1.8;   **(c)** 1.15;   **(d)** 2.17;   **(e)** 2.27;   **(f)** 3.18; **(g)** 4.12.

Discussion and application

5   **(a)** What do you think is the most painful part of being a prisoner?

   (b) What effect does imprisonment have on prisoners? What effect did it have on Paul?

6   Give two examples from the history of the Church, of Christians who were able to serve Christ in difficult circumstances.

7   Give some examples of ways in which God 'works for good' (Romans 8.28) by using what seems to be useless.

8   **(a)** When you yourself think that other Christians are working with wrong motives, how do you behave towards them?

   (b) How do you know what is the right thing to do in such circumstances?

Philippians 1.19–26

Ready to live, ready to die

 Summary

Paul is certain about his deliverance but he also states that, whether he lives or dies, he is ready because it is all about Christ.

 Notes

1.19. Through your prayers: In his imprisonment Paul needed support, and in this verse he says that he is getting support from two sources: the prayers of the Christians and 'the Spirit of Jesus Christ' (see note below).

The help of the Spirit of Jesus Christ Some people say that this means the Holy Spirit which is Jesus; 2 Corinthians 3.17 may possibly support such a view. But all the other relevant evidence of the New Testament is decisively against such an interpretation. Others think that it means the Holy Spirit that is *sent* by Jesus (John 15.26; Acts 2.33). What really matters for Paul is that in his sufferings he can depend on more than human help. He can depend on the very same Spirit of God which filled Jesus himself, and who is sent by Jesus.

This will turn out for my deliverance What sort of deliverance does Paul mean here? The Greek word is usually translated 'salvation' (see note on Philippians 2.12). Clearly he does not mean 'release from prison', because in v. 20 he says that he may soon die. Some interpret it as 'salvation from eternal spiritual destruction' as in 1.28. Probably Paul means deliverance from faithlessness and cowardice during his whole work for Christ, i.e. 'deliverance from being judged guilty in what I am doing'. This is the meaning of the word in Job 13.16 (where the NRSV translation is 'salvation'), which Paul may have been quoting.

1.20. It is my eager expectation: 'Eager expectation' means 'stretching out one's neck to see what lies ahead'.

With all boldness The word translated 'all boldness' means 'speaking freely' (which no one can do unless he or she has courage).

Christ will be exalted … in my body, whether by life or by death The NEB has: 'The greatness of Christ will shine out in my person …' Paul compares his life to a public exhibition, in which passers-by may see the glory of Christ. We see in this whole phrase the way in which Paul is ready to accept anything, including life or death, which may lead others to honour Jesus Christ.

1.21. Living is Christ: As a Jew, Paul had served God since his birth, but it was God-as-shown-forth-in-Christ who had given him what he most valued in life. Whichever way he turned, there was Christ! Christ had changed the direction of Paul's life, had set him on a new way, and had given him his life's work and the strength to do it. Paul had found his true self in Christ. Above all, Christ had given him his own fellowship. 'Living is Christ' was a powerful way of saying what Paul often said about 'living *in* Christ'. See note on Philippians 4.10.

Dying is gain Alongside these words, we should also take note of v. 23b, 'to depart and be with Christ, for that is far better' (see note on that verse).

1.22. If I am to live in the flesh, this means fruitful labour for me: i.e. 'If I am to go on living in this world, then I can go on doing useful work.'
   It is important to note the different meanings of 'flesh' which writers in the Bible give it:

1   Life on earth, human beings using their bodies, minds and spirits in this world. This is its meaning in this verse and in John 1.14.

2   The limited powers and 'weakness' of life on earth, e.g. in Isaiah 40.6: 'All people (i.e. flesh) are grass, their constancy is like the flower of the field.'

3   All of a person's life on earth which is not under the control of God's Spirit. 'Flesh' thus means any thinking or worshipping, any service to our neighbours, any activity at all which we fail to do with regard to God or under his authority (Philippians 3.4; Romans 7.5).

Writers in the Bible do *not* teach that one's physical body is evil and that on the contrary one's spirit is good. Some Eastern religions have taught this. Some Christians also have followed them, teaching for example that it is wicked to enjoy the flesh in sexual intercourse but good to enjoy spiritual conversation. But we do not find such teaching in the Gospels or in Paul's Letters.

1.23. I am hard pressed between the two: This is picture-language. It can be a picture of a traveller in a deep valley who can see no way out. On one side is the steep mountain of 'life', on the other the equally steep mountain of 'death'. Both sides seem to be pressing down upon him. Or it can be a picture of a voter in an election, with members of opposite parties pulling him in different directions. The two directions in which Paul is being pushed are referred to in v. 23b and v. 24.

My desire is to depart The Greek word translated 'depart' is another picture-word. It can refer to pulling up tent-pegs after camping, or releasing a boat from its anchor as it sets out to sea.

To be with Christ This shows that Paul believes that after death he will have fellowship with Christ. This fellowship will be even closer than the fellowship he has by being 'in Christ' on earth. (See 1 Thessalonians 4.16–17, and note on Philippians 2.19.)

1.25. I will remain and continue with all of you for your progress and joy in faith: Although Paul has said earlier that he did not know what would happen to him (and repeated this in 2.17), he adds here the belief that he will be with them again, in order that they may make progress in their faith and have joy in it. He repeats his hope in v. 26.

The word translated 'continue with' means 'remain beside someone who needs you', just as God's Holy Spirit is called *Paraclete*, the one who is 'called in to stand beside' us. See John 14.16 and Philippians 2.1a.

'Progress' is an idea which Paul often uses to describe a healthy congregation (see 1 Thessalonians 4.1). A congregation needs to ask itself from time to time not only: 'Are we maintaining what we have received?', but also: 'In what ways are we developing it to meet the needs of the present time?'

1.26. Share abundantly in your boasting in Christ Jesus: The word in Greek which is translated as 'boasting' in the NRSV could also mean 'jubilation'. This 'jubilation' is in Christ Jesus because Paul's deliverance will demonstrate that Jesus has answered their prayers and is sovereign.

 Interpretation

The language of this part of Paul's Letter is not simple, because he was trying to share his experience of 'being pushed two directions' (v. 23a), and because he was using the language of a lover or a poet rather than ordinary phrases, e.g. 'living is Christ' (v. 21).

His main thoughts, however, were clear.

1   Paul believed that God would deliver him (v. 19 and vv. 25–26).

2   Paul gladly accepted both the outcomes of 'life' and 'death' (v. 20).

3   Paul could say this because for him all living, whether it was living here in this world or living beyond the grave, was in Christ and with Christ (v. 21a).

4   But Paul still had a problem, i.e. what he should ask for (vv. 22–24). He finally decided on life.

What we chiefly notice here is the way in which Paul, while being in a state of great uncertainty, showed a calm and steady acceptance of whatever should happen to him.

Paul believed that the prayers of the Philippians could make a difference for him (v. 19). He also said in several of his Letters that he depended on the prayers of other Christians (2 Corinthians 1.11; Romans 15.30–32). How is it that the prayers of one person can make a difference to others? It is because such prayers are a way of co-operating with God (see note on Philippians 1.9). God wishes to do his work through his body, the Church, and part of his strengthening of those in need is given through the prayers of others. This is why we can say that prayer changes things.

We may add that those who are in need are also strengthened by knowing that someone is praying for them. Once, a group of soldiers were captured by the enemy and were kept in harsh conditions for over a year. Many of them gave up hope and died. Of those who survived, and were eventually released, a large number said they were alive because they knew that people at home were praying for them.

To be sure, being 'pushed in two directions' is very often a part of the suffering which Christians have been told to expect. But for Paul, whatever direction life took or whatever outcomes ensued from his trial, he was ready to accept both life and death. If he lived, it was for Christ. If he were to die, it would be for Christ. The hymn of St Patrick (written in the fifth century AD) captures this beautifully.

> Christ be with me, Christ within me,
> Christ behind me, Christ before me,
> Christ beside me, Christ to win me,
> Christ to comfort and restore me,
> Christ beneath me, Christ above me,
> Christ in quiet, Christ in danger,
> Christ in hearts of all that love me,
> Christ in mouth of friend and stranger.

What may be astonishing to some readers is that Paul believed 'dying is gain' (v. 21). How was it possible for Paul to hold such a belief? No Old Testament writer had ever said this, e.g. see Isaiah 38.18: 'Sheol cannot thank you, death cannot praise you.' The great philosopher Socrates did not believe it either. He said, 'The hour of my departure has arrived, and we go our ways, I to die, you to live. Which is better only the gods know.'

Paul could say it because Christ had come and had died and had been raised to life. As a result he and other New Testament writers held ideas about death of the body such as the following. They thought of death:

1 as *being* with Christ (as in v. 23b);

2 as a *deepening* of relationship with Christ (Romans 6.8);

3 as a *release* from the limits which we experience in this life (2 Corinthians 5.8);

4   as a sort of peaceful *sleeping* (1 Thessalonians 4.13);

5   as an *entrusting* of life into God's hands (see Luke 23.46);

6   as a *completion* of this life (John 19.30: 'It is accomplished!' NEB).

Those who see death in this way and accept it have peace of mind. Those who refuse to think or speak about it are pretending that it will not happen.

No wise person pretends to know what happens after death. Those who wrote the words referred to above, and those who today speak about life after death, do so in hope. They have hope because of what they already know of the love and power of God.

What must not be missed is that it was more important for Paul that he maintained a courageous and good testimony before the people who were going to try him. He expressed in v. 20 that this was his 'hope'. 'Hope' is one of the great words of the New Testament and is worthy of further reflection here.

1   Hope is confidence in God's love and power. Thus it is different from a cheerful outlook or careful calculations (see 2.19).

2   Hope is confidence in God as regards the future. (The word 'faith' e.g. in v. 25 refers to confidence in God as regards the past and present.) The future includes the rest of our lives in this world, our life to come after death, and the completion of God's whole creation (Romans 8.18–25).

3   Hope is based on what God has done. See 1 Peter 1.3: 'he has given us a new birth into a living hope through the resurrection of Jesus Christ from the dead.'

4   Hope is kept alive by our being in touch with the living God (Romans 5.5).

Indeed, it is God's love that is poured out abundantly into our hearts that will sustain hope.

 ## STUDY SUGGESTIONS

Word study

1 **(a)** What is your understanding of the word 'hope' as used by writers in the New Testament?

(b) In what ways does its meaning in the New Testament differ from its meaning used in ordinary conversation today?

Review of content

2 From what two sources did Paul say that he was getting help and encouragement in his imprisonment?

3 In v. 21b Paul says, 'dying is gain'.

   (a) What 'gain' did he believe that death would bring him?

   (b) What enabled him to hold this belief?

   (c) In what chief way did this belief differ from the belief about death held by writers of the Old Testament?

Bible study

4 In what ways did Paul (and his companion Silas) suffer in Philippi, according to Acts 16.19–24?

5 What ideas about death did the writers of the following passages have:

   (a) Psalm 6.5; **(b)** Isaiah 38.18; **(c)** John 19.30; **(d)** Romans 8.38; **(e)** Philippians 1.23b; **(f)** 2 Timothy 1.10; **(g)** Revelation 14.13.

Discussion and application

6 In which countries today are there Christians who are suffering imprisonment for their faith? In what ways can other Christians, including you yourself, give them the 'support' they need?

7 **(a)** Discuss with one or two friends what each of you *really* believes about life after death.

   (b) Do you think that there will be further training or purifying after death?

   (c) What is the teaching of your own church on this subject?

   (d) In what ways, if at all, is your belief different from what most non-Christians in your area believe?

Living worthily of the gospel

 Summary

Paul encourages the Philippians to live lives worthy of the gospel by standing firm together, without being intimidated by their opponents. Their suffering for Christ is actually a God-given privilege.

 Notes

1.27. Live your life in a manner worthy of the gospel: The Greek word which is here translated 'live in a manner' is *politeuomai*, which is the verb of the better-known *politeia*. *Politeia* refers to the rights, privileges and duties of being members of a community or state. As Philippi was a Roman colony, its inhabitants were proud of being Roman citizens. So the verb Paul uses would have arrested the attention of the Philippian Christians in a profound way. In effect Paul is saying, 'you are Roman citizens and you treasure it and therefore you behave in a way that suits Roman customs. But you are also Christians, therefore as you mix with others behave in a way that befits the gospel.' Do note that from *politeia* we get our words 'politics' and 'polite'.

Worthy of the gospel This does not mean that a Christian's behaviour can ever be sufficiently good or could ever *earn* God's approval. Paul had been urging the Philippians to be united. So here his meaning was, 'Let your behaviour fit the gospel which you preach. If you are not reconciled to one another, it does not fit the gospel in which Jesus preached reconciliation between God and human beings, and between one person and another.'

In one spirit This phrase (along with 'with one mind' and 'side by side') refers to the Christian unity which the Philippians needed (see also note on Philippians 2.2). The theme of unity is first sounded here and this theme runs like a thread throughout the entire letter (2.2–4; 3.15–16; 4.2–3).

Striving side by side … for the faith of the gospel In this sentence Paul put many thoughts into a small space, and as a result the whole meaning is not very clear. It probably means 'striving side by side to bring people to put their "faith" in God, faith which they will have through hearing the gospel'. But some scholars think that the meaning is 'striving side by side against evil, supported by your confidence in the truth of the gospel'.

It may be that when Paul wrote this he was thinking of a line of trained spearmen. If they kept side by side in a battle it was difficult for an enemy to overcome them. Philip of Macedon, after whom Philippi was named, had won many battles by the use of such spearmen, and the people of Philippi would have understood this sort of picture-language. Or perhaps Paul was thinking of the games, wrestling and athletics of the Greeks. The word translated 'striving' really means 'being athletes together' (see 2 Timothy 2.5).

1.28. This is evidence of their destruction, but of your salvation: That is, 'this, the confidence which you show and which is God's gift, will be a sure sign to them that it is God himself against whom they are fighting, and that their opposition to God will result in their destruction. But it is a sure sign that you are being saved.' Paul himself had experienced that, when he was attacking Christians before his conversion, he was in fact attacking Jesus himself (Acts 9.5). For 'salvation' see note on Philippians 2.12.

1.29. He has graciously granted: i.e. 'God, out of his generosity, has given you the honour …' The root of the word which is translated 'granted' means 'grace'. The point is that just as the Philippian Christians received salvation by grace so they would also receive suffering as a form of God's grace. This appears abhorrent to many people but it makes sense if we think of being identified with Christ in every way as one of life's greatest honours. See 1.2, 7; 4.23.

1.30. Having the same struggle that you saw I had and now hear that I still have: Paul's readers had seen him engaged in conflict and suffering at Philippi (Acts 16.19–40). Perhaps the jailer who made him suffer was one of these readers. Paul and his readers were engaged in the same 'conflict' in which Christians must be engaged in every generation and in every place. And Paul, like all great leaders, only urged his readers to endure what he himself had endured.

 Interpretation

After explaining his circumstances, Paul now turns to address the situation of the church at Philippi and offer advice on how they may live their lives as Christians in that Roman colony. In this section he writes about unity and suffering as characteristics of lives that are worthy of the gospel.

Unity has always been a difficult problem for many communities, not least the Christian ones. But why was it difficult for the Philippian

Christians to be united? We may notice two reasons (see also 2.1–4). First, the various members of the congregation at Philippi, as happens in many city congregations in the world today, had belonged to different religions and came from different races (see note on Philippians 1.12). Naturally they held different opinions about how to live the gospel. Second, the Philippians were being persecuted. Often, when there is persecution, there are very different ideas as to the right action to take among those who are being persecuted. Those who resist very courageously may feel that they are superior to those who are afraid.

The above leads us to reflect on the topic of Christian unity. What is Christian unity?

1　There is 'unity' when Christians who hold different ideas, or who perhaps do not even like each other, share a love for Jesus Christ, and have the same aims. 'Unity' does not mean holding the same ideas or liking the same things.

2　Unity is necessary so that members can do the work that God intends the Church to do (see note on Philippians 1.5). How can non-Christians believe in Christ the Reconciler if they do not see his followers being reconciled to each other? Christians must be free from fighting against each other if they are to fight the evils which attack the Church.

3　Unity is easily destroyed in a congregation, e.g. when members pay more attention to what they do than to the reasons for doing it, or more attention to which person is doing it than to what he does. When they are so keen on using some special music in worship, or some method of accountancy, but forget the reasons why the worship or the accountancy is done, there is disunity (1 Corinthians 3.4–7). The Corinthians were divided because they paid more attention to the leaders of each 'party' in the congregation than they did to Christ.

In his description of unity, Paul uses language that is connected with struggle and suffering. The Philippian Christians were encouraged to 'strive' together, and the term recalls either the games or battles. Whatever the case may be, Paul saw living as a Christian as a struggle.

If Christians (or congregations) are not engaged in some sort of struggle, it may be a sign that they are failing to follow Christ. An African bishop visiting Britain in 1980 said that English Christians seemed to be too contented. They reminded him of a sleeping lion. 'This', he said, 'is because they are following past heroes instead of Jesus Christ who is alive today.'

The Philippian Christians needed also to be ready for suffering. They must not be surprised at this, but accept it as Paul himself did (v. 30). But the more important reason to bear in mind is that it was connected with their being identified with Christ so that suffering for him became an honour which was graciously given. But how can anyone regard it as a duty or an honour to suffer? How could it be that Peter and the other apostles 'rejoiced that they were considered worthy to suffer dishonour for the sake of the name' (Acts 5.41)? The answer is twofold:

1   By suffering willingly, Christians are sharing in God's own activity. God has treated us as 'family', and family members share in the pains as well as the joys of the family. God became human for our sakes and shared in the sufferings of humankind, and a Christian who also shares willingly in these sufferings is thus 'honoured' and 'blessed' (Matthew 5.11, 12) to share God's life. The philosopher Descartes said, 'I think, therefore I am.' But perhaps it is more true to say, 'I suffer, therefore I am'; I suffer, therefore I become what God created me to become.

2   We see suffering as an 'honour' when we can see a purpose for it. This is why Paul wrote, 'for his sake'. To suffer because we are Christians shows the world how much we value Jesus Christ.

What must not be missed in this section is Paul's vision of the gospel being lived in public. We see from Paul's use of the word *politeuomai* that Christians show their love for God, not in isolation from the rest of the world, but by the way in which they *relate* to the public. They relate to their fellow citizens and so, for example, they go to the wedding of a neighbour's daughter, and they pay their taxes, and they are concerned with their country's politics. They also relate to their fellow Christians, and so they pray and work with them. Unfortunately, there are many Christians who say, 'My religion is a matter between myself and my God.' Clearly they forget that the way they know and trust and join with other members of the congregation is part of being a Christian. Or they may say, 'A truly spiritual Christian is not concerned with the affairs of the world.' But by saying this they are escaping from Jesus' command to be 'salt to the world' (Matthew 5.13, NEB).

 STUDY SUGGESTIONS

Word study

1   **(a)** What does the Greek word *politeia* mean?

    (b) Since the words 'politics' and 'polite' are based on the same Greek word, do you think their meanings are connected, and why?

Review of content

2   Why was it specially important for the Philippian Christians to be united?

3 Explain in your own words why Paul wanted the Philippians to 'strive' (v. 27).

Bible study

4 **(a)** What does 'worthy of the gospel' (v. 27a) mean?

(b) In which four of the following verses does the word 'worthy' mean the same as in Philippians 1.27? What is its meaning in each of the other verses?

(i) Mark 1.7; **(ii)** Acts 5.41; **(iii)** Acts 26.20; **(iv)** Ephesians 4.1; **(v)** Colossians 1.10; **(vi)** 1 Timothy 6.1; **(vii)** Revelation 5.12.

Discussion and application

5 How would you answer a fellow Christian who says, 'A truly spiritual person is not concerned with the affairs of the world'?

6 **(a)** To what extent are the different 'denominations' or branches of Christ's Church working toward greater unity in your country?

(b) How important is it that all the churches become one Church? Give reasons for your answer.

7 **(a)** What would your own answer be to the question: 'How can anyone regard it as a duty or an honour to suffer?'

(b) Is it only Christians who regard suffering as a privilege? Give reasons and examples in support of your answers.

Philippians 2.1–4

Fellowship among Christians

 Summary

Paul encourages mutual sharing in the spirit of unity, which is possible only when self-centredness is eradicated.

 Notes

2.1. If then there is any encouragement in Christ: The word translated here as 'encouragement' is the Greek word *paraklēsis*, and it is used in two rather different ways in the New Testament:

(a) support, comfort, consolation (e.g. in 2 Thessalonians 2.16);

(b) appeal, request, exhortation (e.g. in 2 Corinthians 8.17).

We find a similar Greek word (*paraklētos*) in John 16.7, where it refers to the Holy Spirit. It is there translated as 'comforter', 'counsellor' or 'helper'. Literally it means 'the one called in (like a senior doctor or a legal adviser) to be beside someone in need'.

Just as this word is interpreted in two ways, so the whole of v. 1 can be interpreted in two ways:

1 Perhaps it describes the support which the Philippians had experienced. If this is the right interpretation, then the verse means:

   Seeing that, in your life in Christ, you have received encouragement, and have been comforted by God's love, and have shared the same Spirit, and already have some affection for others and sympathy with them, *then* let this bear fruit and produce unity. So you will complete my joy ...

2 Perhaps it describes the appeal which Paul was making. If this is the true interpretation, then it means:

   If my exhortation given 'in Christ' has any power to influence you, if my appeal which comes from love can move you, if our common participation in the Spirit is important to you, if I can appeal to you on the grounds of my affection for you and sympathy with you, *then* complete my joy by being united ...

Most scholars interpret the verse in the second way.

Any compassion and sympathy The word translated 'compassion' is *splanchna*, and it literally means 'entrails', because people thought that their feelings were actually situated in them (see note on Philippians 1.8).

2.2. Be of the same mind: Note also the phrases 'having the same love', 'being in full accord' and 'of one mind'. In all these phrases Paul is explaining the sort of attitude that is necessary for unity to be possible.

2.3. Do nothing from selfish ambition or conceit: These are the first two words Paul used to answer the question, 'What destroys unity?'

Selfish ambition means the desire above all for one's own personal advantage rather than for the good of the whole Church.

Conceit means false or empty pride. There is a good sort of pride, when someone recognizes the gifts which God has given her and uses them and thanks God for them. And there is also a false sort of pride. A falsely proud 'conceited' person is one who pretends that he is a better, more valuable person than others. Such a person is more anxious to be well-known or admired than to do the work which he has been given.

Humility As in v. 2 Paul here answered the question, 'What produces unity?' A 'humble' person is one who accepts the truth about herself, and does not pretend to have developed as a Christian more than she really has. A humble person is willing to be corrected. The word here translated 'humility' did not exist before the coming of Christ although a related term was often used. This related term was only used in a bad sense, to refer to the 'mentality of a slave'. Christianity made 'humility' a virtue. Hence, only someone who, through Christ, can believe in God's forgiveness can dare to be humble. There are people who pretend to be worse than they are, and refuse all responsibility on the grounds that they are 'nobody'. These are *not* humble people. But the more truly humble people there are in a congregation, the more the members are united. See Romans 12.3–5.

Regard others as better The word translated 'better' does not mean better in character. Paul was not saying here that a Christian should pretend that everyone else is a better Christian or a more expert teacher than she is. He meant that a truly 'humble' person sees Christ in the people whom she meets, and can say 'Praise God that you have qualities which I do not possess.' This agrees with the words of 1 Peter 5.5–6, where it is said that a humble person is first of all humble before God and as a result humble with other people.

2.4. Look not to your own interests, but to the interests of others: Christians are right to make plans and to pray for themselves, their families and their friends, and to rejoice in the gifts God has given them. But always at the same time they must plan and pray for other people and rejoice in *their* gifts.

 ## Interpretation

In these verses Paul again appealed to the Christians at Philippi to be united (see also Philippians 1.27). He made his appeal with gentleness, but he would not have made it at all if there had not been serious divisions in the congregation.

There were many reasons for divisions at Philippi. The church there was composed of people of different tribes and classes: some were well-educated and some uneducated; some were rich and some poor; some were slaves, some were free; some wanted to hold on to old Jewish rituals, some wanted to be free of them (3.1–11); two of the women members were failing to work in harmony (4.2). In addition, the congregation was lively and progressive. Inevitably, there were different opinions as to how its activities should be conducted.

As well as urging them to be united, Paul drew attention here both to those attitudes which produce unity and also to the attitudes which destroy unity. We notice once more how personal this letter was. Paul wrote with authority, 'Be united because you cannot do your work otherwise,' but he added, 'Be united so as to complete my joy' (v. 2).

In the following story we see how a Christian leader appealed to a congregation to be united. There is a village in the north of Israel where the people are all Arabs and all members of the Christian ('Orthodox') Church. Once they were divided against each other so deeply that there were even brothers who would not speak to each other.

In that place Palm Sunday was the most important church festival. On that Sunday the children so much wanted to take part in the procession that they persuaded their parents to come to church. So all the people came together. But one group sat on one side, and the other group on the other side. Neither group looked at the other.

During the service the priest locked the doors and said to them all, 'For a long time I have tried to bring you together, but you refused. Now that you are all here and cannot escape, please either fight each other (and I will conduct the funeral of those who are killed) or be reconciled.'

For ten minutes there was silence. Then one man stood up and said, 'I forgive everyone and I ask to be forgiven by everyone.' The priest went to him and kissed him on each shoulder. Then the man walked across the church and, following the example of the priest, kissed all those on the other side of the church. Then all the people, for more than one hour, kissed one another.

One of the attitudes encouraged by Paul to foster unity is compassion. This is a gift which God has given to all people and not only Christians.

But Jesus Christ, by his coming into the world, made it possible for human beings to be more deeply compassionate than before. We may think here of the compassion of a Christian doctor called Vedabodikam in Tirunelveli, South India. He discovered that there were a great many lepers living in a village called Satan's Pool who could not get treatment from the hospital 12 miles away because the sand was too hot for their bare feet. So, with the help of friends, he built a simple treatment centre in their own district. But the elders of the village fiercely opposed him, and at the same time his own wife died, and the centre had to be closed. It was after ten years' more work, when Dr Vedabodikam was 77, that the centre was finally re-opened, with enough accommodation for 30 men and 30 women to receive in-patient treatment, both Hindus and Christians. They are, as God's children, becoming what God created them to be, through one man's compassion.

 STUDY SUGGESTIONS

Word study

1 With regard to the word 'encouragement' (paraklēsis) in v. 1:

(a) Divide the following words into two lists according to whether they mean 'support' or 'appeal':
console cheer urge comfort incite sustain stir up persuade

(b) Which meaning does the word 'encouragement' (paraklēsis) have in
(i) 1 Corinthians 14.3; (ii) 1 Thessalonians 2.12?

Review of content

2 (a) What two attitudes did Paul describe as *destroying* unity in a congregation?

(b) What two attitudes did he describe as *creating* unity?

Bible study

3 'Pride' can mean two quite different attitudes: false or empty pride on the one hand, or a good sort of pride. Which sort of pride: (a) false or (b) good, is meant in each of the following passages?

(i) Mark 7.21–23; (ii) 2 Corinthians 5.11–12; (iii) 2 Corinthians 7.4; (iv) 2 Corinthians 7.14–15; (v) 1 John 2.15–17.

Discussion and application

4 Give two examples from everyday life of people showing false pride, and two examples of people showing good pride. What was the effect on other people in each case?

5 'We are less useful to others if we can only use our minds and not our hearts.' Do the members of your congregation chiefly use their minds or their hearts, in their relationships with each other and with those outside the church? In what ways, if any, could they be more 'useful to others' if they expressed their feelings of compassion more openly?

Philippians 2.5–11

Jesus Christ the Servant

 Summary

Paul appeals to the example of Jesus Christ, who, although he was equal with God, humbled himself to be a servant for the sake of humans. God exalted Christ and gave him a name that is above every name.

 Notes

2.5. Let the same mind be in you: The Greek word that is translated 'mind' actually refers to a person's attitude or outlook in life. Just as Paul appealed to the Philippian Christians to live public lives worthy of the gospel (1.27), he now appeals to them to have an attitude that is worthy of Christ or patterned after him.

2.6. Who: With this word Paul begins a poem or 'hymn' about Christ. It may be that in vv. 6–11 Paul was quoting from a hymn written by someone else which was used in church services at that time. The reasons for thinking this are:

(a) In Greek this passage divides up into six lines each of the same length and has a rhythm like a poem or hymn.

(b) It refers to the cross of Christ but (contrary to Paul's custom) does not add 'for our sakes'. Also, contrary to Paul's custom, it makes no reference to Christ's resurrection.

He was in the form of God Behind the word 'form' stands the Greek *morphē*. It is hard to find an English equivalent for it. It may refer to the 'outward appearance' or, more probably, the idea of 'having the essence of a thing'. In this sense, the 'form of God' is the 'nature of God', so that this means 'Jesus shared God's nature'. We cannot tell from these words whether, first, the writer meant that Jesus 'had always been God by nature' (Phillips) or, second, he was referring to Jesus' life on earth. Most scholars believe that the first of these interpretations is correct: 'Divine nature was his from the first' (NEB). We find that Paul expressed this belief (that Jesus had existed since the beginning of creation) in other Letters also, e.g. 1 Corinthians 8.6: 'Jesus Christ, through whom are all things and through whom we exist'.

Did not regard equality with God as something to be exploited There is a long history of interpretation connected with this clause mainly because many scholars found it hard to understand the meaning of the Greek word *harpagmos*, which is used here. Many versions reflect this uncertainty through their differing translations. Table 1 will illustrate this. The italics indicate the attempted English translation of *harpagmos*.

Table 1

AV	'thought it not *robbery* to be equal with God'
NIV	'did not consider equality with God *something to be grasped*'
REB	'yet he *laid no claim* to equality with God'
GNB	'but he did not think that *by force he should try* to be equal with God'

The NRSV captures it most accurately. Instead of focusing just on the meaning of the word, it takes into account another word, 'regard' (Greek = *hēgeomai*), and treats them as an idiomatic unit. This results in the translation of 'regard ... as something to be exploited'. Paul is speaking about the type of exploitation connected with powerful people. In contrast to them Christ, who is above all these because he is equal with God, did not use his status or power to exploit others. Instead, he regarded his equality with God as something to be used for service.

What exactly this 'equality' means Paul does not explain. All he wants to do here is to contrast the extremes in order to make a point. There can be no higher status than being equal with God. And yet, Christ emptied himself of this and became a slave. Moreover, in Paul's world where the idea of 'the more powerful a person is, the more he can exploit' is always operating, Paul wants to show that if Christ did not exploit his equality with God for his own gain, no human being, however powerful, should be allowed to do so.

2.7. Emptied himself: These words have been translated in various ways in different Bible versions. e.g. 'stripped himself of all privilege' (Phillips); 'made himself nothing' (NEB); 'gave it all up' (GNB).

Of what did Jesus strip himself? *Not* of his sharing of God's nature. It was God's majesty and dignity and position that he put aside when he became human. (Some think that 'emptied himself' is a quotation from Isaiah 53.12, 'he poured out himself to death'. If this is so, then emptying refers to Christ's death, not to his becoming human.)

Many readers of this verse also ask the question: 'Did Jesus strip himself of God's power and knowledge when he became human?' This is an important question, but it was 'status' and 'dignity' (not power or knowledge) of which Paul was thinking when he said that Jesus 'emptied himself'. However, based on the gospel evidence there appears to be a limitation to Jesus' knowledge and power: 'He could do no deed of power' (Mark 6.5); 'But about that day or hour no one knows ... nor the Son' (Mark 13.32). And he needed to grow as human beings do. 'Jesus increased in wisdom ...' (Luke 2.52). If Jesus had not been limited in these ways we could not regard him as a real human being.

The form of a slave Jesus willingly became a 'slave' or a servant of God and of the world. He did not wear the disguise of a servant, but really was a servant ('form' means 'real nature', as in v. 6). Jesus was not a helpless 'slave', but he did experience humiliation and was always under orders. The writer probably had in mind the 'Servant' of Isaiah 42.1–4, and Jesus may have been referring to Isaiah when he described himself as having come 'not to be served but to serve' (Mark 10.45).

Born in human likeness The words mean that Jesus looked like a man, and everyone could see that he was a human being. This repeats what was said in the first part of the verse. It does *not* mean that he was only 'like' a human being. Paul was not making the mistake of saying that Jesus was God and that he only 'appeared' to be a human being. This mistaken belief is referred to in 1 John 4.2: 'every spirit that confesses that Jesus Christ has come in the flesh is from God.' If Jesus had not been fully human, he could not have mediated between God and humankind.

2.8. He humbled himself: This is achieved not only by becoming human, but also in his life as a human being (see note on humility, in Philippians 2.3b).

Became obedient to the point of death We find one account of this in Mark 14. In Gethsemane Jesus was faced with the decision, whether to escape death or to accept it, and we read of his obedience in v. 36, 'not what I want, but what you want'. Usually in the New Testament, writers point to the results of Jesus' death (Romans 5.19). But in this verse the death of Jesus is a sign that there were no limits to his obedience to the Father and no limits to his self-giving to humankind.

Death on a cross To be put to death would have been terrible enough, but Jesus was put to death *on a cross*:

(a) Philippians, living in a Roman colony, where crucifixion was reserved for slaves and rebels, i.e. the people society deemed to be scum or the most dangerous, could see for themselves what a terrible death it was.

(b) Jews, following Deuteronomy 21.23 ('anyone hung on a tree is under God's curse'), believed that anyone killed on a cross was cursed, and therefore separated from the love of God (see Galatians 3.13). There were thus no limits to the self-giving of Jesus.

2.9. Therefore: The word indicates that what follows is a response of God (the Father) to Jesus' self-giving. With this, the scene changes from humiliation to exaltation. In the New Testament, writers do not regard exaltation as a reward, but as a part of the necessary counterbalance to righteous suffering, which otherwise would be meaningless. Thus Matthew 23.12 puts it: 'all who humble themselves will be exalted.' It is also possible that Paul may be hinting at the connection with Isaiah 52.13, which speaks of the exaltation of the Servant. The next verse certainly shows that Paul has Isaiah in mind. If all this has any significance at all, it means that the 'therefore' is there also to show how prophecy is fulfilled in Christ (see note on Philippians 2.10).

Gave him the name that is above every name What is the name that Jesus received? In the Bible 'name' means much more than the word which distinguishes one person from another, such as 'Joshua', 'Elizabeth'.

(a) It means the character or nature of the person. 'I will do whatever you ask in my name [i.e. according to my character]' (John 14.13).

(b) It often means a new stage of a person's existence, especially being given the power or authority or 'rank' to do some special work. This is its meaning in this verse and in Matthew 16.18: 'you are Peter'. It was a new stage for Abraham when God made a covenant with him and gave him a new name (Genesis 17.5). It was a new stage for Jacob when he met God 'face to face' and God gave him a new name (Genesis 32.28–30).

The name which is above every other name can refer either to the name of Jesus or the sacred name of God, i.e. Yahweh. Since the name 'Jesus' was already given at his birth and since Psalm 8 speaks of God exalting his name above all things, the name here is best taken as referring to the sacred name of God. This name is now granted to Jesus.

2.10. At the name of Jesus: Since the character and nature of Yahweh are now expressed through Jesus, it is this name that will command assent and worship from all human beings.

Every knee should bend i.e. all creation, the angels, and all human beings, both the living and the departed. See also 'every tongue' in v. 11. What is more significant is that these words and the following clause are derived from Isaiah 45.23. This is a prophecy about God finally taking action in our world, resulting in everyone acknowledging him to be the one, true God. It therefore speaks of the defeat of idolatry and the triumph of monotheism. What is so amazing in Philippians 2.10 is the application of the prophecy of Isaiah 45.23 to Jesus. This means that in exalting Jesus, God the Father is now giving the role to Jesus to usher in this final outcome of his programme. When monotheism finally triumphs, the God humans will see and acknowledge is Jesus the servant. In other words, by interpreting the essence of being God to mean humble service, Jesus correctly and fully understood what being God means. This being the case, he will be revealed at the end of history as the one God whom the world will acknowledge. The world will then finally understand who God really is and what his character really is too.

2.11. Every tongue should confess that Jesus Christ is Lord: The theme of vv. 9–10 is the 'exaltation' of Jesus, and it is summed up in v. 11 in the word 'Lord'. We should first note how revolutionary this sentence is. To say that Jesus who 'took the form of a slave' and 'humbled himself' and 'became obedient to the point of death' should be called 'Lord' turns upside down what the world regards as greatness. The world calls people 'Lord' who aim at escaping suffering, live apart from ordinary people, and give orders to others. This sentence is as revolutionary as Jesus' own words to his disciples: 'You know that among the Gentiles those whom they recognize as their rulers lord it over them ... But it is not so among you' (Mark 10.42–43).

What did this word 'Lord' mean to the Philippians?

(a) Greek-speaking Jews used it to translate 'Yahweh' which was the Hebrew name for God;

(b) Romans used the word when speaking of their emperor;

(c) Romans and Greeks used it for their 'gods';

(d) but for all of them the word meant 'master' or 'owner', such as the owner of a ship or house or slave.

From the way we have explained vv. 9–11, the 'Lord' does not just speak of Jesus as the Master of all but also points to his divine identity. What applies to Yahweh may in a profound sense be applied to him.

To the glory of God the Father i.e. Jesus desired that glory should be given to his Father, not to himself. Jesus, the exalted one, was still Jesus the servant, the servant of his Father God. Paul taught that, although Jesus was not 'inferior' to the Father, he was 'subject', 'answerable', and 'obedient' to him (1 Corinthians 15.28).

In v. 11b Paul was summing up the whole passage of 2.1–11. He was saying, 'You must regard Jesus as the willing servant. He was servant of all mankind (v. 7) and he is servant to his Father. If you follow him closely, you will be servants to one another. In this way you will become a united congregation.'

 Interpretation

In Philippians 2.1–4 Paul had urged his readers to be united. But how could this be done? Disunity and war are the natural ways in which humans live. How could unity and peace 'break out'? How could the Philippians learn to regard others as better than themselves'?

Paul answered in vv. 5–11: 'Only by being open to receive the spirit of Jesus Christ, the truly humble one, the servant.'

In these verses he was continuing his teaching about the attitude of Christians towards each other. It may seem at first sight that Paul was trying to describe carefully and fully what sort of existence Jesus had before he became human, or in what way he was both God and human. All this is indeed astonishing but they are mentioned to emphasize something else. But if we study the letter as a whole, and especially 1.27—2.11, we shall see that Paul's chief aim was to change the attitude of church members to each other. He was saying, 'If members have the Spirit of Jesus the Servant within them, they will look for ways of serving each other rather than looking for status and privilege.'

The thoughts are:

1 'Let your attitude to one another be like Christ's attitude to mankind' (v. 5);

2 'Christ accepted humiliation and suffering and death for their sake' (vv. 6–8); and

3 'But in doing so, he was raised to his full self, he was exalted' (vv. 9–11).

The focus then is on the attitude of Christ. His attitude is particularly impressive because, as Paul emphasizes at the start, Christ Jesus is equal with God. How is Christ equal with God? How exactly Jesus is to be regarded as God has tested many theological minds. Although we are in no position to solve every difficult problem connected with this, we must not miss Paul's intention here. As we have seen, in this passage Paul was aiming at changing the Philippians' behaviour rather than explaining these matters to them. It is as if, in writing or quoting these words, he was saying, 'Christ shared and shares God's nature, and God's nature has always been self-giving love. Meditate on this, and you will live in fellowship together.'

That said, it must be emphasized that the really astonishing thing here, which also clinches powerfully Paul's teaching point, is that Jesus understood what the essence of being God means, i.e. the nature of God. The essence of being God is not exploitation but service. It is this that 'qualified' Jesus to bring in the final phase of God's programme for this world, where everyone will worship the one true God by confessing Jesus as Lord. This means at the end of the history of this world, humankind will come to understand that the one true God is indeed a servant. Being a servant, he humbled himself and became obedient even to the point of death. This was no ordinary death but the death of the cross, a death that was extremely painful and humiliating. This means we have a God who has not allowed anything to stop him from loving and saving human-kind. Indeed, the new world that God will bring about will be a world of service, since that world will be patterned fully after God's character. It is this astonishing claim that should lead the Philippian Christians to reassess their attitude towards service and towards one another (see Theological essay 3).

Did the Philippians see the application of this to their own lives, as Paul hoped? Did they for the sake of others give up the desire for position and status? We have no way of knowing this although we know many Christians have repeatedly failed to do so. In the past many British Christians in India believed that Hindus and Muslims would take Christ seriously if he was worshipped in magnificent buildings, and if the Church had special privileges from the government. In fact these Christians found that such 'privileges' made their witness not easier but more difficult, because it is in humble people that most Indians expect to find God's presence.

Jesus' death on the cross was the climax of a life of service and it summed up what service meant for him. This service was prompted by love. There are many non-Christians who see the death of Jesus in this way. The Hindu Gandhi saw the self-sacrifice of Jesus on the cross as a perfect example of *satyagraha*, because Jesus was innocent and yet suffered. It is true that Gandhi saw the death of Jesus only as a supreme 'example' and could never believe that by his death Jesus 'cleanses us from all sin' (1 John 1.7). But Jesus' death always inspired and stimulated Gandhi and his followers, and indeed many non-Christian Indians still go to Christian churches on Good Friday. Buddhists regard quietness and separateness as the most important qualities in life, but many of them are attracted by Jesus who totally let go of his quietness and separateness by dying for the sake of others.

Most Muslims regard the death of Jesus as failure and, because they honour him as a prophet, they say that he did not die (Koran, Sura 4.156–57). But Muslims pay great respect to someone who gives his life for others.

All this means Christian churches can only witness to non-Christians if they follow the self-giving which Jesus showed by his death. As we have seen, this means individuals giving up the desire to get their own way. It may mean churches being willing to give up privileges, and to give up their existence as separate churches in order to achieve the greater unity of the whole Church.

 ## STUDY SUGGESTIONS

Word study

1 Which five of the following words have the same meaning as 'name' as it is used in v. 9?

character   title   nature   power   authority   label   appointment   reputation

2 **(a)** What word is used to translate the word 'Lord' (v. 11) in your own language or any other language you know?

(b) In what other context is that word generally used?

Review of content

3 What question was Paul answering in vv. 5–11?

4 (a) For what two reasons do some people think that in vv. 6–11 Paul was quoting from a hymn?

(b) It may be that there are parts of other hymns in Colossians 1.15–18 and 1 Timothy 3.16. Which of these passages do you think is most like Philippians 2.6–11? In what ways is it similar?

5 With regard to the meaning of 'he was in the form of God' (v. 6a), which interpretation do you accept? Give your reasons.

6 Of what did Jesus 'empty' himself (v. 7a)?

Bible study

7 Read the following passages and then explain what is meant by saying that Jesus became the servant (a) of God, and (b) of the world.

(i) Isaiah 52.13—53.8; **(ii)** Matthew 12.15–18; **(iii)** Matthew 20.25–28.

8 Which of these passages do you think most closely agrees with Philippians 2.7a? Give reasons for your answer.

(a) John 13.14; **(b)** Romans 8.3; **(c)** Hebrews 2.14.

Discussion and application

9 What do people of other religions or of no religion, whom you know, think of the self-giving of Jesus?

10 One student said that in his experience 'being humbled willingly may be exaltation, but it can also lead to conceit'. Another student said, 'For me, being humbled willingly is almost impossible. I am being humbled unwillingly all the time.' Discuss these statements with a friend in the light of your own experience.

11 Why is the statement 'Jesus is Lord' said to be 'revolutionary'?

Theological essay 3
God and servanthood

JUAN CARLOS CEVALLOS

At first glance, it is impossible to unite these two words: 'God' and 'servanthood'. When we look at our churches we do not see good models of servanthood. We are encouraged to understand God as strong and powerful in a way that undermines God's servant qualities. In many biblical texts, however, there is no doubt that both words are intimately linked.

The concept of God and servanthood is a concept strongly rooted in the Old Testament, illustrated in the incarnation of Jesus and exemplified in the New Testament as a model for the mission of the Church.

1 Biblical and theological foundation

Immediately after we think of the words God and servanthood, the texts in Isaiah about the Suffering Servant come to mind.

God and servanthood in Isaiah

There are four passages in Isaiah that generally have been recognized as the 'Servant Songs': Isaiah 42.1-4; 49.1-6; 50.4-9; 52.13—53.12. Some, however, have included in this list the passage of Isaiah 61.1-2, which leads us to Luke 4.18-21, where Jesus applies the fulfilment of the text to himself.

On the other hand, the term 'servant' (*ebed*), used in this section, frequently appears outside of the indicated texts, with reference to the nation of Israel. It is also used in the Old Testament for people closely related to God (e.g. Genesis 26.24; Exodus 14.31; 2 Samuel 7.5; Amos 3.7). But without a doubt, one can clearly see the idea of 'servanthood' personified in the figure of the 'Servant' in the 'Servant Songs'. The distinctive element is the obedient and undeserved suffering on the Servant's part, as a way to remove his people's sin so 'the many will be made righteous' (Romans 5.19).

The problem with these texts is trying to identify the 'Servant'. There are several possibilities.

(a) The identification with Israel. This is explicitly mentioned in Isaiah 49.3; it says that Israel is the Suffering Servant, possibly creating the connotation of a pious remnant with a mission, whose mission includes suffering to redeem all of Israel.

(b) 'Corporate personality'. Here one recognizes in the Old Testament that individuals (e.g. a king or a father) can represent the groups they direct. They are members of the groups but they also lead them. In this manner, the Servant is everything that Israel represents, but is also an individual with a mission *to* Israel (Isaiah 49.5ff.), and its experiences in favour of the nation (53.1-6).

(c) An individual. The later Jewish and Christian tradition has interpreted the Servant as an ideal person, an agent for the redemption of the people: the Messiah. For Hellenistic Judaism the corporate interpretation was more acceptable, since it rejected the idea of a suffering Messiah – the idea of a 'serving' Messiah could not be accepted.

God and servanthood in the New Testament

It has been noted that in the New Testament there are relatively few citations of passages related to the Servant. However, there are also several allusions that must not be ignored and these are central to Jesus' mission. All this will demonstrate that the title 'Suffering Servant' is intimately related to Jesus.

It is Jesus himself who quotes Isaiah 53.12 as fulfilled in himself (Luke 22.37). There are also allusions such as Mark 10.45 or 14.24. The use of the title 'Servant' (*ebed*, Hebrew; *pais*, Greek in the LXX) is found in Acts 3.13, 26 and in the prayer of the Church in Acts 4.27, 30. The allusion in 1 Peter 2.21–25; 3.18 is also clear. The New Testament clarifies the concept by indicating that the Servant in Isaiah is Jesus himself.

There are also several quotes with reference to Jesus and his mission: Matthew 8.17; 12.18–21; John 12.38; Acts 8.32–35; Romans 10.16; 15.21. All of these quotes serve as a testimony to affirm the conviction held by the primitive Church that the figure of the Servant described in Isaiah 53 is the divinely inspired model indicating the messianic mission of Jesus.

A central text: Mark 10.35–45

The passage in Mark points us to Jesus' redemptive task, but it curiously 'mixes' with his mission of service. Within the whole text he mixes words with different connotations: in v. 43, the word translated as servant is *diakonos*; later 'slave' (*doulos*) is used, emphasizing unconditional and submissive obedience. The text describes his task as to serve (*diakonēthēnai*). Mark decided to use *diakonos*, which emphasizes the attitude of voluntary service in 'unimportant' matters.

2 Missiological implications

The biblical–theological dimension is incomplete if its pertinence to the reality of the Church today cannot be found. What better way to see this pertinence than by meditating on the text in Philippians 2.5–11, and comparing it with texts that talk about the necessity of imitating Jesus' mission here on earth. Paul becomes an echo of Isaiah 53 in his magisterial passage that we will treat immediately.

Understanding Philippians 2.5–11

The text of the hymn found in Philippians 2.5–11 lends itself to many forms of appropriation. It is used as a central passage in Christology, yet with good reason it is said to be one of the most complicated passages for theology. Nevertheless, this passage, like the entire Bible, is not a passage with which to make 'pure theology', since such theology does not exist in the Bible. All existing theology happens within the context of the life of the Church, and responds to a current need.

The calling Paul makes in the text is: 'Let the same mind be in you that was in Christ Jesus.' This phrase that introduces the hymn (v. 5) reiterates the theme in v. 2, and presents Christ as a model of the attitude Paul expects will characterize the Philippians. Nevertheless, it is not only about proposing a model of conduct. Christ's attitude can only be imitated if one's life is submitted to Jesus Christ's dominion.

Paul immediately clarifies who Jesus Christ is: he is God ('who, though he was in form of God', v. 5). The next verse affirms that Jesus 'emptied himself, taking the form of a slave, being born in human likeness'. Paul, however, uses a more explicit Greek word for 'slave' here than that which appears in the LXX of Isaiah. Jesus takes the form of a slave (*doulos*), without ceasing to assume the 'form of God'. Both things subsist in the same form: he is God and a slave/servant. This is central in the incarnation, and is explained in the next two verses. It is not a doctrine to be contemplated, but a doctrine to be imitated. There must be, in us, the same attitude Jesus had: that being so great, he humbled himself to be a servant.

The term 'slave', as applied here to Christ, is to be interpreted in terms of Isaiah's Servant passages (Isaiah 52.13—53.12). Thus the phrase 'taking the form of a slave' means 'exactly playing the part' of the Servant of the Lord. It should also be noted that the poem in Isaiah strikes the same theme as is sounded at the conclusion of the Philippian hymn: 'See, my servant ... shall be exalted and lifted up, and shall be very high' (Isaiah 52.13; cf. Philippians 2.9–11). If this is the idea to be attached to *doulos*, then 'slave/servant' is in reality an honorific title. Yet the context demands that 'slave' be understood as a term of extreme abasement, the exact opposite of 'Lord', a title later used to describe the exalted Christ.

This concept is completely contrary to the Gnostic idea that found it impossible to believe God would limit himself in the incarnation. The incarnation constitutes the model for the mission of the Church. The greatness of God is seen in his becoming extremely lowly, and that is also a mandate for the Church.

If the context in which the hymn is inserted presents a call to serve one another, then 'slave' emphasizes that, in the incarnation, Christ entered the stream of human life as a slave, that is, as a person without advantage, with no rights or privileges of his own, for the express purpose of placing himself completely at the service of all humankind (cf. Mark 10.45).

The 'servant' of Isaiah 53 also was 'poured out' or 'emptied himself', though not in the incarnation only, but in death (Isaiah 53.12; cf. Philippians 2.8). The incarnation is both humiliation and mission. By serving people, Jesus is serving God; being a slave of humankind is doing God's will.

Our mission is the 'same' as Christ's

Jesus Christ is the centre, the climax, and the objective of God's revelation. For this reason, it is impossible to fulfil our mission without taking into account what Jesus Christ did. Jesus becomes the model of what it means to do contextual mission, since it can be said that God has contextualized himself in Jesus Christ. The incarnation of God manifests the approach he makes to humankind: participating with human beings in all their vicissitudes by being Emmanuel, a first-century Jew and a servant. The incarnation shows that God's intention is to reveal himself from within the human situation. By virtue of the proper nature of the gospel, we only know the gospel as a message contextualized in culture. Since God became human, it has been constituted in the example of the only way the gospel should incarnate in a culture so that it has the pertinence for humans. It is through the incarnation that God manifests his 'method' of sharing with humankind.

Our mission cannot be separated from service. Two more texts in the Gospel of John point us to the necessity of imitating Jesus in our task: John 17.18: 'As you have sent me into the world, so I have sent them into the world', and John 20.21: 'As the Father has sent me, so I send you.' How does God desire we complete this task?

The incident in which Jesus uses himself as an example of a slave/ servant, and washes his disciples' feet, takes us back to the hymn in Philippians, where the context obliges us to think about service towards the other.

John, in his Gospel, presents Jesus as fulfilling his task of revealing the Father by serving. The pivotal point of the Gospel of John is chapter 13. Jesus is directed towards the passion, but at the same time continues with his pedagogical task of teaching his disciples, by the washing of feet. This is also an example to imitate: 'For I have set you an example, that you also should do as I have done for you.'

There is no doubt that the task of the Church is to follow the example of Christ, the servant God.

3 Contemporary reflections

The practice of the teachings of Jesus should happen in life itself and in its every sphere. Nothing in the behaviour of the believer should be foreign to the model of Jesus.

Reality

Allow me to analyse my experiences in a border city in the United States, about five minutes from Mexico. I have been a pastor for more than 30 years and have served as the president of a theological seminary.

In Latin America, evangelical churches are no longer an insignificant minority. Some have seen phenomenal growth. Nevertheless, the societal influence of evangelical churches is not very noticeable. In many places the presence of an evangelical church has not improved the morals and living conditions of a community. Indeed, sometimes social morals have deteriorated.

This numerical growth is spurred by the establishment of mega churches, some with more than 10,000 members. In general, these mega churches are directed by 'pastors', 'apostles' or 'servants' (a hierarchical title that in many cases is the one of highest order; what a contradiction!) and practise a managerial system of leadership, and not a system of an authentic service following the model of Jesus.

In the United States, mega churches are also on the rise. Several English-speaking churches close every day. Often small congregations close down and 'believers' move to mega churches. Unfortunately, these churches are promoters of an 'artistic show' service where the 'pastoral figure' is exalted, which is far from being a servant figure. In a hedonistic society, the exaltation of the pastoral figure is a great temptation. With a ministry of 'success', it is difficult for people to see that the Church exists to exalt Christ and not a charismatic human being, such as a pastor with great leadership capacity.

The mission of the Church has limited itself to a task of proselytism, which is sometimes masked by contemporary terms such as 'church planting'. Many churches have become agencies to recruit new members. The task of service, the development of a 'ministry of service to the community', is almost nil and, in the best cases, limits itself to actions of benevolence and works of charity.

The 'service crisis' in the churches is so severe that para-church organizations have developed, to do what the Church does not wish to do.

Service in family life and the Church

Leadership and authority in family life and Church should take place in humility, in mutual submission, and in the context of the narrative of how Jesus exercised his authority. As the glorious hymn to Christ in Philippians 2 expresses it: for the incarnation and cross, Jesus deprived himself of his rightful place, humbled and dedicated himself to the needs of others, and finally was unflinchingly obedient to the authority of God the Father (Philippians 2.5–11). This fits in with the virtues of humility, the commitment to God, and Jesus' concept of justice, seen in the Beatitudes. All Christians should imitate this model.

Mutual servanthood places certain limitations on the authority of any Christian in any context. The model of Christ gives form to a perspective in which all authority is employed. Any member of the Christian community can hold any other member responsible – even leaders – according to the example of Christ. Mutual servanthood uses but also limits liberty, releases gifts for responsible use, directs authority, organizes the Christian community, and participates in the kingdom. In love, mutual servanthood creates mutual control over the exercise of liberty and power, which preserves and allows justice to advance. This is the best model for all relationships within the body of Christ.

The congregation in El Paso, of which I am a member, is developing a simple programme of neighbourhood clean-up. It is called 'I Love El Paso' (*Yo Amo El Paso*). The city suffers greatly from the problem of litter in the streets. We have organized ourselves so that every so often groups of members from our church can pick up trash from the city streets. This activity simply transmits the message that we love the city where God has placed us. The possibilities for service are many and will depend on the situation of each congregation. The responsibility lies in searching for ways to live, with the conviction that Christianity is fundamentally to serve as Jesus did.

The serving Church

The call Paul issues to the Philippians is to have the same mind that Jesus had. There is no other way to do mission. The people of God must follow the model of the Suffering Servant, ready to give himself, ready to deprive himself of benefit for the sake of the people. The Church is not here to lord over everyone else. Following the example of Jesus means that we must insert or incarnate ourselves in our society, as Christ did. We must insert or incarnate ourselves in society with the same attitude that Jesus had. The Church exists to serve. We must face our mission from the standpoint of the call to deprive ourselves. Being in the form of the body of Christ with all its privileges, we must take the form of servants, and then the Church will be exalted. True exaltation is not possible without humiliation.

The service vocation of the Church is an urgent imperative. Obeying Christ should impel us to look for ways to serve in our community. The servant attitude of the Church will be a sign of hope for humankind, and also a sign of Christ's lordship. God-service, Christ-service, Christ-lordship are inseparable words.

In a society where being a servant is not common (when has it been?), we have the challenge of the serving God to follow his footsteps. The Church can only be conceived, by the light of the Word, as a serving Church.

I would like to finish by affirming that the mission of the Church in the twenty-first century should return to the model the Word gives us. It is a model that is rooted in the Old Testament, most precisely in the mission of the Suffering Servant, and is concretized in the life of Jesus. It is a model that was proclaimed by Paul, and a model we should keep following. God and servanthood cannot be separated. God is a servant and that is where his greatness lies. The Church is a servant. Christians worship God through their service.

Philippians 2.12–18

Practical implications of salvation

 Summary

Since God is at work in them, Paul urges his readers to live out the practical implications of their salvation, so as to shine like stars in a darkened world. Using different metaphors, Paul explains how he and the readers are profoundly linked.

 Notes

2.12. Therefore: In Philippians 2 Paul first declares a great truth and then says, 'Therefore ...'. This shows his readers how to apply the truth to their lives. He does the same in other letters (e.g. Romans 12.1).

Paul is saying here that if the Philippians really believed that Jesus was the supreme Servant, then they would turn their belief into behaviour. (We do not 'believe' the great statements of the Creed until we live them.)

My beloved In these verses Paul was calling on them to make changes in the way they lived, but he did so with gentleness. Because he loved them, they could see what he meant when he taught that God loved them. So by gentleness he led them forward.

In my absence It was good that Paul had lived among the Philippians, but he could not remain in Philippi for ever. And now that he is absent, they must continue to obey God. This is a test for them. If Paul had pointed to himself rather than to God, if it was Paul only whom they had been obeying, then when he left them they would fall away from living as Christians. But if it was God himself whom they obeyed, then Paul's absence would not seriously affect their lives. What they did when Paul went away showed what they themselves believed.

Work out These words really mean 'work to complete' or 'work hard at'. See note on Philippians 1.6. There was a danger that, having once been established by Paul, some members might think that their task was only to maintain what they had been given. It was as if Paul was saying, 'You are like farmers who have bought some land. Go on working till harvest time!'

Your own salvation In this verse Paul is probably thinking of the spiritual health of the whole congregation. He has referred to it earlier when he wrote about right relationships in the congregation (see notes on Philippians 2.1–4). As a congregation they must learn to do without him, and grow in dependence on God and in their work of being servants to one another and to those around them. This is also how Paul used the word 'salvation' in 1.28. That said, this should not be taken to mean that other important 'dimensions' of salvation are to be excluded: the 'individual', 'corporate' and the 'spiritual' (i.e. the 'eschatological' or the 'final state' of God's programme) are all interrelated.

In the New Testament the word 'salvation' is usually used with reference to the 'individual' or the 'spiritual' (as it was qualified above).

(a) Being rescued from ill health or physical danger or from death (Mark 3.4).

(b) Having 'wholeness', i.e. health of body and soul (see Luke 17.19: 'thy faith hath made thee whole (Greek = has saved you)', AV). New Testament writers thought of a person as a whole person. They did not regard a human being as a collection of separate parts: 'body', 'mind', 'spirit'. See Special note H on 'body'.

(c) Being rescued by God through Jesus Christ from the overwhelming power of our sins (Matthew 1.21) and from being for ever separated from God. See also Mark 8.35.

When does salvation take place? On the one hand writers say that a person 'has been saved' (Ephesians 2.8). This means that this person has gratefully accepted God's offer of salvation. On the other hand, this person still has a long way to go and so he is still 'being saved' (Acts 2.47), and his salvation needs to be completed in the future (Romans 5.9: 'will be saved through him from the wrath of God').

With fear and trembling This is a common biblical expression, which is often used to speak of 'reverence' and 'seriousness' (Psalm 2.11; Ezekiel 12.18; 2 Corinthians 7.15; Ephesians 6.5). Paul is not referring to the sort of fear that prevents a person from taking action, as a rabbit is paralysed by its fear of an approaching fox or a lizard by its fear of a snake. Nor, of course, does Paul want his readers to doubt the love and mercy of God. 'With fear and trembling' means honestly facing our weaknesses as a congregation, and as individuals, knowing our own special temptations, never taking for granted that the way we do things is the way that God wants them done. It means depending on God's grace, as Paul shows in v. 13 (see also 2 Corinthians 7.15).

2.13. For it is God who is at work in you, enabling you both to will and to work for his good pleasure: That is, 'You do not have to do this in your own strength alone. God's Spirit is at work in you. He creates in you the desire (will) to do what he wants done, and the power (work) to do it.' The thought of this verse and that of the previous verse show how biblical writers regard as compatible the notions of divine initiative and human responsibility.

2.14. All things: These words receive the emphasis in the Greek text, conveying the idea of 'in every situation and deed'.

Murmuring and arguing This is the first of the three signs by which, Paul hopes, the Philippians would show that God was at work in them. They would be humble and contented rather than murmuring or arguing. Perhaps Paul was thinking of the murmurings of the Israelites against Moses (Exodus 16). But it seems from 2.1–4 that the Philippians murmured against each other.

2.15. Blameless and innocent ... without blemish: The second sign which, Paul hopes, would show that God was at work in the Philippian Christians was chiefly this: that in their behaviour they would be distinguishable from those who were not Christians. The words 'blameless' and 'innocent' and 'without blemish' do not mean 'perfect' or 'without sin'. They mean 'not being a serious stumbling block to those who are not members of the Church', 'not making it impossible for other people to believe in Jesus Christ'. See note on Philippians 1.10.

Innocent This means sincere, having good motives.

Without blemish This is a phrase which Jewish worshippers used to describe an offering which was fit to be sacrificed (see v. 17 and the references to sacrifice). We could translate it 'fit to be God's servant'.

Children of God ... in the midst of a crooked and perverse generation Using the language of Deuteronomy 32.5, Paul writes that the Christians are the children of God and implicitly warns that they should not be like the Israel of old: for they were a crooked and perverse generation. Israel became like the 'world'; the Philippian Christians must not.

'Crooked' is often used in the New Testament in the figurative sense of being 'dishonest and 'unscrupulous'. The word 'perverse' often refers to the action of someone who wishes to distort the 'straight' ways of God. Used together, the terms express the dishonest and distorting deeds of humankind.

The world The Greek word is *kosmos* and has the following range of meaning in the New Testament:

(a) the whole universe which God has created (Matthew 25.34);

(b) those who fail to acknowledge God's authority: 'The world hates me' (John 7.7). This is the meaning in v. 15b;

(c) those whom God is always working to win back from disobedience to obedience (2 Corinthians 5.19).

You shine like stars in the world Paul urges his readers thus: not only are they to 'stand out' from the world, they are there also to 'shed light', i.e. 'transform society' by good behaviour and deeds (Matthew 5.14–16).

2.16. Holding fast to the word of life: This is the third sign that God was at work in the Philippians. 'Holding fast' means keeping something safe which God had entrusted to them or holding it firmly, like a servant guarding the house carefully while the owner is away. Another interpretation is that it means 'holding it out for all to see; offering it to everyone'.

'Word' in the Bible is used in several ways: e.g.:

(a) God's creative word (Genesis 1.3: 'God *said*, "Let there be light" ');

(b) God's will which he communicates to humankind through his messengers (Isaiah 38.4: 'the word of the Lord came to Isaiah');

(c) God's word as it has been written down in the first five books of the Bible (Psalm 119.42: 'I trust in your word');

(d) Jesus Christ himself who perfectly expressed God's will (John 1.1: 'the Word was with God');

(e) the 'good news' or 'gospel' which Christians preach (Acts 13.44: 'The whole city gathered to hear the word of the Lord'). This is its meaning in this verse. It does not mean the Bible or the New Testament. They did not exist as such when Paul wrote.

The 'word of life' here means 'the good news through which the life of God himself has come to you, and by which you now live'.

I can boast on the day of Christ that I did not run or labour in vain Some readers are surprised or troubled to see that Paul draws attention to himself in vv. 16–18, as he did in 2.2. They believe that a church leader should hide his own feelings from those whom he leads. But one of the reasons why Paul was able to lead congregations was that he treated them as his friends, with whom he could openly and honestly share his joys and his hopes and his fears and his doubts.

Paul writes v. 16 with a feeling which most church leaders have sometimes felt: 'What will all my work lead to in the end? Is it really worthwhile?' Paul gives his own reply: 'I am praying that you, as a congregation, will complete your salvation (v. 12), live in humility (v. 14), be distinctive as Christians (v. 15), and hold firmly to the gospel (v. 16a), so that in the end I shall know that my work was worthwhile.'

He uses the words 'run' and 'labour' because he, like his readers, knew about the Greek games. He had probably watched them. There were many different sorts of athletics, but the chief sort was running. The training for these races was very strenuous indeed. As Paul uses the word 'labour', the readers would be able to picture the sweat pouring off the runner as he went around the course time after time under a burning sun. See note on Philippians 3.14. As the runners hope that they will receive a reward, so Paul prays that he would in the end have a reward, and could 'boast' that he had achieved his object. For 'in the day of Christ' see note on Philippians 1.6b. For 'boast' see note on Philippians 3.3.

2.17. If I am being poured out as a libation: In v. 16 readers could picture the games. As they read v. 17 they pictured a priest pouring a 'libation' (which he did during the games), i.e. spilling wine on to the ground as part of a sacrifice, usually the last part. This was a common thing to see in those days, just as it is a common custom among many tribes and peoples today. In several countries wine is poured out when a new ship is launched or a new house is completed.

Paul clothes his thoughts in words and picture-language which would be familiar to his readers. In writing this verse he has four special thoughts:

1   He might very soon be executed: 'even if I am being poured out ...' (This is a different thought from those in 1.24 and 2.24).

2   If so, his death would be like a sacrifice: 'poured out as a libation'.

3   His death would be in fellowship with the sacrifice which the Philippians were already making: 'over (i.e. following on) the sacrifice and offering of your faith'. Their faith expressed itself in many sorts of service (see 4.14), and so Paul calls it a sacrifice. (He uses the Greek word which is usually translated as 'liturgy', which means a priestly ministry.)

4   He rejoiced and wanted them to rejoice too. The Philippians could rejoice both at the sacrifice which they themselves made and at Paul's death if it should take place soon.

 ## Interpretation

Paul's main thought in this section may be expressed as follows: 'We have seen that Christ was the supreme Servant. You will behave as servants by faithfully continuing with the work which you have begun: work to complete your salvation.' Paul might also have the story of Moses in mind, perhaps feeling that he himself had had a similar experience. He had brought the people out of their old life into a new one, but now they were grumbling and slow to go forward. In helping the Philippian Christians to progress, Paul appealed to God's initiative, outlined the kind of behaviour to be expected of them as they worked out their salvation, and used metaphors to speak of the profound connection he had with them.

All this was needful especially when Paul was absent. When Paul was present with them in Philippi and leading the congregation, they obeyed him. At that time Paul did not merely send them messages, he lived among them. A pastor is someone who is among his people and visiting his people's homes, not one who only preaches from a pulpit. Sadly, this may sometimes lead to a condition of over-dependence on people. To be sure, the work of a church leader is to help members to love and obey God himself, as revealed in the gospel about Jesus Christ. Then when the leader, or the members themselves, must go to live somewhere else, their faith is not weakened.

There is always a danger that church members may give their loyalty not so much to God as to the leader of the congregation (especially if the leader is a strong personality). Or they may depend too much on a friend whom they admire, or on a group of Christian friends who have supported them, or on their family. These are all God-given supports, but they too easily take the place of God himself. An Indian teacher to whom many went for counsel expressed this in the form of a parable: 'I point with my finger and show you the moon. But you gaze at my finger and see no moon.' It was easier for the Philippians when they could let Paul take their decisions for them. In the same way it is simpler for people today to have a powerful church leader or political dictator who takes all the decisions. But when this happens the people are prevented from becoming mature.

In Paul's advice to his readers, concepts of divine initiative and human responsibility are viewed as compatible. How is this so?

1   At first sight there seems to be a contradiction between 'working' (v. 12) and letting God work (v. 13). But when Christians put these two verses into practice, there is no contradiction. We become our best selves when we most fully let God control us, just as a sailor in a small sailing boat catches the wind. He controls the boat, so as to make the most of the wind. But he cannot provide the power that drives the boat along.

    Study group leaders have to work hard to help each member to take a proper share of the study and discussion. They are 'working' (v. 12). But they can at the same time be aware that God's Holy Spirit is there, to come into the group, making it possible for the members to trust each other, or to understand an important truth in a way that at first seemed impossible.

2   No one who really believes that God 'is at work' in them can boast of their own achievements (1 Corinthians 4.7). A boastful Christian is as ridiculous as a student who won the first prize for an essay, but who (it was discovered later) had copied the whole essay out of a book.

3   It is part of the 'good news' of Jesus' teaching that God is at work in us. He is at work in the minds of students as they study, in the hands of builders as they build, in the wills of those who worship him.

Paul's advice to his readers takes into consideration that God has placed his Church 'in the midst' of his world. Jesus prayed that his disciples would be *in* the world, but not *of* the world, i.e. Christians should be in communication with the people around them, but should not depend on those people for leadership and inspiration (John 17.15–16). All members of small Christian congregations know how difficult it is to take a full part in the life of the surrounding community if most members of that community belong to other religions or practise no religion at all. But it is not more difficult for them than it was for that small Christian congregation in the great Greek city of Philippi.

However, Christians are not being faithful to God if they spend so much time on church affairs that they are ignorant of the events taking place elsewhere. When in 2 Corinthians 6.17 Paul wrote 'come out from them, and be separate' (thinking of Isaiah 52.11) he meant, 'Be distinctively Christian. Be different in the way you live.' He was not telling them to retreat from the world into an enclosed society of Christians. There is a church in a Swiss town which has one wall made entirely of glass. The pastor said, 'As we worship we are aware of the people outside whom God will send us out to serve.'

Finally, a word must be said about the way Paul wrote about himself in 2.16–17. These verses sum up what he was saying throughout the whole letter: to accept suffering ('being poured out as a libation') and to be in fellowship with the Philippians ('poured … over the sacrifice and offering of your faith') – this, indeed, is joy ('rejoice with me'). Christians of many nations, and at different times, have shown the same willingness to 'be poured out'. In 1977 Archbishop Luwum of Uganda became convinced that he and the other bishops there must make a strong protest to Idi Amin who was then President of Uganda. The president's soldiers had been allowed to destroy churches and kill Christians and very many others in an attempt to suppress opposition. But to protest was to risk death. As Janani Luwum set out with the letter of protest he said, 'Even if he kills me, my blood will save the nation.' He was killed on 16 February 1977.

STUDY SUGGESTIONS

Word study

1   What three meanings does the Greek word here translated 'world' have in the New Testament?

2   What sort of 'fear' was Paul talking about in v. 12?

Review of content

3   In what way was Paul's absence a 'test' for the Philippians?

4   (a) What were the three 'signs' which would show that God was 'at work' in the Philippian Christians?

(b) What sort of behaviour might prevent them from 'shining like stars in the world'?

5   What is the full meaning of the phrase 'word of life' in v. 16?

Bible study

6   Which verses or phrases in 2.12–18 contain the same or nearly the same thought or teaching as that in each of the following?

(a) John 17.15, 16; **(b)** Matthew 5.16; **(c)** Acts 13.47; **(d)** Philippians 4.4; **(e)** 2 Timothy 4.6.

Discussion and application

7   'Work out your own salvation' does *not* mean 'Be independent of God'. What does it mean?

8   A feeling which most church leaders have sometimes felt is: 'What will all my work lead to in the end? Is it really worthwhile?' Some Christians think that leaders should hide such feelings. What was Paul's attitude? What is your own opinion?

9   Paul clothed his thoughts in words and picture-language which were familiar to his readers. What sort of picture-language would you use today to express the idea of 'sacrifice' if you were speaking:

(a) to a village congregation in a mainly Muslim area of West Africa;

(b) in a seamen's mission in a busy port in South-East Asia;

(c) in a large industrial city of Europe or America;

(d) to your own congregation (unless included above)?

Philippians 2.19–30

Co-workers

 Summary

Paul commends Timothy to the Christians at Philippi and returns Epaphroditus to them, both of whom he regards highly and offers them as examples of good disciples of Jesus Christ.

 Notes

2.19. I hope in the Lord Jesus: This statement in its context refers to Jesus as both Lord and assurance of Paul's hope. In other words, what Paul hopes to do is to be submitted to Christ's lordship and Christ as the true Lord means for Paul that he can 'hope' without being ashamed. Usually, Jews would have said, 'I hope in God' but Paul has substituted Jesus for God in this statement, revealing to his readers what he thinks of Jesus Christ in relation to God.

To send Timothy Timothy is sent in order to gather news about the Philippians. Paul first met Timothy in Lystra (Acts 16.1), and had him circumcised so that Jews as well as Gentiles would accept him. After that Timothy was with Paul on many of his journeys, as we see from Acts 17—19; and he was with Paul in prison (1.1).

2.20. Genuinely concerned for your welfare: Paul believes Timothy is really interested in the well-being of the Philippians.

2.21. All of them are seeking their own interests, not those of Jesus Christ: At first sight it seems that Paul is angrily condemning the whole local congregation, and must be exaggerating. But 'all' probably means 'all the Christians in this place (i.e. Rome) whom I have so far approached'. Paul's point is: 'The only way to encourage the Philippians to live in fellowship is to send a messenger. Letters of advice are not enough. But that messenger needs to be someone who loves Jesus Christ and loves the Christians more than he loves his own advancement.' Timothy fits the bill.

2.22. Like a son with a father: This describes the close spiritual relationship between Timothy and Paul.

2.25. To send to you Epaphroditus: The Philippians had sent Epaphroditus to Paul with a monetary gift (see 4.18), and so that he could look after Paul in prison. While Epaphroditus was there he became very ill (v. 27). The Philippians heard about his illness and were distressed. Then Epaphroditus heard about their distress and, having recovered from his illness, wanted to return to Philippi and to show them that he was well again (v. 26). Paul encouraged him to go. He did this probably for two reasons: first, because Epaphroditus wanted to go; second, because Paul thought that Epaphroditus was the right sort of person to work for unity in the congregation (v. 28).

The name 'Epaphroditus' is interesting because it contains the name of the pagan Greek goddess 'Aphrodite'. It seems that when Greeks became Christian, they did not think it necessary to throw away a name which they had used before being baptized.

My brother and co-worker and fellow soldier These are words which, as we have seen, describe the relationship between Paul and one of his junior colleagues. The words point to the way in which Christians share relationships and share work.

Your messenger and minister to my need Epaphroditus was a *messenger*. The Greek word is *apostolos*, which means someone who is 'sent'.

(a) Usually in the New Testament it means one of the 12 apostles whom Jesus sent to be his representatives (Mark 6.30).

(b) There were others later who were called 'apostles', along with the Twelve, e.g. Paul and Barnabas (Acts 14.14).

(c) In two places (here and 2 Corinthians 8.23) it refers to other people who were sent to represent a congregation officially. It was in this way that Epaphroditus was an 'apostle'.

Epaphroditus was a *minister*. The Greek word is *leitourgos*, which meant someone who offered service to God. In Greek cities it meant someone who served the public by making a generous gift to a city, e.g. by paying for the training of their athletes, and who was therefore very much honoured. Paul uses the word here probably to show that Epaphroditus' service has many parallels with a Greek *leitourgos*. He carried the gift of the Philippian Christians, and offered his life in service to God, and hence is to be honoured.

2.27. God had mercy on him: Paul means that God has enabled Epaphroditus to recover from his illness.

2.30. He came close to death for the work of Christ: Epaphroditus was to be honoured because he worked for Christ and in doing so nearly died. It was his desire to work for Christ and the work which he did for which they should honour him; not his serious illness.

Risking his life to make up for those services The word translated here as 'risking' is a word used by gamblers. Epaphroditus had 'gambled with his life' by being the friend of Paul who might soon be executed.

 Interpretation

We discover in these verses the special reason why Paul wrote this letter: because he was so anxious (v. 20) about the lack of unity among the Philippians, he had decided that as he could not go himself he must send Timothy and Epaphroditus to them, as his representatives. But since the Philippians might not welcome them, he had to prepare them for the visit. So he wrote this letter.

This passage, then, focuses on Paul's two co-workers: Timothy (vv. 19–24) and Epaphroditus (vv. 25–30). One of them was chosen by Paul as his companion in his missionary journeys; the other was sent to him. It will become clear later that one reason why they were commended to the church at Philippi was that they showed good examples of love modelled on Christ. This is seen principally in the way their qualities were highlighted in vv. 20–21, 25–27.

Regarding Paul's co-workers, we may note, first of all, the sort of relationship Paul had with those with whom he worked from phrases such as the following: 'co-worker' (v. 25), 'father' and 'son' (v. 22), 'brother', and 'fellow soldier' (v. 25). It is likely that by nature Paul did not find it easy to work with other people (see note on Philippians 1.15). But in spite of this, and because of the help of God, he did work with them effectively.

Timothy was an important companion of Paul in his missionary work. In this passage, his qualities are being held up as worthy of being followed. We may note especially:

(a) Timothy's *faithfulness.* He genuinely cared about the well-being of the Philippians (v. 20). He sincerely wanted to give honour to Christ (v. 21). People had discovered these qualities over a long period – 'Timothy's worth you know' (v. 22a). This is the reason why Paul planned to send him.

(b) His *willingness to take second place.* Messengers and junior typists are not treated as important people in most communities. But Timothy was happy to be Paul's messenger (1 Corinthians 4.17; 16.10; 1 Thessalonians 3.6); and to help Paul with many of his letters (2 Corinthians 1.1; 1 Thessalonians 1.1; 2 Thessalonians 1.1; as well as Philippians 1. 1). Those who take the lead and those who take second place are equally 'important' in the Church.

Timothy's two other qualities may be found in other New Testament writings:

(c) His *overcoming of disadvantages.* We see from 1 Timothy 4.12 that some people were unwilling to listen to Timothy because he was young. Also it may be that, because he was the child of a mixed marriage (Greek and Jew), neither Greeks nor Jews fully accepted him, although he had the advantage of inheriting the best traditions of both races. Whatever disadvantages there were, he overcame them.

(d) His *willingness to suffer* for the gospel. Like Paul he was imprisoned (see Hebrews 13.23).

Paul's other colleague was Epaphroditus. This person was sent by the church at Philippi to minister to Paul's needs. Being the 'sent one', he might be designated as 'apostle'. What was impressive about his service was that he was willing to serve to the point of death. In this way, his example is patterned after that of Jesus Christ. Furthermore, Epaphroditus was a *leitourgos*. Referring probably to what a *leitourgos* would do in the context of ancient Greek culture, Paul was stressing how Epaphroditus served him not only by carrying the generous gift of the church at Philippi but also by offering his own life without hesitation, in service to God. Not surprisingly, Paul asked that he be honoured.

 ## STUDY SUGGESTIONS

Word study

1 (a) What does the word 'apostle' mean'?

   (b) Identify the types of people the word 'apostle' is used for in the New Testament.

Review of content

2 What do we learn from this passage about the special reason why Paul wrote to the Philippians?

3 What do we learn from this passage about Paul's relationship with his fellow workers?

4 Why had the Philippians sent Epaphroditus to Paul, and what had happened to him as a result?

Bible study

5 In what way did people experience the 'mercy' of God or humankind in each of the following passages?

   (a) Deuteronomy 7.9; (b) Luke 1.50–55; (c) Luke 10.33–37; (d) Luke 18.35–42; (e) 1 Peter 1.3.

Discussion and application

6 In Paul's description of Timothy (v. 19a) we note four qualities that made him a good helper and messenger. What *other* qualities, if any, do you think can help to make a person a good helper and messenger or representative?

7 **(a)** In what way should a Christian be a 'fighter'?

   (b) What are the benefits and dangers of thinking of the Church as an 'army' and Christians as 'soldiers'?

8 What risks, if any, have you yourself ever taken on account of being a Christian?

Philippians 3.1–11

The old and the new

 Summary

Just before concluding the letter, Paul warns his readers against those Jews who desire to impose Jewish ways on Gentile Christians. Paul uses his own personal experience to bring home some important points. These concern mainly how the new has replaced the old.

 Notes

3.1 Finally: Why does Paul write 'finally' but not bring his Letter to an end? Scholars have made various suggestions, as follows:

(a) Some have suggested that Paul, having written 'Finally', remembered that he had something else that he wanted to say. We all do this in writing letters, especially if we are dictating to a secretary as Paul was. In this case he wanted to add a warning to his readers. So without crossing out 'Finally', he gave his warning, beginning at v. 2. It seems that he also did this in his first Letter to the Thessalonians (see 1 Thessalonians 4.1).

(b) Others think that Paul was just about to end his Letter when a messenger arrived from Philippi with news about false teaching which the Christians were receiving, and that he immediately attacked this false teaching.

(c) Others believe that 3.2–19 are part of a different letter which Paul wrote at another time. They think that, when Paul's Letters were being collected together, editors mistakenly included these verses with this chapter.

Option (c) appears to be quite improbable and most scholars today would opt for option (a).

Rejoice in the Lord: Paul wrote about rejoicing in 1.18 and 2.18. But here and in 4.4 he writes 'Rejoice *in the Lord*', meaning 'Be glad with the gladness that comes from depending on the Lord himself rather than on changing circumstances' (see note on Philippians 4.4). Some translations have 'Farewell' instead of 'Rejoice'. The Greek word can have either meaning (see Theological essay 4).

To write the same things What were these 'things' about which, it seems, Paul had already written to the Philippians? Paul may have been referring to his teaching, (a) about rejoicing, or (b) about unity (as in chapters 1 and 2), or (c) about the false teaching which he later described in vv. 2–11. We cannot tell.

Whatever teaching Paul was thinking of, he had probably given it to the Philippians in one of the letters which he wrote but which we do not have. Paul was travelling round the Eastern Mediterranean, visiting congregations and writing to them, for about 16 years, but we have only a few of his letters. He may have written many more letters which have since been lost.

Not troublesome i.e. 'I never get tired of saying this.'

3.2. Beware of the dogs: By 'dogs' Paul is probably referring to non-Christian Jews who were persecuting the congregation in Philippi and trying to persuade the members to join (or return to) the Jewish faith. But some scholars believe that by 'dogs' Paul meant Christians who taught that it was necessary for followers of Christ to keep the old Jewish laws.

In the ancient world, the word 'dogs' often conjured up the picture of the half-wild dogs who lived on rubbish outside the city. Hence, dogs were often regarded negatively as exemplifying ill discipline, sloppy and vile behaviour. By using such language, Paul appears to be very offensive. This is rather surprising because he usually spoke about the Jews respectfully (see Romans 10.1; 11.1–2). Why then does he compare these people to dogs? Two considerations may lessen the offensiveness of Paul's tone. The first is that Paul was very worried the Christians in Philippi might be won over to the teaching of these people. It appears that the problems that affected the Galatian churches were also present in other churches although not to the same degree. Hence, Paul uses strong language here to indicate how critical the issue is. Second, the use of the term may be ironical. The Jews in Paul's day often regarded Gentiles as ritually impure and referred to them as dogs (compare the verbal exchange between Jesus and the Syrophoenician woman in Mark 7.27–28). The irony then is that it was not the Gentiles but those Jews, who wanted to impose Jewish understanding of purity on them, who were really the 'dogs'.

Beware of evil workers, beware of those who mutilate the flesh Evil workers and 'those who mutilate' are two more phrases with which Paul refers to that Jewish group in Philippi. 'Mutilate the flesh' is Paul's angry way of referring to circumcision (compare this with Galatians 5.12).

3.3. For it is we who are the circumcision: According to Genesis 17.9–11, Jews were circumcised as a sign of the covenant between God and Abraham. Paul used the word 'mutilate' in v. 2 rather than the proper word for Jewish circumcision, because he wanted to teach that it was the Christians (not the Jews) who were practising true circumcision. Old Testament prophets had long ago shown what real circumcision is: 'the Lord your God will circumcise your *heart* and the heart of your descendants, so that you will love the Lord your God with all your heart and with all your soul ...' (Deuteronomy 30.6). But later many Jews forgot that teaching. According to Romans 2.29, 'real circumcision is a matter of the heart – it is spiritual and not literal.' This means facing our own sinfulness, letting God forgive it, and sincerely intending to cut it out.

This is a very important verse for the Philippians to read. It explains clearly that it is *not* necessary to be physically circumcised in order to be accepted by God. The Jews, as we know, taught that circumcision *was* necessary. This was the main difference between the 'new way' Paul teaches the Philippians to follow, and the 'old way' of those Jews who do not accept his teaching.

Worship in the Spirit of God This is how Paul referred to true circumcision, i.e. spiritual circumcision rather than physical. In some manuscripts the phrase is 'worship *by* the Spirit of God'. The NRSV translation offers us the possibility of seeing how this verse is linked with John 4.23–24.

The Greek word translated 'spirit' is *pneuma*, and it has many meanings in the New Testament:

(a) wind or breath (John 3.8);

(b) a person's 'self': his heart, his soul, his thinking, his feeling (see Luke 1.47: 'My soul magnifies the Lord, and my spirit rejoices in God my Saviour');

(c) an invisible force for good or evil (Acts 5.16); and

(d) the spirit of God, or the Holy Spirit, i.e. the very life of God himself flowing into the lives of human beings (as in Philippians 2.1 and in this verse).

Boast in Christ Jesus and have no confidence in the flesh There is a contrast in this sentence:

(a) Some of the Christians were proud of what Christ Jesus had done, and relied on him because it was through him that they were acceptable to God. This is 'boasting in Christ'.

(b) Others relied chiefly on their own outward performances, and their effort to keep the religious rules, and did not admit that they depended totally on God's grace. This is 'putting confidence in the flesh'. See note on 'flesh' in Philippians 1.22; and note on 1.26 for 'boast'.

187

3.4. If anyone else has reason to be confident in the flesh, I have more: Paul is saying in effect: 'It is not because I have failed to fulfil the Jewish laws and ceremonies that I am criticizing them. I have not become a Christian just because I was an unsuccessful Jew.' In vv. 5–6 he goes on to say he has kept the Jewish law more strictly than most Jews. He makes a list of six ways in which he was a strict Jew:

1 *Circumcised on the eighth day* (v. 5a), i.e. 'I come from a family who kept the law strictly' (see Leviticus 12.3).

2 *A member of the people of Israel* (v. 5b), i.e. 'I was a Jew by birth. I was not one of those Gentile "proselytes", who had been welcomed into the Jewish community from outside.'

3 *Of the tribe of Benjamin* (v. 5c), i.e. 'I belong to the tribe which gave the Jewish nation its first king, Saul.'

4 *A Hebrew born of Hebrews* (v. 5d), i.e. 'Both my parents were Hebrews who trained me in the use of the Hebrew language, even though we lived in a Greek city.'

5 *As to the law, a Pharisee* (v. 5e), i.e. 'I am a member of the sect whom everyone respected because the members kept both the written law and the traditions more strictly than anyone.'

6 *As to zeal, a persecutor of the church* (v. 6a), i.e. 'I was so keen to be a faithful Jew that I used violence to attack the followers of Jesus.'

From the verses that follow (vv. 6–11) it is clear that Paul made this list only in order to show that nothing that he himself did could make him accepted and forgiven by God. Something different, something more, was needed (Matthew 5.20).

3.6. As to righteousness under the law, blameless: In these words Paul sums up his list of ways in which he has kept the Jewish law. Two words stand out as important here. The first is 'righteousness'. Paul has found another sort of righteousness, that is the true 'righteousness which is through faith in Christ' (see note on v. 9). On this further see Special note C.

By being 'blameless' Paul does not mean he kept the Jewish law perfectly. Instead, he means he has done so conscientiously and consistently. If he did transgress any of the commandments, he would make recourse to the Jewish sacrificial system for absolution of sins or restoration. In this light, being 'blameless' means Paul has followed the *system* of the law fully: i.e. without deviating from its system of commandments and sacrifices for restoration.

3.7. Whatever gains I had, these I have come to regard as loss because of Christ: In vv. 7–8 Paul compares what he has 'lost' with what he has 'gained' or may gain in the future. The language Paul uses is treasurer's language; it is 'profit-and-loss' language, which may be set out as shown in Table 2.

Table 2

Loss	Profit
'Whatever gains I had' (v. 7)	'Christ'
'Everything' (v. 8a)	'Knowing Christ Jesus'
'All things' (v. 8b)	'Gain Christ and be found in him'

But Paul saw things in this way only after his conversion. Before his conversion he put the privileges (which he had because he was a strict Jew) on the side of 'profit'. Afterwards, he felt that they were 'loss', because they encouraged him to rely on his own efforts. In this way they actually prevented him from relying on Christ, through whom he had found a right relationship with God.

3.8. Loss: Paul never ceased to be a Jew, but he was glad to have given up his 'old' way of living, i.e. trying to gain God's approval by keeping the law. He was like a man who has been working all night with an oil lamp, then the dawn breaks and the lamp is no longer needed. The sun has risen.

Knowing Christ This is an unusual phrase. Most writers refer to 'knowing God' (Galatians 4.9). But see a similar occurrence in Philippians 2.19.

I have suffered the loss of all things, and I regard them as rubbish Paul is chiefly thinking here of the loss of his position and status as a strict Jew. It may be that he also has in mind the loss of his property, since he may well have been disowned by most of his family when he became a Christian.

He calls his old position as a strict Jew 'rubbish' or 'refuse' because it is useless. To Paul's Jewish contemporaries, this would have been an astonishing and deeply offensive statement. It is not surprising that the Jews became so angry with him that they failed to understand what he was saying. They thought that he was attacking *all* religious rules and regulations.

That I may gain Christ and be found in him The two phrases 'gain Christ' and 'be found in him' mean nearly the same thing. Paul has this great hope or aim that, at every moment in his life and whatever happened to him, he would be 'in Christ' and would be seen ('be found') to be part of Christ (see note on 'in Christ' in Philippians 4.10).

3.9. Not having a righteousness of my own that comes from the law, but one that comes through faith in Christ, the righteousness from God based on faith: Paul again makes a comparison.

1 He has tried to reach 'righteousness' (or a right relationship with God) through his own effort, and to be a good Jew in keeping the law strictly. Paul has rejected this because it gave a false self-confidence before God and was often used to exclude non-Jews.

2 Now he has found a different way to righteousness. He describes this way by two phrases:

(a) 'Through faith in Christ' can be taken to mean either 'faith in Christ' (NRSV, NIV, NJB) or 'faithfulness of Christ'. The latter notion is becoming more popular among scholars today. But we need not be over-precise over this because the two ideas are not mutually exclusive (see Special note B). Scripture does teach that the faithfulness of Jesus was important in bringing salvation to humankind (Romans 5.18–19) and humankind must respond in faith in order to receive this salvation. Bearing this in mind, we may say that Paul believed that righteousness was available to him because of what Christ did and if he were to believe in him.

(b) 'From God', i.e. righteousness was God's free gift of forgiveness, given to him although he did not deserve it (see Romans 3.21–24).

3.10. I want to know Christ and the power of his resurrection: In the previous verses Paul has shown his readers the way in which he became a Christian. In verses 10 and 11 he explains in four phrases what he is now aiming at. 'I want to know' refers to his aim and goal.

This, the first of the phrases, means 'I want to get to the stage where I not only know Christ (see note on v. 8a), but can be more open to his power, the power of Christ who is risen and alive.' Although Paul says that this is his goal, he has of course already begun to learn how to accept this 'power'. It has raised him out of spiritual death, out of the temptations of the world, and out of physical exhaustion as he made his journeys.

The sharing of his sufferings Paul's second aim is to be in such close union with Christ that he may see his own sufferings as part of Christ's sufferings. It is as if he were saying,

> Christ could not do his work for humankind without suffering. Nor can I (or his other followers) work 'for him and in him' without suffering. But I am not just imitating what Christ did long ago; I am letting his life flow into my life.

(See also Colossians 1.24 and 2 Corinthians 4.10.)

Becoming like him in his death Some people think that in this sentence Paul is referring to his own physical death (which indeed may have taken place soon after he wrote this Letter), and that he is saying, when he dies, he will be following in Christ's footsteps. But it seems more probable that he is referring to dying to 'sin' (Romans 6.2–11). The difference between that passage in Romans and the phrase we are studying is that in Philippians 3.10 Paul is talking of a goal (Paul's third aim) towards which he is moving, or of a change in himself that he hopes to see, not as an event that has once happened. In effect he is saying: 'May I increasingly and every day reject (die to) all that is un-Christ-like in me.'

Perhaps Paul is here intentionally using the language of the mystery religions which flourished all over the Greek-speaking world at that time. In some of these religions, candidates shared in a ritual in which a god symbolically died and rose again. They believed that their own natures would thus be transformed, as they united themselves with the god by means of their ritual. The great difference between this 'transformation' and the change that Paul is referring to is that in the mystery religions people believed that transformation took place 'magically', i.e. as the result of the right words being said and the right actions performed. Paul's 'dying to sin' is an inner surrender of himself to the will of God and is based on a historical event: the death and resurrection of the Lord Jesus Christ.

3.11. If somehow I may attain the resurrection from the dead: Paul knows that he already has a new life, life 'in Christ'. In this verse he writes about his fourth aim or hope, that after his physical death he may be given a fuller form of life in Christ.

There are many passages in Paul's Letters where he expressed his belief in life after death (principally 2 Corinthians 5.1, but see also Romans 8.38–39; Philippians 1.22–23; 1 Corinthians 15.12).

We may ask why Paul in this verse writes with such hesitation: 'if somehow'. Did he have doubts about life after death? The answer is twofold. First, there were times for Paul, as for all Christians, when it was easier to be confident, and times when it was less easy. No one, however deeply committed to Christ, lives permanently in the clear daylight of certainty. Second, in these verses (and still more in vv. 12–16) Paul was pointing out with humility how much more he still needed to learn, and that he had no 'claim' on life after death. In everything he depended on God's grace.

 Interpretation

In the first two chapters Paul wrote mainly about the need for the Philippian Christians to be united. In chapter 3 he changed the subject. The subject is now a comparison between the 'old' way and the 'new' way.

The 'old' way was the way in which Paul had previously approached God and in which (in his experience) many Jews still did approach God, principally through their own good deeds, and by being circumcised. He referred to all this as 'confidence in the flesh' (vv. 3–4). The 'new' way was that in which Paul now approached God. Christians believe (Paul said) that God accepts them because of what Jesus did and in spite of their sinfulness, and that their being accepted into the family of God is based on faith. This would then put the Jew and Gentile on equal footing. Paul also compared these two ways, but much more fully, in his Letters to the Galatians (see Galatians 3.1–4) and Romans (see Romans 8.1–8).

We are now in a position to see how Paul presents his case. The passage can be summarized as follows. Verse 1 stands on its own and is not connected with vv. 2–11. But in vv. 2–3, Paul issued a *warning* against a group who were trying to bring the Christians in Philippi back to the old way. This was reinforced by Paul's appeal to his *past experience* (vv. 4–7), and the failure of the 'old way' to bring him righteousness. Finally, Paul spoke about his *aims*: that he might grow in the righteousness which he had found through Christ (vv. 8–11).

Although Paul was contrasting a Jewish way of behaving with a truly Christian way, his teaching applies also to Christians. All Christians can be tempted at one time or another to 'put confidence in the flesh'. When they give in to this temptation, their way of life shows that they believe they will be more acceptable to God if they perform enough good deeds, pay their church subscriptions, attend church services regularly, marry one wife only, or say their prayers every day. Paul taught that these are good and necessary things to do, but that God accepts people and enters into fellowship with them because of faith in Jesus Christ, not because of their good deeds.

Paul's new way is the way of faith (v. 9). It was through faith in Christ that Paul believed he would find righteousness. Abdul Masih was the first Muslim in India who became an ordained Christian minister. When he was converted, five senior Muslims made a long journey to persuade him to change his mind. In the following conversation between them we are further helped to see the meaning of this verse:

Abdul Masih: God bless you for having taken such trouble for a poor sinner like me, who has no refuge but Christ.

One of the Muslims: God has not such a shameless creature anywhere on earth.

Abdul Masih: That is true. I am even worse than you describe.

Another Muslim: How will you answer this before God?

Abdul Masih: Indeed, I do not know what I can answer. But I hope in the word that the Lord Jesus Christ has himself spoken: 'I came, not to call the righteous but sinners to repentance.' I firmly trust that he and no one else will answer for me.

After further conversation, one of the visitors said, 'May God give you understanding,' to which Abdul Masih said, 'Amen.' This story illustrates powerfully what it means to have faith in Christ without being offensive.

In the new 'way' that was presented by Paul, knowing Christ and what he had achieved was key (vv. 7–10). To know God, to know Christ, means to put oneself at his service, to love him, to be loyal to him, to commit oneself to him. This is how Paul used the word in this verse.

Finally, we must note that the juxtaposition of 'power' and 'suffering' is stark in v. 10 and would have been regarded as rather astonishing by ancient people. To know power usually meant to be able to escape suffering. But for Paul, 'power' and 'suffering' do often go together, especially if the suffering meant participation in Jesus' sufferings.

Although we may say that Paul's sufferings were not extreme or unique, they *represent* all human suffering that is endured for the sake of Christ, and therefore we can learn from them. How do human beings behave when suffering comes to them? Some are angry and puzzled and complain to God; some look for someone else to blame; some begin to notice other people's sufferings and try to lessen them; some discover other ways in which God can use them now that they are suffering. Others, like Paul, find that they can suffer in the company of Christ.

 ## STUDY SUGGESTIONS

Word study

1 Paul used the word 'righteousness' three times in this passage, once in v. 6 and twice in v. 9. What were the two sorts of 'righteousness' that Paul compared in this passage?

2 What did Paul mean by 'knowing' Christ (vv. 8, 10)?

Review of content

3 **(a)** Who was it that Paul was telling the Philippians to 'beware of' in v. 2?

(b) Why was he so discourteous as to call them 'dogs'?

4 **(a)** In vv. 5–6 Paul listed six ways in which he was a strict Jew. What were they?

(b) Why did Paul count as 'rubbish' all that he gained from being a strict Jew?

5 In what ways did Paul expect to share Christ's sufferings and become 'like him in his death' (v. 10)?

Bible study

6 Which sort of circumcision did the writers refer to in each of the following verses, physical or spiritual?

(a) Jeremiah 4.4; **(b)** Luke 1.59; **(c)** Acts 7.51; **(d)** Acts 15.5; **(e)** Colossians 2.11–12.

7 How did people show that they had faith, according to each of the following passages?

(a) Mark 2.3–5; **(b)** Mark 10.46–52; **(c)** Luke 7.2–9; **(d)** Galatians 2.14–16; **(e)** Hebrews 11.8.

Discussion and application

8 Think about some ways in which you yourself are tempted to live 'according to law', and then make a 'profit-and-loss table' to show what would be the 'gain' or the 'loss' for you of trying to follow Christ instead.

9 'No one can work for Christ or live "in Christ" without suffering.' What is your opinion?

10 By 'I may attain the resurrection from the dead' (v. 11), did Paul mean that he hoped to 'rise again' and be seen on earth after his death, like Jesus after his crucifixion? If not, what did he mean?

 ## Special note F
Power

Paul mentioned in Philippians 3.10 that one of his hopes in connection with 'knowing' was that he might 'know' the 'power of Christ's resurrection. What might 'power' mean in this context, and as used in the Bible? This is especially relevant in our time because of the frequent abuse of power.

1 Writers in the Bible had two great truths in mind when they wrote about 'power': first, that human beings are by nature not strong enough to live without God; second, that God possesses power and offers it to people. Hence, the real source of power is God and all power ultimately belongs to him.

2 Thus it is God's power of which we chiefly read in the Bible. Writers referred to his power because of the things which God had done in the world, e.g. Psalm 150.2: 'Praise him for his mighty deeds.' Note that this was a very different way of thinking about God from the old Greek ideas, and from the ideas of religions such as Hinduism. The Greeks believed that a 'High God' existed but that he would have lost dignity if he had concerned himself with the activities of human beings. Indeed, there are people in the world today who model themselves on such a god! Hindus do not call God 'creator' of the world because in their view he is so completely removed from the world that he could never become involved in it.

3 A special action of God showing his power in the world was the raising of Jesus from the dead (see Acts 2.24, 32; Ephesians 1.19–20). Jesus' resurrection meant more than just making a corpse alive. It meant the dawning of a new age, which involved God's gracious call and remaking of humankind.

4 But a result of God's raising of Jesus was that his power became available for humankind. This is what Paul meant by 'the power of his resurrection' in Philippians 3.10. So Paul could preach effectively to the Gentiles because of that power (see Romans 15.18–19). It is this power that really counts in gospel work and not empty rhetoric or the persuasive words of people (1 Corinthians 2.1–5).

5 This power that is made available is not for the elevation of a person's status but for service, and especially for the work of the gospel (Romans 15.19; Colossians 1.28–29; 2 Timothy 4.17).

6 The power that God gives is often evident in the midst of weakness. Most ancient people would have regarded power and weakness as contradictory to each other. But for Paul, experiencing the power of the resurrection must also go with sharing in the sufferings of Christ (Philippians 3.10). Indeed, Paul could write, 'whenever I am weak, then I am strong' (2 Corinthians 12.10). This does not mean that weakness on its own is a good thing. Rather, it is in weakness that the grace of God is clearly manifest. Weakness drives a person to rely on the grace of God. It is this grace, and not human ability, which is powerful (2 Corinthians 12.9). Human pride would then be prevented from rearing its ugly head.

Philippians 3.12–16

Pressing on

 Summary

Paul speaks about how he presses on toward the prize of God's heavenly calling, not resting on past attainments.

 Notes

3.12 Not that I have already obtained this: 'This' refers to the state of completeness which Paul wrote about in vv. 8–11, using such phrases as 'gain Christ' (v. 8), 'be found in' Christ (v. 9), 'having a righteousness from God' (v. 9), 'know Christ' (v. 10), 'know the power of his resurrection' (v. 10), 'sharing of his sufferings' (v. 10), 'becoming like him in his death' (v. 10). 'All this' (v. 12, NEB) was 'the prize'.

Reach the goal The Greek word literally means 'perfect' or 'mature' (as in v. 15).

1 Members of the mystery religions, which were popular in Philippi and other Greek towns, used this word. When one of them had taken part in all the ritual purifications and sacrifices, that member was called 'perfect', i.e. he had reached the highest grade. It did not mean that he was without sin.

2 For other Greek writers it usually meant 'suited to the work you are doing at present'. So a workman using an axe to cut down a tree could call his axe 'perfect' for the job even if its handle was scratched and dirty.

3 For most of the New Testament writers it had several other meanings:

    (a) The sort of person that a Christian can become at the end of this world: 'when the perfect comes' (1 Corinthians 13.10, RSV). Probably this is its meaning in v. 12.

    (b) Sharing to some extent (though not completely) in God's absolute goodness (see Matthew 5.48).

(c) An adult, i.e. anyone who is no longer an infant; also a baptized member of the Church, i.e. one who is no longer a probationer (see 1 Corinthians 2.6: 'among the mature we do speak wisdom'). Such people do *not* think that they have reached their goal. They are more aware than other people of their own incompleteness and ignorance and sinfulness. They are growing in their awareness of Christ's will and of other people's needs (Ephesians 4.13–15). They are becoming able to 'distinguish good from evil' (Hebrews 5.14). They 'hunger and thirst for righteousness' (Matthew 5.6).

I press on to make it my own i.e. 'I press forward in order to take hold of the prize, because Jesus once took hold of me.' Paul is like a runner in a long-distance race, who kept on running towards the finishing post, even though there was still a long way to go. See note on Philippians 2.16 about Paul's use of the language of athletics.

Made me his own What Paul is doing was the result of what Christ had done. Christ took the first step. Paul has in mind the time when he was on the road from Jerusalem to Damascus and Christ made him 'his own' or 'took hold' of him (NEB).

3.13. One thing I do: This is like a modern athlete saying, 'I have to decide whether I shall train for the 100 metres race or the long jump. If I try to do both, I shall not win either. I have to do "one thing".' For Paul the 'one thing' is 'running toward the goal', in the words of v. 14. He has described the goal in vv. 8–11, and he sees it clearly.

Forgetting what lies behind Paul clearly does not mean that he has ceased to remember his past life as a strict Jew (he remembered it well in vv. 4–7). Nor does he forget his early years as a Christian (he remembered them in v. 12 and in passages such as 1 Corinthians 15.3–10). He means that it is even more important to fix his mind on the goal ahead than to look back and remember what God has done for him in the past. In other words, Paul does not rest on his laurels or depend on his past achievements.

Straining forward to what lies ahead Again Paul uses the language of athletics (see note on v. 14). In the early stages of a long race, some runners may be somewhat relaxed, but in the later stages they 'strain forward'.

3.14. I press on toward the goal: This is one of the many verses in which Paul compares living as a Christian to taking part in the Greek games or athletics. There were the Olympic Games, the games at Ephesus, and the games at Corinth. In all of them the competitors performed many different sorts of sports, such as boxing (1 Corinthians 9.26), chariot-racing and running.

Prize For Paul the 'prize' is complete fellowship with Christ himself, as Paul has said in v. 8, 'that I may gain Christ'. The difference between

Christians aiming at this prize and Greek runners aiming at their prize is that all Christians can share the prize. One Christian getting the prize will not prevent others from getting it. In the Greek games, 'only one receives the prize' (1 Corinthians 9.24).

Heavenly call This means that God, who is in 'heaven', calls us to share his own life. We know that 'God is Spirit' (John 4.24), and therefore is not situated in any one place, so that heaven is not really 'above' us. But human beings have to use picture-language when they are talking about God. 'Heavenly call' does not mean God telling someone that his or her life on earth is over.

3.15. Let those of us then who are mature be of the same mind: Who were the 'mature'? Some people think that Paul is referring to the baptized members of the church who were growing in their faithfulness to Christ. But it seems more likely that he is being sarcastic:

> There are some who are so puffed up that they think they are complete Christians, or are without sin, or have reached the end of the course already. These people should note what I have said. They have a long way to go before they reach their 'prize'.

Paul treats his readers in the same way in 1 Corinthians 8.1, as people who thought they knew everything.

If you think differently … God will reveal to you: Paul is saying in effect: 'If you do not agree with me, there is one who will guide you into all the truth, namely God' (see John 16.13).

3.16. Only let us hold fast to what we have attained: Paul means that all Christians have understood something about God and about themselves. It may only be a very small part of the whole truth. But if they put into practice ('hold fast') that part which they have grasped they can grow in their understanding. 'Those who have will be given more' (Matthew 13.23, NEB). Do note that the Greek word translated 'hold fast' really refers to a group of people standing in line. So Paul is thinking of the whole congregation (and of its need for unity), not of any one separate individual.

 ## Interpretation

Paul wrote these verses for two reasons. First, he wanted to prevent his readers from misunderstanding vv. 2–11, where he had said that through Christ he had found righteousness. A reader might think that Paul was satisfied with his own life as a Christian. So in vv. 12–16 he said, 'No! I am still a long way from being the sort of person that God means me to be.' Second, Paul wrote these verses to correct those who were too easily satisfied with their own lives. His thoughts were: 'God, in Christ, invited me to enter for a race and to win a prize. I have accepted his invitation and I am running towards the goal. But I have not yet reached it.' All this translates as a message about the need for all Christians to have a clear goal.

What hampers a person from having or achieving a goal is often the past. Like Paul, Christians today cannot forget their past lives. But, as far as their past sins and failures are concerned, they can accept God's forgiveness instead of continually accusing themselves. As far as past success is concerned, they can thank God and be open to God's Spirit, so that they can learn from him what to do at this present time, and in the years ahead.

Indeed, finishing well is so important in all endeavours. There are Christians who have begun well and given their lives to Christ, but have no goal lying ahead. They are much more interested in what God once did for them than the ways in which God now wants them to grow and develop. Others are enthusiastically pursuing a goal, but they find it very difficult because they have never made a break with the past and begun a new life. Others are like Paul and have made a break with the past, but are chiefly interested in 'what lies ahead', i.e. what God wants them to become.

In presenting the need to press on, Paul used the language of the games, which was familiar to his readers. Teachers or preachers cannot do their work effectively unless they understand the things which their hearers do. A minister born and educated in London went to work in a country town where many people kept pigs. 'I watched the pig-farmers at work for many months before I could usefully preach the gospel to them,' he said.

In vv. 12–14 there are five phrases from which we see that Paul understood the Greek games. He used these phrases to teach that a Christian needs to be self-disciplined and keen above everything else to reach his goal. The phrases are:

1   'I press on' (vv. 12, 14).

2   'Forgetting what lies behind' (v. 13). In a track event it is important not to look back to see who is behind.

3   'Straining forward to what lies ahead' (v. 13), i.e. not slowing down until the end is reached. How many runners have lost a race by stopping a yard from the end!

4   'Toward the goal' (v. 14). There was a pillar at the end of the course.

5   'For the prize' (v. 14). The prize was a crown made from the leaves of wild olive or laurel or green parsley. Runners could see it on the finishing post as they ran towards it.

Finally, what needs to be taken to heart is that the possibility of pressing on to reach a goal has come about only because of God's initiative, i.e. God's 'heavenly call'. Paul did not enter this race of his own accord. It was graciously granted by God through Christ Jesus. The word 'call' is one of the most important words in the Bible and it can carry the following shades of meanings:

1 It always means that God's loving actions come first. The good that human beings are able to do comes afterwards.

2 God's call is a call to repentance (see Luke 5.32), to obedience (see John 1.43), and to 'wholeness' (i.e. 'salvation' as in this v. 14).

3 God calls all human beings (see 1 Timothy 2.4).

4 We hear God's call in many different ways, e.g. through other people (Luke 14.17), in a dream (Matthew 1.20).

5 We need to answer his call (see Hebrews 3.7–8).

6 He calls some people, but not all, to positions of authority, e.g. in the church (see 2 Timothy 1.6–9).

 STUDY SUGGESTIONS

Word study

1 (a) What is the meaning of the word 'call' in v. 14?

(b) How would you translate it in your own language?

Review of content

2 (a) Why did Paul want to forget (v. 13)?

(b) Why is it more important for a Christian to look forward to the future rather than back to the past?

(c) When Christians do look back to the past, what should they do about it?

3 (a) What was the 'one thing' which Paul said that he did (v. 13)?

(b) What do you yourself aim at doing above everything else?

Bible study

4 In 3.12–14 Paul used the language of the Greek games in order to illustrate his teaching. What sort of games or athletics do the writers refer to in each of the following passages?

(a) 1 Corinthians 9.26; (b) Galatians 2.2; (c) Philippians 2.16; (d) 2 Timothy 4.7–8; (e) Hebrews 12.1–2.

Discussion and application

5 How does a congregation discover the directions in which God wants it to grow and develop?

6 'People often say that it is better to live a Christian life because you love Christ than because you hope for a reward.' Which do you think is better, and why?

7 In your experience, how far is it necessary for a Christian minister to understand the occupations of those to whom he or she ministers?

Philippians 3.17—4.1

Waiting for Christ's coming

 Summary

Paul instructs his readers to follow good examples so that they may not pattern their lives after the enemies of the cross of Christ. Instead, they are to live in preparation for Christ's coming.

 Notes

3.17. Join: Paul is again urging the Philippians to behave as a united congregation: 'join'. A strong congregation is one where, although members hold different opinions, the congregation as a whole shares the same aims.

Imitating me In the ancient world, the primary method of learning was to imitate a teacher, both his teaching and life. Paul knows that the Philippians will 'imitate' someone or other (as we all do). The question is, 'Who?' Paul's answer is, 'The example you see in myself and my colleagues, Epaphroditus and Timothy and others.'

What does Paul want them to imitate? He does not want them to copy everything he did, but to follow the way in which he lived, the way in which he faced persecution and hardship, the way in which he relied on the Spirit of Jesus Christ.

Live The Greek word here translated 'live' means 'walk'. In the Old and New Testaments, 'walking' often refers to the sort of life we live, the way we behave. It also refers to the fact that believers have a goal towards which they are travelling: we walk in order to get somewhere (Psalm 119.1; Isaiah 30.21; Romans 6.4).

3.18. Many live as enemies of the cross of Christ: In Philippians 3.2–11, Paul warned his readers against those who wanted them to return to Jewish ways. But in v. 18 he refers to a different group of people. These were not enemies of Christ himself, but of his 'cross'. They had refused to accept the way in which Christ had done his work: they refused to accept persecution and suffering. They regarded the church as the place where they ought to receive comfort and support. They were unhappy to belong to a church whose sign was a cross of death, and in which belonging meant suffering.

3.19. Their end is destruction; their god is the belly; and their glory is in their shame: No one is sure who these people were, of whom Paul says that their 'end is destruction'. They may have been a group of Christians who had wrongly interpreted his teaching about 'freedom'. Paul writes, for example, in Romans 7.6: 'Now we are discharged from the law.' As a result there were some who thought that they could reject all rules and discipline and responsibility. They said, 'Live as you please and God will always forgive and forget' (see Romans 6.15).

Or they may have been Christians who had been influenced by some strains of Greek philosophy, which taught that the human spirit was good, but that all material things (including the human body) were evil or unimportant. Therefore people could do whatever they liked with their bodies and their possessions.

Their god is the belly We saw in the note on v. 18 that there were people who rejected Christ's way of suffering. In this verse Paul adds something else about them: their greed, or more precisely, that they are controlled by their appetites.

Minds ... set on earthly things Paul does not despise earthly things. In Philippians 1.24 and 2.15 we see that he fully accepted the duties of living in this world, and the importance of obeying the laws of the Roman Empire. But he was also a citizen of an invisible world (see 3.14 and note on Philippians 3.20).

The people to whom Paul refers here would trust only the things of this world, things they could know through the senses of their physical body. Only the things which they could touch or smell or hear or taste or measure were real to them. So it became impossible for them to trust the invisible God.

3.20. But our citizenship is in heaven: The Greek term for 'citizenship' here is *politeuma*. Here is more language which (like the references to the games in vv. 12–16) the Philippian Christians could well understand. Philippi was a Roman colony (Acts 16.12). In its population were many old Roman soldiers who had been rewarded by being made full citizens of the empire and by being given houses in this colony. In their speech and dress and morals they behaved just as they would have done if they had been living in Rome. Paul himself was a full Roman citizen. When he was visiting Philippi he was imprisoned without a trial, and was only released when the magistrates learned that he was a Roman citizen (Acts 16.38).

The point Paul is making then is, 'Just as a Roman citizen living in Philippi never forgets that he belongs to the great Roman Empire, do not forget that you also belong to an even greater empire which is "heaven".' Indeed, the term *politeuma* also suggests that the church at Philippi was actually a colony of heaven even though it was located in the Roman Empire. Accordingly, the Christians should know to whom they owe their loyalty. On the meaning of 'heaven' see Special note G.

From there ... we are awaiting a Saviour, the Lord Jesus Christ Paul, having referred to God's invisible empire, heaven, now added that it was from God himself that salvation would come. This is one more phrase in which he made it clear that salvation is a gift from God, and not something which human beings can produce or can earn for themselves.

It is true that when Christians have accepted God's offer to rescue them from the overwhelming power of their sins we can say that they 'have been' saved (Ephesians 2.8). But Paul often emphasizes that this salvation needs to be completed. In 1 Corinthians 1.18 he writes about 'us who are *being saved*' (see also note on Philippians 3.12). So we 'await' a Saviour. We should also note that Paul is not writing about the salvation of individuals at the time of their death, but about 'the end', i.e. the time when Jesus would be finally victorious over all evil (see Acts 3.21: 'Jesus must be received into heaven until the time of universal restoration', NEB).

Saviour Paul hardly ever uses this word when he is referring to Jesus. The reason for this is probably that at that time people often used the word to describe the Roman emperor or a military leader who, by the use of armies, defeated a national enemy. Or they used the word to describe some individual who rescued the country from chaos by overthrowing the existing ruler by a coup. It was because Jesus used other means than force that Paul did not usually call him 'Saviour'. Jesus reconciled us to God ('saved' us) by dying on the cross, and brings us to a completed salvation by living in us (Romans 5.10). See also note on Philippians 2.12 about 'salvation'.

3.21. He will transform the body: God will change, not annihilate, people's 'bodies', so that they can have a different way of expressing themselves (see Special note H on 'body'). Greek philosophers taught that at death the 'body' was destroyed and the 'soul' survived. But Hebrew thinkers refused to split the 'body' from the 'soul': they regarded a person as a whole person. Therefore Paul writes that God will change or transform 'the body', not destroy it.

Body of ... humiliation i.e. the body that is powerless in so many ways, the body that becomes ill and decays. Paul himself probably suffered from some bodily illness which he called his 'thorn in his flesh' (2 Corinthians 12.7). He knew the ways in which his body prevented him from doing what he wanted to do. But nowhere did he ever call the body 'evil'. The AV translation 'vile' is very misleading.

Conformed to the body of his glory i.e. to share the power and the freedom of Christ's risen life. The phrase 'the body of his glory' shows clearly that the 'body' referred to here does not mean flesh and blood.

By the power Here again we see how different were the beliefs of Greek philosophers and Paul's beliefs. First, the Greeks taught that human beings are by nature immortal, that their 'souls' endure for ever. Paul taught that life after death (and sharing God's life at the end of time) is due to the power of God, it is his gift. Second, the Greeks taught that gods exist but take no action in human affairs. But Paul (like all writers in the Bible) believed that God had 'power' and took action in the world (see note on Philippians 3.10a). 'Power' is the word Jesus used when the Sadducees told a story in order to ridicule the belief in life after death. He said, 'You know neither the scriptures nor the power of God' (Mark 12.24).

To make all things subject to himself Paul must have brought great hope to his readers by writing this. They were living in a city where the forces of evil seemed much stronger than the forces of good. They were being persecuted, and the persecutors seemed more powerful than the Christians. Then Paul says: 'But in the end God will be victorious over all evil.'

4.1. Therefore: i.e. 'Because we have such a glorious future ahead of us, we should respond in the following manner.'

Whom I love and long for These words remind us of Paul's strong feelings of affection for his friends.

My joy and crown In 3.12–16 Paul referred to athletes who took part in the games and who hoped to receive the 'prize' or 'crown'. Here he compares himself to a runner who has the 'joy' of receiving the 'crown' from the hands of Christ. This crown is the Philippian congregation.

Stand firm in the Lord There are very many temptations into which the Philippians might fall, and Paul has referred to some of them in Philippians 3. They might follow the example of the 'dogs' (3.2) who were trying to persuade them to return to the old Jewish ways, and might make the keeping of regulations take the place of personal loyalty to God himself. They might imitate those who thought that they were 'mature' and had no more to learn (3.15). They might refuse to accept the suffering which comes to all faithful Christians, and might fall into despair, and use the Church only as a place of consolation (3.18). Or they might be so much concerned with the things of this world that they forget that they belong to the invisible kingdom of God (3.20a). It is in order to help them to stand firm against temptations like these that Paul writes this verse. He wants them to stand firm 'in the Lord' (see also note on Philippians 4.10), i.e. to keep the company not only of each other, but of Jesus Christ himself.

 Interpretation

In the light of the goal he has described in 3.12–16, Paul appealed to Christians to have proper conduct by imitating good examples. He certainly had in mind himself, but also probably Timothy and Epaphroditus.

205

Why should Christians imitate other Christians? This is so because we learn best from role models. Furthermore, what most people want to know about Christians is not 'Are your ideas true?' but 'Can you *live* what you believe?' For human beings cannot learn about living except from seeing how other people live. In places where there has been a church for a long time, traditions grow up concerning the way in which Christians should live, and from these traditions Christians receive some guidance. Parents hand down to their children the customs which they received from their parents, and the children do not fully realize that that is happening. But where the church is young (as the church in Philippi was), and where there are very few traditions, it is especially important for members to watch ('mark') living people. So Paul told his readers to watch him and his colleagues to see that it was indeed possible to live as Christians.

This prompts the question about how a Christian can be an example without becoming conceited. Paul has shown us three ways.

1 'Follow my example as I follow Christ's' (1 Corinthians 11.1, NEB), i.e. 'we all need to follow the same example, namely that of Christ'.

2 'Not that I have already obtained' (Philippians 3.12), i.e. 'I am still a learner'.

3 'Those who live' (4.1), i.e. there are others whose example you should follow.

Paul used language and terms that were relevant to the Philippians' colonial context to speak about a greater reality: a Christian's true *politeuma* is in heaven (3.20). Of course we have to submit to the authorities on earth; but we also belong to the invisible empire, of which the eternal God is the head. We owe loyalty to him, and by him we are inspired and supported. For similar teaching see Ephesians 2.19: 'you are citizens with the saints and also members of the household of God'.

In an important sense all Christians owe this same sort of 'double loyalty'. There are times when it does not seem possible to fulfil both loyalties, and we have to decide how to put first the *politeuma* of heaven.

 ## STUDY SUGGESTIONS

Word study

1 (a) What might the word 'Saviour' mean to the Philippians in Paul's day?

   (b) What does it mean today in your culture?

2 (a) What meaning do people give the word 'heaven' when they use it in ordinary conversation?

(b) How different is this from the biblical usage?

Review of content

3 What was Paul's chief teaching about the 'body' (i.e. our physical form):

(a) during life on earth;

(b) after death?

4 Paul exhorted the Philippians to 'stand firm in the Lord' (4.1).

(a) Against whom or what, according to Philippians 2 and 3, did they need to stand firm? (Give references.)

(b) In what way might Paul's words in 3.21b help them to do this?

Bible study

5 The Greek word which is translated 'live' in v. 17 means 'walk'. How is it translated in each of the following passages (a) in a modern translation, (b) in another language which you know?

(i) John 8.12; **(ii)** John 12.35; **(iii)** Galatians 5.16; **(iv)** Ephesians 2.2; **(v)** 1 John 1.6–7; **(vi)** 1 John 2.6.

Discussion and application

6 Paul exhorted the Philippians to 'imitate' his example and that of his fellow workers (v. 17). Why should Christians imitate other Christians? In what ways, if any, should they *not* imitate other Christians? Whom do the young men and women whom you know imitate today?

7 Whom did Paul mean by 'enemies of the cross of Christ' (3.18)? Whom do you see as the 'enemies of the cross of Christ' today? In discussing this question remember that Paul referred to these people 'with tears'. Why did he do so?

8 Give an example of Christians finding that their loyalty to God conflicts with their loyalty to their country. What was the outcome?

Special note G
Heaven

How is the term 'heaven' understood in the Bible? Most people today would think of 'a place in the sky' when that term is used. Some Christians think of it as the place they would go after death. The Bible, however, presents a far more challenging and exciting concept. The term is often plural in Greek (*ouranoi*) but the Hebrew is always plural (*shamayim*). Why this is so has not been explained to everyone's satisfaction. The best guess is that it is a 'majestic' plural or a plural due to 'spatial extension'.

1   In some places in the Bible 'heaven' simply means 'the sky'. Take, for example, Luke 9.16: 'taking the five loaves ... he looked up to heaven' (Luke 9.16).

2   Many ancient people, including the Jews, thought of God as being in one place rather than in another, and thought of the sky as that place. Scripture sometimes uses such language (Psalms 14.2; 102.19; Isaiah 63.15) but we must not think of it as being a crass indication of where heaven is.

3   The Jews, through reverence for God, did not want to use his name and often used the word 'heaven' when they meant 'God', e.g. 'Father, I have sinned against heaven' (Luke 15.18).

4   The chief teaching of the New Testament writers about God is that he is Spirit (John 4.24), and therefore does not live in any one place. Thus 'heaven' is not a place. It is fellowship with the eternal and invisible God. When God meets a human being and a human meets God, that is heaven. Or alternatively, we may call heaven a 'dimension' of true reality, which is often hidden from humankind but may be revealed from time to time by the grace of God (Philippians 3.20). It takes place, as it were, when the 'veil' is lifted and we get to see what the true reality of the situation around us is (see 2 Kings 6.15–19; Revelation 4.1). We pray for heaven to come on earth principally to mean that all on earth may truly perceive and experience the true reality of God and his world, where God reigns as the Lord. In this sense we pray that God's will be done 'on earth as it is in heaven' (Matthew 6.10).

5   Heaven is for us now, and not a gift which God gives us after we die. John's purpose in the book of Revelation was not to describe life after death. He was giving us in symbolic language his vision of the triumph of God over evil.

6   The Christian's hope then is not about going to heaven when he or she dies but for God to bring in the new heavens and the new earth (Revelation 21.1), i.e. where the full dimension of true reality, where God is seen to be, and is obeyed as, the Lord of the universe, is fully realized on earth. This must mean a great transformation of the state of our world. This takes place at Christ's second coming, an event which also involves the resurrection of the dead (Philippians 3.20–21).

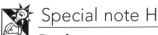

Special note H
Body

The term 'body' occurs in the Letters attributed to Paul 91 times. The Greek word is *sōma* and it is used in a variety of ways.

1 In the Bible the word 'body' sometimes means the flesh and bones of a person. 'Do not fear those who kill the body but cannot kill the soul' (Matthew 10.28; also Matthew 6.25).

2 Although this physical body suffers weakness, and decay, it is not evil in itself. Jesus did not regard the physical body as evil; nor did Christians, until some of them were led astray by religious groups from Asia, such as the third-century Manichaeans, and so began thinking of the body as 'a prison house of the soul', i.e. made of material that is inferior, and thus needs to be discarded in order to gain entry into God's paradise.

3 But 'body' usually means 'a person'. As we have seen, writers in the Bible did not regard the 'body' as separate from the whole 'self' or personality. 'Present your bodies as a living sacrifice' in Romans 12.1 means 'Present yourselves'. Paul also writes: 'whoever is united to a prostitute becomes one body with her' (1 Corinthians 6.16) to mean sexual union is not simply the union of two physical bodies but of two personalities.

4 Paul also taught that the 'natural body' (the flesh and bones) ceases at death, and that God changes it into another sort of body at the resurrection. He called it a 'spiritual body' (1 Corinthians 15.44). It is called thus not because it is immaterial but rather it is a body belonging to the powerful realm of the Spirit, i.e. the new world where everything is energized and led by God's Spirit. It is also called the 'resurrection of the body' in the Creeds. 'Body' thus means the means by which a person expresses him- or herself.

5 Paul also used the word to refer to the Church, because it is the means by which Christ expresses himself in the world. The Church is 'the body of Christ' (1 Corinthians 12.27).

Philippians 4.2–9

God's peace

 Summary

Paul urges Euodia and Syntyche to put aside their differences, and offers final advice on what virtues all the Christians at Philippi are to have in order for them to experience truly the peace of God.

 Notes

4.2. Euodia and Syntyche: We do not read about these two anywhere else, but it is clear from v. 3 that they were women and that they were good and sincere Christian workers in Philippi.

To be of the same mind in the Lord The implication is the two prominent women have quarrelled. What was the reason for their quarrel? Paul does not tell us. We may guess that perhaps each one felt what she did for the congregation, and the gifts God had given her, made her superior to the other. Then, probably, members of the congregation took sides, and so a serious division existed. Something like this has happened in most Christian congregations. What can be done about it? This division could be healed if they had 'the same mind in the Lord', i.e. an outlook and attitude that is submitted to Christ's lordship (see note on Philippians 4.10a).

4.3. I ask you: Paul does not issue a command here, just as he did not command the women to agree. Instead he urges them to help each other to heal their divisions, because he loved them and was concerned about them.

Loyal companion Who was the person whom Paul addresses like this? Either he is a member of the congregation who has once worked with Paul in Philippi, or his name is Syzygos (which in Greek means 'yokefellow' or 'true comrade').

These women There are many references in Acts to the important part which women played in the church in that district of Greece (see especially Acts 16.13–14; 17.4, 12). The position of women in Philippi was probably higher than it was in most Greek cities because Philippi was a Roman colony. In Rome women were often influential in society. So it is not surprising to read of women being prominent in the church at Philippi.

For they have struggled beside me in the work of the gospel The congregation to which Paul writes this letter was, as we have seen, a tiny minority living among neighbours of whom many were against them.

Whose names are in the book of life Greek cities had a register of their citizens, as some modern cities have. So in several passages in the New Testament those who accept the sovereignty of God are mentioned as having their names 'in the book' (Luke 10.20; Revelation 20.15). Here Paul means that God has accepted their work and made their work a part of his own.

4.4. Rejoice in the Lord always: This can be translated: 'Farewell; I wish you all joy in the Lord' (NEB), but it is more likely that it means, 'May you always be joyful as you live your life in the Lord' ('always' means 'in all circumstances'). Paul returns to the theme of joy, which he first announced in 1.18–19 (perhaps even as early as 1.3). Paul believes it is this theme that can help the Philippian Christians develop a proper attitude towards themselves and others.

4.5. Gentleness: It is not easy to find a word to translate the Greek word which Paul uses here. We may see its meaning by describing people who have 'forbearance' or 'gentleness'. They are ready to believe that they may be mistaken, they do not always insist on their rights, they are considerate and gentle to others, they are ready to forgive others and to be forgiven by them, they are generous in praising others and merciful in judging them, they are more keen to turn their opponents into friends than to attack them. They are not obstinate or stiff in mind or resentful. See Matthew 5.41–42.

Be known to everyone Paul hopes that when people talk about the Christians in Philippi they will say, 'They have a name for being "forbearing",' just as when they talked about the Romans they said, 'They have a name for being good administrators.' He was not encouraging them to boast about themselves, but urging them to represent Christ faithfully (Matthew 5.16)

The Lord is near This is the fifth time in this letter that Paul has referred to the 'coming' or 'day' of Jesus (see note on Philippians 1.6). So v. 5 means, 'Be forbearing and don't repay evil for evil, because Jesus is coming to be the judge of everyone.' But some scholars think that it means: 'The Lord is always present or near at hand' (as in Psalm 119.151: 'you are near, O LORD'). If this is the case, Paul is in effect saying: 'You can bear suffering and persecution because the Lord is alongside you and with you.'

211

4.6. Do not worry about anything: The Greek word which is translated as 'worry' is like the English word 'care'. Sometimes it means 'loving attention', e.g. in Paul's 'anxiety for all churches' (2 Corinthians 11.28). See also note on Philippians 2.20. Here and in many other passages it means 'worry'.

But in everything by prayer and supplication ... requests Whatever the Philippian Christians were worried about, whatever they were hoping for or fearing, whether they were experiencing pain or pleasure, they could take it to God by praying to him.

The word translated 'prayer' means prayer of all sorts. The words 'supplication' and 'requests' refer to one sort of prayer, namely the prayer of asking. Asking may be for our own needs, or it may be for the needs of others.

With thanksgiving These words are connected with the words 'in everything', i.e. be thankful whatever happens. Once again we need to remember that Paul was in prison when he wrote this, and that his readers were living in very difficult circumstances. His teaching was that, whatever happens, God's love for us is continuing and totally reliable, and that this is what we can be thankful for in all circumstances (Romans 8.28).

Be made known to God Christians 'make known' their needs to God not because he requires the information, but because they are sharing their whole lives with him.

4.7. The peace of God: i.e. the peace which God gives. This refers not just to the absence of conflict but the wholeness that God gives to humans and the world. It is based on the Jewish idea of *shalom*. See Special note I.

Surpasses all understanding This means *either* 'peace that is better than anything which we could create for ourselves', *or* 'peace which gives us more than we had expected', *or* 'peace which is so marvellous that we cannot understand why God has given it to us'.

Will guard The Greeks used this word to describe a body of soldiers 'keeping guard' over a city, as the Roman soldiers kept guard over Philippi to ensure that there was peace in the city. Paul is once again using language that will be familiar to the Philippian Christians.

Your hearts and your minds God will guard and protect their 'heart' (i.e. their feelings and their freedom of choice), and keep guard over their 'minds' (i.e. what goes on in their minds: their thoughts; see 2 Corinthians 10.5).

In Christ Jesus i.e. all this is true for someone who lives 'in Christ'. See note on Philippians 4.10a.

4.8. Whatever is true ... honourable ... just ... pure ... pleasing ... commendable ... think about these things: All the words in this verse are words which Greeks and Romans of that time (who were not Christians) used in order to describe a 'good' person. As we have seen, most people in Philippi were Romans. The meaning of these words in brief is as follows.

- 'True': those who follow the truth, especially as it has been revealed in Christ, rather than following what most people think or what is convenient to think.

- 'Honourable': those who rightly earn respect from others.

- 'Just': those who treat their fellow humans with fairness.

- 'Pure': those who are single-minded and loyal, and not divided in their loyalties.

- 'Pleasing': the Greek word *prosphilē* occurs here only in the entire New Testament. Its basic meaning is 'that which is love-inspiring'. They thus appear 'pleasing' to people.

- 'Commendable': those whom others rightly speak well of.

If there is any excellence The Greek for 'excellence' here is *aretē*, and is used in Greek philosophy to denote the highest virtue that is found in a truly good person. We may translate it more accurately as 'moral excellence'.

Think about these things i.e. 'let your mind continually dwell on these things'. Focusing on these qualities will help the Christians attain the kind of exemplary life that God desires them to have.

4.9. Keep on doing the things that you have learned and received and heard and seen in me: It may seem that Paul is boasting in this verse. But this is not so. He is actually saying:

> What I have written above, about joy and forbearance and prayer and peace, is not just a collection of good ideas or theories. I was describing a life that a person can live, and it has been my responsibility to live it as best I can, and you have seen it. Now put it into practice.

From the five verbs of this verse we see how Paul has taught the people at Philippi (and also how any good teacher does his work):

1 They 'learned' because he taught them out of his experience.

2 They 'received' because he also handed on the tradition of past Christians.

3 and 4 They had 'heard' and 'seen' because he practised what he taught.

5 They should 'do'. He had a practical aim, i.e. that they should not only know what it means to be a Christian, they should also live it.

Interpretation

In this paragraph Paul urged two prominent women to be 'of the same mind' and takes the opportunity to teach the Philippian Christians on the things that nurture peace in their community.

What may strike some modern readers today is the prominence women had in the church at Philippi, and indeed, in many first-century churches. A person may then ask, 'Are women today being given the full opportunity to serve God in the Church?' In places where the Church does not give women such opportunity, there may be good reasons for this. For example, in some cultures it is not the custom for a woman to take a leading part in any public events. A woman who did so would be regarded as 'immoral'. This is probably the reason why Paul said that it was 'shameful' for a woman to speak in church (1 Corinthians 14.35). But sometimes the reasons for excluding women from positions of responsibility are not good, e.g. if the reason is simply that people do not want changes of any sort, or the men in the congregation want to dictate to the women. This is not an easy problem for churches to solve. They face the question, 'To what extent should the Church lead the rest of society, and to what extent should it accept the present conventions of society?' We can only pray for more understanding and more courage to do what is pleasing and right (Philippians 4.8).

Paul also dealt with the problem of anxiety in helping his readers to experience the peace of God. Jesus teaches that with regard to anxiety we do have to make a choice. The choice is between trusting chiefly in what we ourselves can do, and trusting chiefly in what God can do. An anxious Christian, he said, is like someone trying to serve two employers at the same time: 'No one can serve two masters ... Therefore I tell you, do not worry about your life' (Matthew 6.24, 25).

Jesus also spoke of those who are anxious about the present (Matthew 6.25). He also spoke of those who were anxious about the future, for example those who were worried about what they should say if they were persecuted (Mark 13.11). Note that none of the New Testament writers teach that Christians should forget about feeding and clothing themselves and their families, or that they should refrain from making plans for the future. What they teach is 'Do not make your plans in such a way that you trust God less.'

However, the big question is, 'How can we get rid of anxiety?' In the next sentence Paul answered this question. He said, 'By praying.' By praying we turn our attention to God's love and power, rather than to ourselves. We realize each time that his love and power are greater than our needs.

In prayer we place ourselves as we really are in God's presence. It is letting his authority challenge us. It is letting his love surround us as we rediscover each time that God is to us as a father is to his children. We may be alone or with others. We may be silent or speak aloud. We may put prayer into words or pray without words. When we are in great pain our prayer may be, 'Lord, I cannot pray.' We may sit or stand or kneel or lie still.

Paul spoke specifically about one sort of prayer: the asking type (4.6). In this sort of prayer:

1   We are showing that we depend upon God. We are not like the Stoics of Paul's time who said, 'We are not affected by circumstances. We have no need of help.'

2   We tell God without any pretence or holding back what we and others need.

3   We do not only pray for his help for the world in general, but we make particular requests: 'Take away my pain.' 'Show us how to heal this quarrel.'

4   But we leave the result of our asking in God's hands. He knows what we *need*. So we sum up all our asking prayers in the words, 'Your will be done' (Matthew 6.10).

5   Paul linked such prayers with thanksgiving.

Finally, Paul spoke about how Christians needed to 'train' their minds to focus on things of moral excellence and praise. We may ask, 'Why is it important for Christians to do this?'

1   Christians grow in character by enjoying and being grateful for goodness, rather than by fixing their attention mainly on the evil in the world. We all tend to become what we most often see. This is why it is useful to think of good men and women, and especially of Christ himself, when we meditate.

   A man who had memorized the Beatitudes (Matthew 5.3–10) used to repeat them just before he went to sleep at night. In this way he fixed his mind on the goodness in the world, and especially on God's goodness.

2   Christians learn that God is alive and at work throughout the world and not only in the Church. God 'has not left himself without a witness' (Acts 14.17).

3   As Christians appreciate the goodness of non-Christians, they can grow in humility.

? STUDY SUGGESTIONS

Word study

1   How has the word 'gentleness' in v. 5 been translated into another language which you know? What is the full meaning of that word? How good a translation is it?

Review of content

2 'What writers in the Bible call "peace" is different from what most people in the world call "peace".' How would you describe 'the peace of God' (v. 7)?

3 What did Paul say about prayer in this passage?

Bible study

4 What do we learn from this passage, and from the following verses, about the position of women in the Church in Paul's time?

(a) Acts 16.13–14; **(b)** Acts 17.4, 12; **(c)** Acts 18.26;
(d) Romans 16.1–6; **(e)** 1 Corinthians 16.19; **(f)** Colossians 4.15.

5 Several times in this Letter Paul said he was rejoicing or would rejoice. According to each of the following verses what was the reason for his joy:

(a) 1.18; **(b)** 2.17; **(c)** 4.10.

Discussion and application

6 What opportunities are given to women in your church to 'struggle in the gospel' (v. 7)? How do they compare with the opportunities given to men? How do they compare with the opportunities given to women in other churches in your area?

7 **(a)** What did Paul tell the Philippians to do in order to get rid of their worries (v. 6)?

(b) To what extent can Christians of today get rid of worries in the same way?

8 **(a)** Think of people you know in whom you see one or more of the sorts of 'goodness' which Paul listed in vv. 8–9.

(b) Ask yourself what you have learnt about God as a result of thinking about such people.

 Special note I

Peace

'Peace' is such an important word in our world. We may ask, 'What is peace? What does the Bible have to teach about it?'

1 In a few passages in the Bible 'peace' means 'absence of conflict' (Acts 12.20). But see point 7.

2   Often it is a greeting (e.g. in Philippians 1.2; Luke 10.5), just as the words for peace, *salaam*, *shalom*, etc. in many modern languages are greetings.

3   Usually it means a gift which God offers to humankind. Sometimes it is called 'God's' peace (as in Philippians 4.7, 9). Occasionally it is called 'Christ's peace', e.g. 'let the peace of Christ rule in your hearts' (Colossians 3.15); 'my peace I give to you' (John 14.27).

4   This gift is a 'completeness' or 'wholeness' which comes to a group of people or to individuals when they are in a right relationship with other people. This is the basic meaning of the Hebrew *shalom*.

5   A right relationship with God comes when we accept the forgiveness which he offers to us, and when we depend on his purposes rather than our own. 'Therefore, since we are justified by faith, we have peace with God through our Lord Jesus Christ' (Romans 5.1). A right relationship with other people comes when we are able to forgive them and to accept forgiveness from them (Ephesians 4.3). But there can be real peace among Christians even when they disagree with one another, e.g. when they serve the same Lord, but by different methods.

6   God calls on those who have received this gift of peace to share it with others, i.e. to be peacemakers (Matthew 5.9).

7   What writers in the Bible call 'peace' is different from what most people in the world call 'peace'. For most people, 'peace' depends mainly on outside circumstances, e.g. the absence of noise or the absence of conflict. For writers in the Bible it comes from a right relationship with God. We see the peace that Jesus himself had when we read the account of his trial by Pilate in John 19.5–14. Jesus who was about to be condemned to death, not Pilate, had the peace of God.

Theological essay 4
Joy in Philippians

LOUSIALE UASIKE

Do not be afraid; for see – I am bringing you good news of great joy for all the people: to you is born this day in the city of David a Saviour, who is the Messiah, the Lord. (Luke 2.10–11)

1 Introduction

The good news proclaimed by the angel in Luke is the core message of the New Testament. It is the message of God's saving work in Jesus Christ, the Saviour, the Messiah. It is a message of great joy. Whoever

217

believes in God's salvific work revealed in Christ, and abides in him, experiences great joy. Joy is a gift offered by God to all people and experienced in a unique way by those who accept the gift of the gospel of Christ.

Paul received this gift of joy when he encountered the Resurrected Christ on the Damascus road. In building a close relationship with Christ, Paul experienced the wellspring of joy that flows from Christ, and he knew after his conversion experience that being 'in Christ' means being filled with joy, despite whatever circumstances of suffering and hardship one may undergo.

Joy is, in fact, the keynote of Paul's entire Letter to the Philippians, which was one of his letters written from prison. We may well ask what sense it makes to be joyful in an unpleasant, harsh situation such as prison, where one's daily life is severely restricted, hope threatened, medical care limited, and where one lives with constant fears of mistreatment by other inmates or prison staff. We can imagine that Paul went through some of these experiences during his imprisonment, but in reading his Letter to the Philippians we discover that his response to his situation is one of joy, because of his union with Christ and his solidarity with the Philippians.

This essay probes this phenomenon of joy in Paul's Letter to the Philippians and appropriates its message for today, with special reference to the experience of joy in the Pacific Islands context. We will examine four representations of Paul's joy in his Letter to the Philippians, concluding with a hermeneutical reflection on a Tongan concept for joy (*fiefia*), as it relates to Paul's concept of joy in Philippians.

2 Joy in suffering (1.12–18)

The essence of Paul's life and ministry is to know Christ and make him known, in living and in dying. Paul's present circumstance in this Letter to the Philippians is his confinement in prison. This situation troubles his friends in Philippi. Yet Paul assures them that all is well, despite his imprisonment. For what matters to Paul, what gives him great joy in the midst of suffering, is that his imprisonment serves to advance the gospel.

The gospel advanced through Paul's exposure to the prison guards and other people who visited the prisoners. All of these contacts provided opportunities for Paul to talk about the Christ for whom he was taken into captivity, and to respond in a 'Christ-like' manner in relation to others in prison (1.13).

Another means of spreading the gospel was through other believers who witnessed Paul's faith and courageous endurance of his confinement. They thereby gained the strength to preach the Word of God fearlessly, in spite of opposition (1.14). Although some preached at least partially out of a sense of competition with Paul, others preached in a spirit of good will. What mattered to Paul was that 'Christ is proclaimed, whether out of false motives or true; and in that I rejoice' (1.18).

It is unusual to find joy in those who are suffering in such dire straits. In fact, Paul confronted various hardships, troubles and opposition. Yet he found joy in the midst of these struggles, because they provided him with an opportunity to advance the gospel.

3 Joy in partnership – *koinōnia* (1.4–7; 4.10, 14–15)

The Christians in Philippi were well known for their special bond with Paul. They had been sharing in Paul's ministry for about ten years, from the earliest stages of his ministry in Macedonia (Acts 16 and 17) until his present imprisonment – 'from the first day until now'. Now, in his time of trial and tribulation, the Philippians were his 'friends in need'. They shared in Paul's problems because of their oneness with each other in Christ. Because of their compassion, Paul was filled with joy. He thus found himself 'constantly praying with joy' for all of the believers in Philippi. This joy resulted from their *koinōnia*, which we roughly translate into English as 'partnership' or 'fellowship'.

Koinōnia in its Old Testament connotation suggests a joint participation in a common mission or interest. At times, in the New Testament, *koinōnia* can refer to a commercial partnership, in the sense of the giving of monetary contributions. This is the sense in which Paul uses the term in his prayer for the Philippians, as he expresses joy and gratitude for their generosity and kindness to him in sending the gift which Epaphroditus had brought to him. This gift was a visible sign of their partnership with him. It was a concrete outworking of the gospel. It allowed them to be partakers with him in the grace of God.

This was a cause of great joy for Paul. It is natural to rejoice in the receiving of gifts. In this instance Paul rejoiced also 'in the Lord' because he understood the gifts and the sending of Epaphroditus to be connected with the cause of the gospel. This connectedness was living proof of the Philippians' Christian love and empathy for Paul. Such partnership in the gospel enabled them to have mutual fellowship through shared suffering for the sake of Christ (4.14). Thus they helped Paul to carry and lighten the burden of his captivity by means of their material giving, their shared interest in the gospel, and their willingness to make sacrifices.

4 Joy in recovery from sickness (2.25–29)

Epaphroditus was sent by the church from Philippi to Paul, with a gift and a charge to minister to Paul. Epaphroditus' service to Paul was acknowledged as a ministry. While Epaphroditus was ministering to Paul in prison, he became seriously ill and came near to death. The news of his illness became known at Philippi and brought worry and sorrow to the church. Thankfully, by God's love and mercy, he was healed from his sickness and restored to health.

The anxiety of the Philippian church led Paul to send Epaphroditus back to the Philippians as soon as possible, so that they might 'rejoice at seeing him again'. The Philippians' rejoicing at seeing Epaphroditus also made Paul full of joy. And Epaphroditus likewise rejoiced to meet his fellow Christians in Philippi. Paul urged the Philippians to welcome Epaphroditus 'in the Lord', in gratitude that God in his mercy had restored him to health. In addition, they were to honour him with respect, for he had carried out the work of Christ in a sacrificial manner. He even worked to point of death as he sought to fulfil his ministry to Paul in prison. Epaphroditus' recovery stirred the Philippians, Paul and Epaphroditus himself with a joyful spirit, and the Philippians welcomed him home with joy.

5 Eschatological joy (1.10; 1.28; 3.20; 4.1)

There is also an eschatological element to the experience of joy in Paul's Letter to the Philippians. Paul anticipates the fullness of life in Christ – the fullness of the kingdom of God ushered in by Christ. Eschatological joy derives from the expectation of being with God in Christ and living in God's presence for ever. Such hope continues to infuse Paul's life with joy, and this joy is at the heart of his teaching. Here are several examples of this anticipation of the coming of Christ in Philippians.

Paul rejoices in anticipation of the 'day of Christ' which the Philippians will experience if they remain 'pure and blameless' (1.10). The 'day of Christ' refers to Christ's promised return, in the fullness of time. Paul here prays for abounding and discerning love, so that the Philippians may be favourably judged on the day of Christ's return. Such discerning love is coupled with knowledge and understanding. Christians achieve this by putting themselves to the test in real-life situations and making moral choices in matters that count. Paul wanted the Philippians to discern what was most virtuous and to lead an inwardly and outwardly pure and moral life. He wanted them to ensure that their conduct was blameless, never being a stumbling block to others. In so living they would experience great joy.

Paul challenged the Philippians to be mindful of the day of Christ by realizing the plan of God for their lives and participating in God's way of salvation (2.12). God's way of salvation in Jesus Christ is worked out concretely, in history, and Paul desired that the Philippians would take part in working out their own salvation. This is a matter of being a responsible believer in the presence of God. The believer is called to participate in pursuing the will of God and realizing the virtues of the Christian life, for God's grace is not an excuse for doing nothing: we as believers must work out what God's grace means in our everyday lives – and therein lies true joy.

Believers indeed are co-workers with God for their salvation, and Paul further identified the believers in Philippi as citizens of heaven, even while living on earth (3.20–21). He wanted to convince them that their citizenship in heaven meant that they had to help make earth like heaven. The ideals of heaven had to be applied to life on earth.

Christians continue to live in this world, and sorrows are still experienced through struggles such as the 'war on terror', many forms of violence, global warming, the pain of the poor through the negative aspects of globalization, the devastation caused by AIDS, and so on. But the joy and hope of the community of faith and struggle derives from the Source of Life and Giver of Joy.

Paul links this divine reality to our growing awareness of the 'day of Christ', when eyes turn heavenward in anticipation of the fullness of the in-breaking of the new creation. This blessed hope exerts a powerful impetus for righteous living and Christian activity. The reign of God in Christ is always coming in power, and is already here in the hearts of those whose heavenly citizenship nourishes their hope and joy on earth. Paul rejoices in this knowledge and considers the Philippians his joy and crown (4.1). They will become a crown of victory in the day of Christ, and this reminds Paul that he has not laboured in vain (2.16). For this, Paul also rejoices.

We will now conclude the essay with a brief reflection on joy in relation to the Tongan concept of *fiefia*.

6 Hermeneutical reflection on joy in the Tongan concept of *fiefia*

Fiefia is a Tongan word which can be translated as 'rejoice', 'be happy', 'be glad' or 'be joyful'. It consists of *fi-e* and *fi-a*, which come from the art of making sinnet (woven ropes) in Tonga and the other island nations of the South Pacific. In the making of these woven ropes, a skilled artisan teaches apprentices how to interweave the individual strands made of coconut fibres. The expert starts plaiting two or more threads together and that is the *fi*; then, giving the strands to the beginner, the mentor directs him or her to *fi e* (to plait or twist this). The training of *fi e* (to plait or twist this) continues until the trainee is capable of having the skills and proficiency to *fi* (plait) a finished product. For that stage, the expert instructs the trainee to *fi a* (to plait, then). What the expert means is that the apprentice is now knowledgeable enough to make the sinnet and no longer needs to be taught to *fi e* (to plait this and twist that); he or she is skilful enough to *fi a* (to make sinnet on his or her own). The *fi e* and *fi a* together produce *fiefia* joy – and in fact the trainee is filled with great joy when beholding the finished work of art. It also causes the experts, who have helped to bring the work to completion and fulfilment, to rejoice.

It is Paul's *fiefia* – the joy of bringing learning and struggle to completion – to see the Philippians accept his teaching of the gospel and to live and grow in the gospel, from their earliest days together to the time of writing this Letter, the period of his imprisonment. 'Rejoice and again rejoice in the Lord' is Paul's message for the Philippians. He rejoices in the advancement of the gospel in spite of suffering, hardship, trouble and difficulties.

Some Christians still face the threat of death or persecution even today, in countries where Christians are a minority. Others find it difficult to live a life of joy because of oppression, poverty, violence or personal struggles. But Paul's joy in the face of suffering can continue to nourish the joy of many today, much as the joy of the sinnet mentor spreads to the sinnet apprentices when their weaving-in-faith results in a beautiful and useful product. Our joy as Christians derives from our being 'in Christ' and this enables us to endure every affliction in a joyful spirit, which spreads in turn to others.

Joyful living is an end product of koinōnia, and this is what Paul experiences in his fellowship and partnership with the Philippians. This is also a core reality of living in the Pacific islands, where people routinely share with one another and live for the benefit of all. Pacific islanders live in a fellowship of service as they 'bear one another's burdens' by contributing willingly to everyone's needs. Such fellowship and sharing creates communities of joy.

But that does not mean that Pacific islanders are detached from conflicts and social unrest, nor are they cut off from the strong negative waves of so-called 'development' associated with globalization. The people of the South Pacific face many difficult challenges today, socially, environmentally and relationally. Yet, just as Paul finds joy in his partnership with the Philippians, so too the Christians of the Pacific can experience a sense of profound blessing and joy if they honour their heritage of communal living and rejoice in the sharing and fellowship koinōnia which has long defined the Pacific Islands ethos, and which finds full expression in the gospel. Indeed, perhaps their greatest joy is shared joy – joy in communal celebrations, feasts and times of mutual sharing. These same gifts of koinōnia can be identified and nourished in every culture in the human family.

Sharing the joy of living together paves the way for working together and striving together to be in union with Christ here on earth, as we journey towards the fullness of the kingdom. This can fill our hearts with joy as we celebrate the many ways in which this kingdom has already come to fruition.

With our hearts full of joy, we can join together with the apostle Paul and his brothers and sisters in the Philippian church, giving thanks to God for the hope and fulfilment we have in Jesus Christ. We can also join together with the children of the South Pacific, and many other parts of the world, who love to sing this well-known song:

Rejoice in the Lord always, and again I say rejoice.
Rejoice in the Lord always, and again I say rejoice.
Rejoice! Rejoice! And again I say rejoice!

Philippians 4.10–23

Giving and receiving

 Summary

Paul finishes his letter by thanking the Philippians for the gift sent to him. He does not want them to misunderstand that he is desirous of a gift because he has learned to be content before God. However, he accepts it, but only because it is an offering to God.

 Notes

4.10. I rejoice: Paul had been taken to Rome as a prisoner, after a voyage of great danger and discomfort. He was a prisoner for two years, and there were at first very few friends. And then 'at last' the gift and the letter came from the Philippians. Paul thus writes that he rejoices.

In the Lord In this Letter we find the following phrases: 'in Christ Jesus' (eight times), 'in the Lord' (eight times), 'in him' (twice), 'in the Lord Jesus' and 'in Christ'. See Special note J for a brief discussion of what Paul means by them.

No opportunity When Paul writes 'at last you have revived your concern', he is not complaining about a delay. In order to make this clear, he adds here that they have not previously had an opportunity. Either they had no messenger or they could not collect enough money to send. In 2 Corinthians 8.1–2 we read that the churches of Macedonia (which included the Philippians) were suffering 'severe ordeal'.

The Greek word translated 'opportunity' means 'the right time', the opportunity which God has given and which may not come again. We find the same word in Jesus' question to the multitudes: 'Why do you not know how to interpret the present time?' (Luke 12.56).

4.11. I have learned to be content with whatever I have: The Stoics and the Christians used the Greek word which is here translated 'content' or 'contented' with different meanings.

1   There were a great many Stoics in Tarsus, Paul's home town, and he understood their teachings well. They were taught to find 'contentment' by wanting fewer and fewer things, and by needing fewer and fewer other people, and by feeling pain and pleasure less and less. This they did by the strength of their own wills. So from childhood they did hardship exercises and disciplined themselves, severely controlling the amount that they ate, wearing only a few clothes in cold weather and hiding any pain they felt.

2   It is clear that there was much in the life of a Stoic which Paul and other Christians could praise and imitate. Jesus taught that 'one's life does not consist in the abundance of possessions' (Luke 12.15). And Paul has said that he did not depend on circumstances in order to find joy (4.4). But while Stoics emphasized what they could *do without* through their own will power, Paul emphasized what he could *do with* the help of Christ.

4.12. I know what it is to have little, and I know what it is to have plenty: In v. 11 Paul said that he could be 'content' in whatever state he was. In v. 12 he gave two examples: (a) when things were going badly ('hunger'); and (b) when things were going well ('plenty'). He says that he has at last discovered how to keep in fellowship with Christ in either situation.

I have learnt the secret Paul uses a word which members of the mystery religions used (see note on Philippians 3.12). In those religions anyone could join in the usual worship, but only those who had 'learnt the secrets' could take part in the more important events. The word was also used by common people to refer to 'learning' in general. If Paul has in mind the usage of the mystery religions, the point he wishes to make is that 'contentment' does not come naturally. It is possible only when a person gains insight into God's ways. Paul explains this insight in the next verse.

4.13. I can do all things in him who strengthens me: Of course Paul is not saying that he could do everything. The six Greek words simply mean 'I am strong – everything in him who strengthens me'. Other translations of this verse are: 'I have the strength to face all conditions by the power that Christ gives me' (GNB); 'I am ready for anything through the strength of the one who lives within me' (Phillips). For the meaning of 'in him' see Special note J.

4.14. It was kind of you to share my distress: The words mean 'you performed a beautiful deed in sharing my troubles'. The Philippians had not been sure if Paul had valued their gift, and so he assures them here that he certainly does value it. The word for 'sharing' is the Greek *koinōnia* (see Special note E). Paul's readers could not remove his trouble, but they could share it. This sharing is one important way of expressing fellowship and it can be done with or without words, by letter or a visit or by a deed.

4.15. Early days of the gospel: Paul is thinking of the beginning of his work in Philippi, when he first preached the gospel there (see Acts 16).

When I left Macedonia i.e. when Paul left Philippi and was on his way to Thessalonica (see Acts 17.1).

In the matter of giving and receiving These words sum up the truth which Paul most wants to express in vv. 10–23. There are different possible ways of understanding it:

1 *Reciprocity in general, i.e. giving and receiving go together in the sense of a partnership* They went together as Paul and the Philippians first met and later formed a partnership. Each gave to the other, each received from the other. See 1 Corinthians 3.8 where Paul wrote that an exchange of this sort was good and important in people's daily work. See also Romans 15.25–27, where he explains how the congregations in Macedonia have received the gospel from Jerusalem and, as a reciprocal action, would like to send contributions to the church in Jerusalem.

2 *Reciprocity in financial matters in particular* 'Giving and receiving' was a standard commercial term for many people of the Roman Empire. It means when money is given, lent or supplied, a return in monetary form or as goods is expected.

3 *Reciprocity as a social convention* There was a very powerful social convention at work at many layers of Greek and Roman societies of Paul's day. When a favour was granted or when money was given, reciprocity in the form of loyalty was expected. This was the way many 'friendships' of that period were based on and nurtured. Paul's hedging about in verses such as 11, 13, and 17 can then be explained. Paul is rather unwilling to receive gifts of any sort because he may be afraid there may be 'strings attached'. However, he recognizes that God has transformed these Philippian Christians and they may not have that motive in mind, i.e. to make Paul their 'debtor'. Nevertheless, to prevent any misunderstanding Paul states that he receives the gift brought by Epaphroditus (v. 18) only because it is an offering to God (vv. 17–18).

4.16. Even when I was in Thessalonica, you sent me help: This is another example of Paul's receiving help from the Philippians. As we have seen, after his first visit to Philippi, he went on to the seaport of Thessalonica. There it was the Philippians, not the people of Thessalonica, who gave him help – and gave him help twice.

4.17. Not that I seek the gift: i.e. I am not anxiously waiting for a gift.

I seek the profit This word is usually used for the 'profit' or 'interest' which people can get when they invest their money or put it into a bank. So Paul was saying: 'Believe that giving that gift will bring you even more advantages than it has brought me. You are now open to many blessings from God.' (He repeated this in v. 19.)

Paul was not saying that the Philippians had *earned* God's blessings by their goodness. That would have contradicted the clear teaching of such a passage as Romans 3.23–24. We can see what Paul meant by looking at 1 Corinthians 9.6–11. A person who behaves generously becomes open to others and to God. Therefore he is open to receive greater gifts from others and from God than before.

4.18. I have been paid in full and have more than enough: i.e. 'If there was a debt which you owed me, then I tell you that it has been more than fully paid.' This may seem an unfriendly way in which to write to friends. But it is likely that Paul is doing nothing more than continuing the language of trading, which we noticed in vv. 15 and 17. His readers probably understood it in that way.

I am fully satisfied, now that I have received from Epaphroditus the gifts you sent, a fragrant offering, a sacrifice acceptable and pleasing to God In this verse Paul is again making it clear that he is grateful for the Philippians' gifts. But he adds that, in sending him a gift, they were also making an offering to God. 'Fragrant' or 'sweet-smelling' offering is a phrase which Old Testament writers use for a sacrifice which worshippers believed to be 'acceptable and pleasing' to God. We read in Ephesians 5.2 that when Jesus 'gave himself up for us' it was 'a fragrant offering and sacrifice to God'. See also Exodus 29.18.

4.19. My God will fully satisfy every need of yours according to his riches in glory in Christ Jesus: This verse is like a box of books which you cannot read till they have been unpacked. Paul is so overflowing with gratitude to God and with hope for his readers that he does not stop to write down his thoughts carefully. The thoughts are crowded together in one short sentence.

The best way to interpret this sentence is probably: 'My God will generously supply every need of yours as you live in Christ thus showing forth his glory.'

Riches See Romans 2.4 for another verse where Paul wrote of God's 'riches'.

Glory This is one of the great Bible words.

(a) Usually it means the showing forth of God's being and power. 'The heavens are telling the glory of God' (Psalm 19.1).

(b) In the New Testament it is usually the 'showing forth of God's being in Jesus Christ' (John 1.14).

(c) In the Fourth Gospel, 'glory' sometimes means the showing forth of God's being when Jesus gave himself to die for humankind (John 17.1).

(d) 'Giving glory to God' (as in Philippians 4.20) means acknowledging his being and his power (see also Revelation 19.7).

(e) Human beings can partially share in God's being and power, and therefore can share in God's glory (John 17.22; 1 Corinthians 2.7).

(f) There is glory which human beings cannot share until Christ's second coming (Romans 8.18).

(g) We should also note that in Old Testament times 'glory' often meant 'weight', 'status', 'wealth', 'beauty', 'shining-bright'. See Genesis 45.13.

4.21. Greet every saint in Christ Jesus: It seems to have been Paul's custom to write the last few verses of a Letter himself, although he had dictated the rest of it. This seems likely from 1 Corinthians 16.21: 'I, Paul, write this greeting with my own hand.'

The friends who are with me greet you This refers probably to Timothy and Epaphroditus, and some Christians who stood by Paul.

4.22. Emperor's household: It was a remarkable event which Paul mentions here, and one for which he is rejoicing as he writes this. There in Rome, among the officials of the great Roman Empire, were people coming secretly to Paul in their free time, to talk and pray and sing, and eat together. They came secretly because they could have been dismissed or punished in other ways if they had been discovered. It was known that Christians served a King and called him the 'King of Kings' (Acts 17.6–7; 1 Timothy 6.15). So it was not surprising if they were thought to be disloyal to the emperor.

Who were these people 'of the emperor's household'? They were not the emperor's own family, but officials who served the Roman Empire. There were palace officials, secretaries, treasurers, and bodyguards. Some were slaves, others free citizens; some were Romans, but there were also Greeks, Syrians, Egyptians and others. It was from this 'household' that the 'saints' came.

Probably they could well understand the position in which the Philippians were placed, because they too were a tiny minority living among people who were hostile to Christians.

4.23. The grace of the Lord Jesus Christ be with your spirit: In church services today, Christians sometimes end with this sentence, but often forget what it means because it has become so familiar. When Paul first wrote it to the Philippians, he probably meant this, 'I will end my letter with a prayer: may God who in Jesus Christ loves us and treats us so much more generously than we deserve (in his "grace") live in you all ("with your spirit").'

 ## Interpretation

Why did Paul not thank the Philippians for their help more eagerly, and why did he wait until the end of his letter before thanking them at all? One possible reason is that by placing this 'thanks' at the end of the letter, Paul was in effect saying that saying 'thank you' was not his main reason for writing. There were, indeed, more pressing issues that Paul must deal with, such as the lack of harmony in the church at Philippi and the enticing message of some Jewish preachers. Thus Paul wished to prevent a misunderstanding from arising – and we all know how money and gifts can bring this about. In other words, Paul's relationship with the church at Philippi was founded not on money or favours; it is founded on something far more secure: their common life and experience 'in Christ'.

That said, Paul still wished to thank the Philippians but he did so in the context of Christians' relationship with God and with each other. Hence, he made the following points:

1 'Your gift and your love did indeed make me joyful. You did more than anyone else (vv. 14–16)!'

2 'But I must say clearly that I can be full of joy without receiving gifts (vv. 11–13).'

3 'Yet your gift was very important, especially the love with which you sent it. It was more than a gift to me, it was an offering to God (vv. 17–20).'

What strikes many modern readers when Paul's words are read is his contentment in changing circumstances. How was it that Paul could be so contented? The answer he gave is found in v. 13: 'the Christ who strengthens me'. Of course, this does not mean he did not appreciate the partnership provided by other Christians. Indeed, he believed that God had made human beings to depend on one another in many ways (v. 15).

In many countries today there is a 'partnership' or 'exchange' between one congregation and another. In a part of London where there is much unemployment and violence, the members of one congregation have become very courageous in helping people in their sufferings, and they are able to share this spirit of courage and caring with another congregation 30 km away with which they are linked. This other congregation has more 'material blessings', and they share these with the Christians in London. There are a great many ways in which each of us can give to the other.

A group of experts from many countries produced a report which showed that rich countries need to reduce poverty in the world, not only to help the poor but in order to prevent the destruction of the world's environment. Some richer countries have asked, 'Why should we care?' The experts' reply was, 'Because if you care you will enable other countries and future generations to meet their needs, and at the same time to meet your own needs.' God has made the world one world.

 STUDY SUGGESTIONS

Word study

1 (a) How is the phrase 'giving and receiving' in v. 15 to be understood?

(b) Is there a similar phrase in your language or culture?

Review of content

2 In what ways did Paul's 'contentment' (v. 11) differ from the contentment of the Stoics?

3 'It was kind of you to share my distress' (v. 14). To what 'distress' was Paul referring when he praised the Philippians in this way?

4 **(a)** Who were 'those of Caesar's household' (v. 22)?

   (b) Why was it remarkable that members of 'Caesar's household' should send greetings to the Philippians?

Bible study

5 Paul, like Jesus, was grateful for help he received from others. What was Jesus willing and glad to receive according to each of the following passages?

   (a) Luke 5.3; **(b)** Luke 7.37–38; **(c)** Luke 10.38–42; **(d)** Luke 14.1; **(e)** John 4.6, 7; **(f)** John 6.11.

Discussion and application

6 Describe from your own experience some of the ways in which a Christian can 'learn' to be content.

7 What are some of the ways in which a minister and his or her congregation can enter into a partnership by giving to each other?

Special note J
In Christ

The phrase 'in Christ' is a favourite of Paul and it occurs frequently in his Letter to the Philippians. It may be regarded as summing up in a nutshell a Christian's relationship with God and with other Christians. It has a wide spectrum of meaning and so it is hard to pinpoint exactly what it means without taking into account the context. If a concise statement is needed, the following may be considered: 'in Christ' defines the Christians' 'mode' of existence, 'resource' for mission, and their 'corporate' identity. Below is a modest attempt at describing its various usages in simpler terms.

1 'In Christ' was Paul's way of saying that a person lives as a Christian by being in fellowship with God who has shown himself in Jesus Christ, now risen. If Paul was confident, it was because he was 'in the

Lord' (1.14). If he was hopeful, it was because he was 'in the Lord Jesus' (2.19). If he could overcome adversity, it was because he was 'in him' (4.13).

Some readers have been surprised that Paul gave so little detailed instruction in this Letter about Christian behaviour. We find the reason for this in the phrase 'in the Lord'. Paul meant 'live in the Lord and work out among yourselves how to live as a Christian in the world.' Compare this with 2.12.

2 Although no one except Paul used these phrases about living '*in* the Lord' or '*in* Christ', we read of the same experience in other parts of the Bible. According to John, Jesus told his disciples, 'Abide in me as I abide in you' (15.4). So Christians have Christ as the 'atmosphere' in which they live. As a fish is in the sea, and the sea is in the fish, so a Christian is in Christ and Christ is in him or her.

3 But being 'in Christ' does not mean enjoying a private and isolated fellowship with him. Being 'in Christ' is at the same time being in his body, which is the Church: 'you are the body of Christ and individually members of it' (1 Corinthians 12.27). Those who are 'in Christ' share that with all others who are 'in him'.

4 God does not force that fellowship upon us which comes from being 'in Christ'. We need to 'receive' it (see note on Philippians 4.15).

Key to study suggestions

Galatians 1.1–5

1 See p. 11, note on 1.1.
2 See p. 12, note on 'and peace'.
3 See p. 13.
4 See pp. 13–14.
5 See p. 13.
6 (i), (iii) and (vii) refer to (a); (ii), (v) and (vi) refer to (b); (iv) refers to (a) or (b).

Galatians 1.6–10

1 Distort, deform, misteach.
2 See p. 17, note on 1.8, 9.
3 See p. 16, note on 1.6–7.
4 See p. 17.
5 See p. 18.
6 See pp. 16, 17.

Galatians 1.11–24

1 See p. 20, note on 1.13.
2 See p. 21.
3 See p. 22.
4 See p. 22.
5 See p. 20, note on 1.12, and notice especially Acts 9.3–5, 13–16.

Galatians 2.1–10

1 See p. 26, note on 2.3.
2 See p. 27, note on 2.4.
3 See p. 26, note on 'To make sure …'; and pp. 28–9.
4 See p. 26, note on 2.3; and pp. 27–8.
5 See pp. 27–8.
6 All four passages are about richer Christians helping poorer ones.

Galatians 2.11–21

1 See p. 32, note on 'By works … through faith'.
2 See p. 35.
3 See p. 35.
4 See pp. 34–5.
5 See p. 36.
6 (a) See p. 32, note on 2.16; and p. 36.
  (b) See p. 34, note on 2.21.
7 See p. 36.
8 See p. 32, note on 2.14.
9 Peter seems to have been rather impulsive, and inclined to act without thinking.

Galatians 3.1–5

1 (c); see p. 41, note on 3.3.
2 See p. 42.
3 See p. 42.
4 See p. 42.
5 The gospel was offered without any conditions.

Galatians 3.6–9

1 See p. 44, note on 3.7.
2 (a) See p. 45.
2 (b) Paul's opponents insisted that the law was necessary for salvation.
3 See p. 44, note on 3.6.
4 All three passages teach that righteousness, and God's blessing, do not depend on the law.

Galatians 3.10–14

1 See p. 51, note on 3.13; and p. 54.
2 See p. 50, note on 3.10; and p. 53.
3 See p. 54.
4 See pp. 51–2, note on 3.13; and p. 53.
5 See p. 54.

Galatians 3.15–22

1 See p. 56, note on 3.15.
3 See p. 56, note on 3.16.
4 See p. 58, note on 3.22.
5 See p. 59.

Galatians 3.23—4.7

1 See p. 67, note on 4.5.
2 See p. 66, note on 4.1.
3 See p. 66, note on 4.1; and p. 68.
4 See p. 65, note on 3.24.
5 See p. 67.
6 See p. 67, note on 4.3.
7 Both passages teach that Jesus sets people free, and makes their position in the family secure.

Galatians 4.8–20

1 See p. 78, note on 4.9.
2 See p. 78, note on 4.10.
3 See p. 80.
4 See p. 80.
5 Verse 12; see also p. 79.

Galatians 4.21–31

1 See p. 82, note on 4.24.
2 See p. 85.
3 Isaac represented those who relied on God's promises; Ishmael represented those who relied on 'works of law'.
4 See pp. 83–4, note on 4.26; and p. 85.

Galatians 5.1–15

1 See p. 88, note on 5.6.
2 See p. 90.
3 See p. 89.
4 See p. 90.
5 (a) The love for God is not mentioned in Galatians 5.14.
  (b) See p. 90.

Galatians 5.16–26

1 See p. 101, note on 5.22; and p. 103.
2 See p. 100, note on 'jealousy'; and p. 103.
3 See p. 102.
4 See p. 103.
5 See p. 101, note on 'love, joy'; and p. 102.
6 (a) vv. 22, 23; (b) v. 24.

Galatians 6.1–10

1 See p. 106, note on 6.2; and p. 108.
2 See p. 107, note on 6.5.
3 See p. 108.
4 (a) See p. 107, note on 6.5.
5 (a) v. 2; (b) v. 3.

Galatians 6.11–18

1 See p. 111, note on 6.16.
2 See p. 111, note on 6.17.
3 This made the letter more personal.
4 See p. 110, note on 6.12; and p. 112.
5 See p. 112.

Philippians 1.1–2

3 See pp. 119, 121.
4 See p. 122.
5 See pp. 120, 122, note on 'with the bishops and deacons'.
7 See p. 120, note on 'God our Father ...'

Philippians 1.3–8

1 (a) See p. 126.
2 See pp. 127–8.
3 (a) Four. (b) See p. 125, note on 'all of you'.
4 See p. 126, note on 1.6.
5 (a) refers to (vi); (b) to (i), (iii) and (v); (c) to (ii) and (iv).

Philippians 1.9–11

2 See p. 133, note on 'full insight'.
3 See p. 133, note on 1.9.
4 See p. 133, note on 1.10.
5 (a) (i) Peter. (ii) That his faith should remain firm.
  (b) (i) Those who crucified him. (ii) That they should be forgiven.
  (c) (i) Philip and other disciples. (ii) That they should receive the Holy Spirit.

    (d) (i) His disciples. (ii) That God would keep them safe and that they might be united.

    (e) (i) Those whom the disciples helped to believe. (ii) That they should be united.

Philippians 1.12–18

2 See p. 138, note on 1.14.
3 See p. 139.
4 (a) Imprisonment.
    (b) Separation from friends.
    (c) Hearing bad news from Philippi.
    (d) Knowing that he might soon be killed.
    (e) Worrying about Epaphroditus' illness.
    (f) Seeing the un-Christ-like behaviour of some Christians.
    (g) Being abased, hungry, and in want.

Philippians 1.19–26

1 (a) See p. 146.
2 See p. 142, note on 1.19.
3 See p. 145.
4 They were dragged into the market place, accused of breaking the law, had their clothes torn off them, were beaten, put in prison, and had their feet put in the stocks.
5 (a) No remembrance or prayer is possible.
    (b) No prayer, no hope.
    (c) It is a completion of life.
    (d) It cannot separate us from the love of God.
    (e) It means being with Christ.
    (f) Christ has abolished its terror.
    (g) It means being with the Lord and being at rest.

Philippians 1.27–30

1 (a) See p. 148, note on 1.27.
    (b) Both words concern how society may be properly ordered.
2 See p. 150.
3 See pp. 150–1.
4 (a) See p. 148, note on 1.27.
    (b) In (i), (iii), (iv), (v) 'worthy' means the same as in Philippians 1.27. In (ii), (vii) it means 'good enough'.

Philippians 2.1–4

1 (a) *Support*: console, cheer, comfort, sustain. *Appeal*: urge, incite, stir up, persuade.
    (b) (i) Support. (ii) Appeal.
2 (a) Selfish ambition, conceit. (b) Having the same mind (goal), humility.
3 (a) (i). (b) (ii). (c) (ii). (d) (ii). (e) (i).

Philippians 2.5–11

1 Character, nature, power, authority, appointment.
3 How can we have unity? See p. 162.
4 (a) See p. 158.

6 See p. 159, note on 2.7.
7 (a) He was God's servant (Isaiah 52.13 and Matthew 12.18) because he was obedient to God.
(b) He bore the sufferings of the world (Isaiah 53.4) and did not come to be served but to serve (Matthew 20.28).
8 (a) Like Philippians 2.7a, it shows Jesus as a servant.
(b) and (c) Like Philippians 2.7a, these verses show that Jesus was a real human being.

Philippians 2.12–18

1 See p. 174, note on 'the world'.
2 See p. 173, note on 'with fear and trembling'.
3 See p. 172, note on 'in my absence'.
4 (a) See pp. 174–5, notes on 2.14–16.
(b) See pp. 177–8.
5 See p. 175, note on 2.16.
6 (a) v. 15. (b) v. 15. (c) v. 16. (d) v. 18. (e) v. 17.
7 See p. 173, note on 'your own salvation'.

Philippians 2.19–30

1 See p. 181, note on 2.25.
2 See p. 182.
3 See p. 182.
4 See p. 181, note on 2.25.
5 (a) By seeing that God keeps covenant, that he is faithful.
(b) By seeing that God supports the weak.
(c) By having his wounds bound up.
(d) By receiving his sight.
(e) By being born again into a living hope.

Philippians 3.1–11

1 See Special note C.
2 See p. 192.
3 See p. 186, note on 3.2.
4 (a) See p. 188, note on 3.4.
(b) See p. 189, note on 3.8.
5 See pp. 190–1, note on 3.10.
6 (a) Spiritual. (b) Physical. (c) Spiritual. (d) Physical. (e) Spiritual.
7 (a) By carrying the man on to the top of the roof (Mark 2.3–5).
(b) By keeping on calling out (Mark 10.46–52).
(c) By believing that Jesus could heal his servant (Luke 7.2–9).
(d) By trusting in what Christ had done rather than in their own achievements (Galatians 2.14–16).
(e) By going out without knowing where God was leading him (Hebrews 11.8).

Philippians 3.12–16

1 (a) See p. 198, note on 'heavenly call'.
2 (a) See p. 197, note on 'forgetting what lies behind'.
3 (a) See p. 197, note on 3.14.
4 (a) Running and boxing (b) running (c) running (d) boxing and running (e) running.

Philippians 3.17—4.1

1 (a) See p. 204, note on 'Saviour'.
2 See Special note G.
3 See Special note H.
4 (a) See 2.15; 3.2; 3.18.
   (b) See p. 205, note on 'to make all things subject ...'

Philippians 4.2–9

1 See p. 211, note on 4.5.
2 See Special note I.
3 See p. 212, note on 4.6; see also pp. 214–15.
4 That women often held leading positions, especially among Christians.

Philippians 4.10–23

1 (a) See p. 225, note on 4.15.
2 See pp. 223–4, note on 4.11.
3 Being in prison.
4 See p. 227, note on 4.22.
5 (a) Simon's boat.
   (b) The woman's ointment and her tears.
   (c) Hospitality from Mary and Martha.
   (d) Dinner from the Pharisee.
   (e) Water from the Samaritan woman.
   (f) Loaves and fish from the boy.

Index

This index contains only the more important names of people and places and the main subjects occurring in the two letters. The names of God and Jesus, and of Paul are not included as they appear on almost every page. Similarly, commonly occurring words such as, 'faith', 'Gentile', 'gospel', 'grace', and 'love' are not listed unless there is a discussion of the concept. **Bold print** shows where a subject is discussed in some detail.